Dimensions of Radical Democracy

Pluralism, Citizenship, Community

EDITED BY CHANTAL MOUFFE

V

VERSO

London · New York

First published by Verso 1992
© Verso 1992
Second impression 1995

Verso
UK: 6 Meard Street, London W1V 3HR
USA: 180 Warwick Street, New York, NY 10014-4606

Verso is the imprint of New Left Books

British Library Cataloguing in Publication Data
A catalogue record for this book is available from the British Library

Library of Congress Cataloging-in-Publication Data
A catalogue record for this book is available from the Library of Congress

ISBN 0–86091–344–9
ISBN 0–86091–556–5 (pbk)

Typeset by Leaper & Gard Ltd, Bristol
Printed and bound in Great Britain by
Biddles Ltd, Guildford and King's Lynn

Contents

Sources

'Outline of a Theory of Citizenship', was first published in *Sociology*, vol. 24, no. 2, May 1990, pp. 189–217, and is reprinted with permission. 'Context is All: Feminism and Theories of Citizenship', was first published in *Daedalus*, vol. 116, no. 4, Fall 1987, pp. 1–24, and is reprinted with permission. 'The Civil Society Argument', was first read as the Gunnar Myrdal Lecture, University of Stockholm, October 1990. 'Eastern Europe's Republics of Gilead', was first published in *New Left Review*, no. 183, September–October 1990, and is reprinted with permission. 'What Revolutionary Action Means Today', was first published in *Democracy*, vol. 2, no. 4, Fall 1982, pp. 17–28, and is reprinted with permission.

Democratic Politics Today

On the eve of the twenty-first century, amid the upheavals the world is witnessing, the task of rethinking democratic politics is more urgent than ever. For those who refuse to see 'really existing' liberal democratic capitalism at the 'end of history', radical democracy is the only alternative. If the Left is to learn from the tragic experiences of totalitarianism it has to adopt a different attitude towards liberal democracy, and recognize its strengths as well as reveal its shortcomings. In other words, the objective of the Left should be the extension and deepening of the democratic revolution initiated two hundred years ago.

Such a perspective does not imply the rejection of liberal democracy and its replacement by a completely new political form of society, as the traditional idea of revolution entailed, but a radicalization of the modern democratic tradition. This can be achieved through an immanent critique, by employing the symbolic resources of that very tradition. Indeed, once we acknowledge that what constitutes modern democracy is the assertion that all human beings are free and equal, it becomes clear that it is not possible to find more radical principles for organizing society. The problem therefore is not the ideals of modern democracy, but the fact that its political principles are a long way from being implemented, even in those societies that lay claim to them. Because of the wide gap between those professed democratic ideals and their realization, the general tendency on the Left has been to denounce them as a sham and aim at the construction of a completely different society. This radical alternative is precisely what has been shown to be disastrous by the tragic experience of Soviet-style socialism, and it needs to be discarded. However, this does not mean that we have to resign ourselves to democracy in its present form. Instead of proclaiming the ideological and illusory character of so-called 'formal bourgeois democracy', why not take its declared principles literally and force liberal democratic societies to be accountable for their professed ideals? This is the path advocated by those who favour 'radical and plural democracy', and I shall argue that this is the only hope for the renewal of the left-wing project.

This is certainly far from completely new, and one can easily show that the modern democratic principles of liberty and equality have furnished the language in which most democratic struggles have been waged. Since the moment when Mary Wollstonecraft took hold of it in 'Vindication of the rights of woman', the discourse of rights has provided the means that have made it possible for different forms of inequality to be presented as illegitimate and anti-natural; equivalent to forms of oppression. Democratic advances have usually been the result of a process of displacement of rights along a double axis: either new groups have claimed access to rights already declared, or new rights have been demanded in social relations hitherto considered 'naturally' hierarchical, such as those concerned with race, gender, etc. Radical democracy must acknowledge that the articulation of the ideas of popular sovereignty and civic equality with the liberal themes of natural rights, constitutional government and separation of powers — an articulation that is constitutive of liberal democracy — has made it possible for new rights to be claimed, and new meanings, new uses and new fields of application to be created for the ideas of liberty and equality. It is within such a framework that the struggle for a free and equal society has to be waged. It is high time to adhere to Norberto Bobbio's long-held conviction that liberal democratic institutions should be an essential part of any democratization process, and that socialist goals can only be achieved in any acceptable way within a liberal democratic regime.

One objection to a strategy of democratization conceived as the fulfilment of the principles of liberal democracy is that capitalist relations constitute an insuperable obstacle to the realization of democracy. And it is true that liberalism has generally been identified with the defence of private property and the capitalist economy. However this identification is not a necessary one, as some liberals have argued. Rather, it is the result of an articulatory practice, and as such can therefore be broken. Political liberalism and economic liberalism need to be distinguished and then separated from each other. Defending and valuing the political form of society specific to liberal democracy does not commit us to the capitalist economic system. This is a point that is increasingly recognized by liberals such as John Rawls, whose conception of justice does not make private ownership of the means of production a prerequisite of political liberalism.

The aim of this volume is to provide a range of reflexions on rethinking the politics of the Left in terms of extending democracy within the framework of a liberal-democratic regime. In order to achieve this aim the liberal tradition is examined to identify the areas where it needs to be reformulated, so that the great contribution of political liberalism to modern democracy can be freed from the individualistic and rationalistic premises that have become fetters to democracy in its present form. The notions of citizenship and community have been stripped of much of their content by liberal individualism, and we need to recover the dimension of active participation that they hold in the classical republican tradition. Now this tradition needs to be made compatible with the pluralism that is central to modern democracy. The contributions to the present book are intended to address from different angles the following challenge: How can the maximum of pluralism be defended — in order to respect the rights of the widest possible groups — without destroying the very framework of the political community as constituted by the institutions and practices that construe modern democracy and define our identity as citizens?

Radical Democracy and Citizenship

If we agree that radical democracy is the only viable alternative for the Left today, and that it consists in trying to extend the principles of equality and liberty to an increasing number of social relations, an important question is raised: What kind of political identity does it require? In other words, since within such a perspective the creation of a common political identity can no longer be conceived in terms of *class*, what kind of political identity can contribute to the constitution of the 'we' of the radical democratic forces?

There is a degree of consensus on the Left that we should revive the idea of *citizenship*. Such an idea, it is said, could recover the radical character that it possessed during the struggle against absolutism, and it might provide the rallying cry of all democratic forces in the attempt to defeat neo-liberalism. I believe that the idea of democratic citizenship is a very promising one for radical democracy, but it must be properly elaborated.

The question we need to ask is: 'What kind of citizen?' As Bryan Turner's overview of sociological debates about citizenship reveals, there are many different ways in which citizenship can be understood. According to the perspective presented here, a purely defensive strategy of reasserting the liberal view of the citizen as a bearer of rights is inadequate. It may help us to resist the neo-liberal onslaught on existing rights, but it is not enough. A citizen cannot properly be conceived independently of her insertion in a political community. In order to formulate a satisfactory concept of the political community, we must go beyond liberal individualism to questions of justice, equality and community.

Besides, since we are concerned with a modern democratic political community, the crucial question of *pluralism* must also be addressed. In recent discussions about citizenship the theme of rights has been presented as central. It is indeed important to reassert the view of citizenship as a system of rights constitutionally guaranteed to all members of a political community, and to affirm that these rights should not only be political but also social. In this way one can re-establish the link between social and political citizenship, which was the great contribution of social democracy and which neo-liberalism has attempted to break. However, since our aim is not simply to restore social democracy but to foster radical and plural democracy, we need a conception of citizenship adequate to such a task. If the idea of citizenship is to serve as the point of convergence for the current endeavour of rethinking the politics of the Left as an extension of democracy, it has to be responsive to the new political demands, which social democracy was unable to address and which have contributed to its crisis. In short, it has to meet the challenge of the 'new movements' and acknowledge concerns relating to ecology, gay issues, ethnicity and others, as well as the struggles around class, race and gender.

Citizenship and Community

A radical, democratic citizen must be an active citizen, somebody who *acts* as a citizen, who conceives of herself as a participant in a collective undertaking. The citizen, as Sheldon Wolin rightly emphasizes, requires that we think from a perspective of commonality: this is incompatible with an individualistic framework.

This is why the current debate in political philosophy between Kantian liberals and their communitarian critics is highly relevant to our purpose. What is at stake is the possibility and desirability of a return to the civic republican tradition in order to restore the idea of politics as the realm where we can recognize ourselves as participants in a community. The issue that is addressed in several of the contributions to this volume concerns the adequacy of the civic republican emphasis on the 'common good' and the way it can be made compatible with the pluralism of modern democracy. How can we defend the gains of the democratic revolution and acknowledge the constitutive role of liberalism in the emergence of a pluralistic democracy, while trying to redress the negative consequences of individualism? That is arguably the central issue in the present debate.

The rediscovery of citizenship is undoubtedly a very positive move, but we should be careful that we do not go back to a pre-modern conception of the political; and we need to be alert to the dangers of nostalgia for the Greek *polis* and *Gemeinschaft* types of community.

Using the tools of Lacanian psychoanalysis, Slavoj Žižek shows how the desire for a community conceived as *Gemeinschaft* is fraught with dangers. Examining the recent developments in Eastern Europe, he helps us to understand the role played by the desire for an organic community in the growth of authoritarian nationalism. The victory of democratic pluralism, he argues, requires the acknowledgement that the multitude of dreams is irreducible. An organic unity can never be attained, and there is a heavy price to be paid for such an impossible vision.

Important as it is, recovering some of the concerns of the civic republican tradition, with its richer conception of the political, and recapturing our insertion in a political community and our identities as citizens, should not be done in such a way that the modern recognition of pluralism is made void. The individual is not to be sacrificed to the citizen; and the plurality of forms of identities through which we are constituted and which correspond to our insertion in a variety of social relations, as well as their tension, should be legitimized.

On the other hand, we must recognize that the current search for a more active conception of citizenship is a response to the limitations, not only of the liberal conception that has reduced citizenship to a legal status, but also to the bureaucratic and statist conception of politics that has for many years been the principal alternative presented by the Left. The shortcomings of such a view should also come under scrutiny. To affirm that citizenship should be accorded a certain pre-eminence among our different identities, and that it is the democratic political identity *par excellence*, does not imply that we should either deny the importance of our other forms of membership or defend a state-centred conception of politics. In 'The Civil Society Argument' Michael Walzer proposes a conception of 'critical associationalism' in which citizenship, while being only one among our several commitments, one of the many associations to which we belong, nevertheless has a crucial role to play because it enables us to mediate among the others and act across them.

Citizenship and Social Justice

Alongside the question of rights, another current topic of discussion concerns the notion of social justice. This is highly relevant to our enterprise. Indeed, a democratic and pluralistic citizenship requires a theory of social justice that can serve as a framework for regulating the diversity and plurality of demands and rights claimed by the various participants in the political community.

It is from that point of view that we should evaluate the work of John Rawls, whose argument for distributive justice in *A Theory of Justice*[1] has been very influential because it combines a defence of individual liberty with a strong commitment to equality. As I have already indicated, it is a type of liberalism that does not make private ownership of the means of production a necessary component of the doctrine, and for this reason it is attractive to progressive liberals. It has also been well received by social democrats because it provides them with a philosophical defence of the welfare state.

There is no doubt that, against theories like Hayek's and Nozick's, who reject the notion of social and distributive justice as meaningless, Rawls's attempt to reconcile individualism with social justice has merit. Nevertheless, I consider that his views are insufficient for a radical democratic project. For, despite their merit, Rawls's proposals do not go beyond liberal individualism. He defines citizenship as the capacity for each person to form, revise and rationally pursue his or her conception of the good. Citizens use their rights to promote their self-interest within certain constraints imposed by the exigency to respect the rights of others. However, Rawls's approach precludes viewing the citizen as one for whom it is natural to join with others in common actions. As communitarian critics have pointed out, it leaves no place for a notion of community that would be constitutive of their identity. According to

Rawls, citizens in a liberal democracy need share only beliefs about procedural matters, about rules concerning getting along together. This is of course consistent with the mainstream liberal tradition, but it is precisely here that the problem lies. As Sheldon Wolin shows, liberalism's exclusive concern with individuals and their rights cannot provide content and guidance for the exercise of those rights. This has led to the devaluation of civic activity which is at the heart of our predicament. The current neo-liberal reduction of the common good to a question of 'wealth-creation', 'tax-payers' freedom' and 'efficiency' has been made possible by that individualism. We cannot successfully challenge their views if we remain on the same terrain.

Another shortcoming of Rawls's thesis, as Quentin Skinner shows, is his reliance on a tradition that considers that the best way to guarantee the individual liberty of citizens is to minimize the exigencies of social responsibility. His approach to social justice in terms of the priority of liberty is therefore inimical to the idea of active political participation. Drawing his arguments from the classical republican tradition, Skinner argues that this is a flawed conception and, against Rawls, he defends the view that it is only through public service that we can ensure and maximize our personal liberty.

There are other problems with Rawls's perspective. For instance, his theory of justice was formulated in the context of a politics that is now in crisis. The emergence of new political subjects, and the creation of new forms of identity and new types of community, has rendered inadequate a conception of justice centred principally on economic inequality. Its failure to address other means of domination makes it inappropriate for capturing the imagination of the new movements.

For a different way of thinking about social justice, one more in tune with the point of view defended here, one can turn to Michael Walzer's *Spheres of Justice*.[2] Walzer argues that we can no longer conceive of the egalitarian ideal in terms of 'simple equality', by which he means a concern to make people as equal as possible in all respects. According to Walzer such a view does not provide modern societies with a sufficient level of differentiation. Furthermore, it would require constant intervention on the part of the state to coordinate the distribution of all goods, and that would jeopardize liberty. To make equality a central objective of a politics that also respects liberty we must, says Walzer, think in terms of 'complex equality'. This means that different social goods should be distributed in accordance with a variety of criteria reflecting the diversity of those goods and their social meanings. He proposes distinguishing several spheres of justice as well as different distributive principles: free exchange, desert and need. Justice would consist in not violating the principle of distribution that is specific to each sphere, and in assuring that success in one sphere is not allowed to exercise dominance in another sphere, as is the case today with wealth. Walzer's approach provides a pluralistic framework that enables us to address different forms of domination. His theory of justice is compatible with a society that would be both egalitarian and heterogeneous. For that reason it is better suited to the democratic and pluralistic conception of citizenship that we require.

Indeed, as Jean Leca argues, the challenge that we are facing today is precisely that of developing a view of citizenship which is adequate for multi-ethnic and multi-cultural societies. We have to accept that national homogeneity can no longer be the basis of citizenship, and that pluralism must allow for a range of different ethnic and cultural identities.

Approaching this question from the point of view of a European identity, and taking his bearings from the situation in France, Etienne Tassin argues in favour of dissociating citizenship from nationality. He declares that the creation of a European public space requires breaking away from the dogma of the nation-state and the confusion that it establishes between general will and national will. That, according to Tassin, is the necessary condition for the existence of Europe as a political community.

These questions are of particular relevance today because of the current process of European integration. The need to envisage what form a European citizenship would take which allows for different national affiliations, is pressing. If Europe is not to be defined exclusively in terms of economic agreements and reduced to a common market, the definition of a common political identity must be at the head of the agenda, and this requires addressing the question of citizenship. European citizenship cannot be understood solely in terms of a legal status and a set of rights, important as these are. It must mean identifying with a set of political values and principles which are constitutive of modern democracy.

Citizenship and Identity

A radical democratic conception of citizenship, which aims at expressing the demands of the 'new movements', cannot ignore the criticisms that have been made by some feminists against the very idea of citizenship. Their argument is that modern citizenship has been constructed on the negation of feminine values. For that reason, and following Carol Gilligan, some feminists oppose a feminist 'ethics of care', which promotes a set of values based on the experience of women *as* women, i.e. their experience of motherhood exercised in the private realm of the family, to what they see as the male, liberal 'ethics of justice'. It is in that vein that the current known as 'maternal thinking' defends a type of politics guided by the specific feminine values of love, care, recognition of needs and friendship.

While acknowledging the insights presented by a number of feminist critiques of the liberal conception of citizenship, the position defended here is different. In her analysis of feminism and theories of citizenship, Mary Dietz criticizes what she calls the 'maternalist' bias in feminist politics and its claim that motherhood should provide the model for a new type of politics and citizenship. She argues that democratic politics is linked to the existence of a public sphere where people act as citizens, and that this cannot be fashioned on the type of intimate bond that exists between mother and child. Agreeing with the important criticisms made by feminists the private/public distinction and its role in women's sub-ordination does not imply that we should reject such a distinction. What we need is a new way of understanding the nature of the private and of the public, as well as a different mode of articulation between them.

Hannah Arendt's notion of the 'public sphere' can help us to do precisely that, since, as Maurizio d'Entrèves shows, the practice of citizenship is, in her view, intimately linked to the existence of a public sphere where members of civil society can exist as citizens and act collectively to resolve democratically the issues concerning their life in the political community.

For Arendt, one's identity as a citizen should not be made dependent on one's ethnic, religious or racial identity. Following the same line of reasoning, we can also affirm that gender should be irrelevant to the practice of citizenship. It is true that the modern category of the citizen has been constructed in a way that, under the pretence of universality, postulated a homogeneous public, which relegated all particularity and difference to the private, and that it has contributed to the exclusion of women. But that does not mean that the answer is to introduce women's so-called specific tasks into the very definition of citizenship. The fact that sexual difference has been central to the structure of modern citizenship, and that it has had negative consequences for women, can also be redressed by constructing a new conception of citizenship where such a difference becomes truly irrelevant. Within the perspective of a project of radical and plural democracy such a 'non-gendered' conception of citizenship is more promising because it allows for the articulation of many democratic demands and does not focus solely on the exclusion of women. But it requires a non-essentialist framework, which implies that there is no fixed identity corresponding to men *as* men or women *as* women. All identities, including sexual identities, are forms of identifications and are necessarily precarious and unstable. This precludes any possibility of reaching their 'essence'. Recognizing the precariousness of identities does not render political agency impossible on the part of women, contrary to what a number of feminists opposed to post-structuralism are saying. According to Kirstie McClure, it allows a resituating of political agency within the plurality of the social, which open the possibility for the political articulation of relations of race, class, ethnicity and sexuality. For that reason, she considers that it is necessary to acknowledge the important insights provided by post-structuralism for the elaboration of a democratic and pluralistic conception of citizenship. McClure indicates how post-structuralist contributions to political theory reconstitute questions of political identity and agency in a way that creates the conditions for a much more radical type of democratic pluralist politics.

Citizenship and Pluralism

A theoretical approach that incorporates the critique of essentialism, which is present in different forms in the more innovative currents of twentieth-century philosophy, is indispensable if we are to tackle the question of pluralism satisfactorily. Indeed, pluralism can only be formulated adequately within a problematic that conceives of the social agent not as a unitary subject but as the articulation of an ensemble of subject positions, constructed within specific discourses and always precariously and temporarily sutured at the intersection of those subject positions. This requires abandoning the reductionism and essentialism dominant in the liberal interpretations of pluralism, and acknowledging the contingency and ambiguity of every identity, as well as the constitutive character of social division and antagonism.

This last point is decisive: we would have made no advance at all if we were simply going to replace the notion of a unified and homogeneous subject by a multiplicity and fragmentation in which each of the fragments retains a closed and fully constituted identity. As we have argued in *Hegemony and Socialist Strategy*,[3] such an essentialism of the 'elements' remains within the problematic that it tries to displace, because a clearcut identity presupposes a *determinate system of relations* with all the other fragments or 'elements' — and what is this but the reintroduction of the category of totality whose elimination was the meaning of the whole operation? It is therefore important not to visualize the dialectics of unfixity as a dialectic of *separation*, but as a dialectic of *subversion* and *over-determination*. And this is possible because the subject does not have an original identity (of either a holistic or a fragmentary nature) but is primarily the subject of a lack. As a result, whatever identity s/he has can be constituted only through acts of *identification*.

Understanding the nature of pluralism also requires a vision of the political as a discursively constructed ensemble of social relations, a vision that is at variance with the philosophy of liberalism. Yet, it is only within such a perspective that it is possible to grasp the specificity of modern democracy as a new political form of society. Modern democracy as a new 'regime' is constituted by the articulation between the logic of democracy and the logic of liberalism; by the assertion of popular sovereignty together with the declaration of a set of fundamental human rights that need to be respected. It therefore establishes a particular form of human coexistence, which requires the distinction between a sphere of the public and a sphere of the private as well as the separation between church and state, civil law and religious law. This is the great contribution of political liberalism to modern democracy which guarantees the defence of pluralism and the respect of individual freedom. It is therefore inconsistent to pretend that such a distinction should be abandoned in the name of pluralism, as some fundamentalists have been arguing during the Salman Rushdie controversy.

This last point indicates that any reflexion on modern democratic citizenship must recognize the limits of pluralism. While it is important to defend the widest possible pluralism in many areas — culture, religion, morality — we must also accept that our participation as citizens in the political association cannot be located on the same level as our other insertions in social relations. To recover citizenship as a strong form of political identification presupposes our allegiance to the political principles of modern democracy and the commitment to defend its key institutions. Antagonistic principles of legitimacy cannot coexist within one single political association; to accept pluralism at that level automatically

entails the disparition of the state as a political reality. And this
— contrary to what some believe — would not mean more democracy
but the very negation of its possibility. Modern democracy, far from
being based on a relativist conception of the world, as it is sometimes
argued, is articulated around a certain set of 'values', which, like equality
and liberty, constitute its 'political principles'. Those who conceive the
pluralism of modern democracy as being total and as having as its only
restriction an agreement on procedural rules do not realize that there can
never be pure, neutral procedures without reference to normative
concerns.

It should be clear by now why a radical democratic perspective requires
a view of the political that is different not only from the liberal but also
from the communitarian one. The pre-modern view of the political
community unified around a substantive idea of the common good
which is found in some communitarians is antithetical to the pluralism
that defines liberal democracy as a new political form of society. Radical
democrats agree on the need to recover such ideas as 'common good',
'civic virtue' and 'political community', but they believe that they must
be reformulated in a way that makes them compatible with the recognition of conflict, division and antagonism. This is indeed, as I argue
in my contribution to this volume, one of the key areas for the elaboration of a modern democratic political philosophy.

On the other side, a reflexion on citizenship reveals the profound
misunderstanding involved in the liberal tenet of the neutrality of the
state. In order to respect individual liberty and pluralism, a liberal democratic state must certainly be agnostic on questions of religion and
morality, but it cannot be agnostic on political values since, by definition,
it postulates a certain set of those values, which constitute its ethico-
political principles. But those political values are not to be conceived on
the mode of a substantive common good: that would leave no place for a
plurality of different conceptions of the good life. They only provide a
framework of common practices to guide political conduct.

Such a critique of a supposed neutrality of the state is also suggested
by Louise Marcil-Lacoste, who analyses the paradoxes of pluralism. She
indicates how in many of its current liberal versions, pluralism is often
reduced to the simple fact of the plurality of opinions. This is certainly
the case not only in Rawls, who constantly refers to the 'fact of
pluralism', but also in all those liberals who insist on the neutrality of the
state and conceive democracy simply as a set of procedures to deal with
the plurality of interests and opinions. Marcil-Lacoste argues that

pluralism should instead be conceived as the institutional expression of a value, i.e. individual liberty.

The understanding of radical democracy presented here should not be conflated with other views which, under a similar name, propose a view of politics which is quite different. This is, for instance, the case with several versions of radical democracy formulated within the framework of a Habermasian problematic. While sharing with us the critique of the traditional conception of socialism, those forms of radical or participatory democracy belong to another philosophical universe and these theoretical divergences have important political consequences. Those universalistic versions of radical democracy are grounded on an evolutionistic and stagist conception of moral development, and they require the availability of an 'undistorted communication' and of a final rational reconciliation of value claims. In other words, they envisage the possibility of a politics from which antagonism and division would have disappeared. Our understanding of radical democracy, on the contrary, postulates the very impossibility of a final realization of democracy. It affirms that the unresolvable tension between the principles of equality and liberty is the very condition for the preservation of the indeterminacy and undecidability which is constitutive of modern democracy. Moreover, it constitutes the principal guarantee against any attempt to realize a final closure that would result in the elimination of the political and the negation of democracy.

To acknowledge the limits of pluralism also means that all differences cannot be accepted and that a radical-democratic project has also to be distinguished from other forms of 'postmodern' politics which emphasize heterogeneity, dissemination and incommensurability and for which pluralism understood as the valorization of all differences should be total. Such an extreme form of pluralism, according to which all interests, all opinions, all differences are seen as legitimate, could never provide the framework for a political regime. For the recognition of plurality not to lead to a complete *indifferentiation* and *indifference*, criteria must exist to decide between what is admissible and what is not. Besides, as Marcil-Lacoste points out, for pluralism to be made compatible with the struggle against inequality, one must be able to discriminate between differences that exist but should not exist, and differences that do not exist but should exist. Clearly, such criteria cannot be provided by the traditional liberal pluralists or by the recent forms of postmodern exaltation of differences and paralogies.

In the end what is always necessary for a democratic society to

function is a set of institutions and practices which constitute the framework of a consensus within which pluralism can exist. It is in such a way
that a modern democratic political community should be conceived, as a
discursive surface of inscription, not an empirical referent. Within such a
framework there will always be competing interpretations of the shared
principles of equality and liberty and therefore different views of citizenship. If our aim is the extension of those principles to the widest possible
set of social relations, a radical democratic conception of citizenship has
to be constructed through identification with a radical democratic
interpretation of equality and liberty. But the tension between those
principles has to be acknowledged and a radical and plural democracy
rather than trying to resolve it should enhance and protect it. Between
the democratic logic of identity and equivalence and the liberal logic of
pluralism and difference, the experience of a radical and plural democracy can only consist in the recognition of the multiplicity of social logics
and the necessity of their articulation. But this articulation should always
be recreated and renegotiated, and there is no hope of a final reconciliation. This is why radical democracy also means the radical impossibility
of a fully achieved democracy.

Chantal Mouffe

Notes

1. John Rawls, *A Theory of Justice*, Oxford 1971.
2. Michael Walzer, *Spheres of Justice: A Defence of Pluralism and Equality*, Oxford 1983.
3. Ernesto Laclau and Chantal Mouffe, *Hegemony and Socialist Strategy. Towards a Radical Democratic Politics*, London 1985.

PART I

1

Questions on Citizenship

Jean Leca

An Intelligible Society

Modern citizenship is generally conceived as an ideal ensemble of three features. First, it is a juridical status which confers rights and obligations *vis-à-vis* a political collectivity. According to the classical division proposed by T. H. Marshall in 1948,[1] this status is divided in turn into three elements: the civil element, the rights which are necessary in terms of individual freedoms — freedom from arbitrary detainment, freedom of speech, freedom of thought, freedom of belief, property and contract rights, and access to an egalitarian justice system; the political element, the right to participate in the exercise of government, either as members of a governing body or as participants in their nomination; and the social element, a minimum share in economic wealth and social security through the distribution of the goods which are available and valued in a given society.

Citizenship is also a group of specific social roles which are unlike the private, professional and economic roles. Through these roles, each citizen, regardless of her place in the division of political work, is placed in a position to make choices (or to accept them, or to participate in them) between contradictory propositions, even if they appear to her as equally legitimate. (It is perhaps perfectly legitimate to ask that the state does not interfere in the citizen's management of her private life and is more active in the protection of and subsidization for her; but there is, after all, a limit to the violation of the principle of non-contradiction.) The

17

constitution of the citizen's role depends on an adequate political culture which facilitates in particular the intelligibility of the state: the recognition of the necessity of an authority which is rational, that is, non-arbitrary and non-contradictory; loyalty *vis-à-vis* the 'universal' institutions, as opposed to exclusive groups; and an interest in public affairs. In scholarly language, this feature is sometimes designated as 'political competence'. It implies the possibility for the citizen to utilize her role to advance her interests successfully as a member of various social groups, defined in terms of occupation, gender, residence, social class, etc., in the political arena.

Citizenship is, finally, an ensemble of moral qualities which are considered necessary to the character of the 'good' citizen. In French, in both scholarly and popular languages, these moral qualities are termed 'civisme'. In reviewing the few French works devoted to this subject,[2] it is striking that, according to French public opinion (however vague this term might be), much more importance is given to the qualities which are relevant to social morality than to the qualities which are relevant to political morality. Qualities of conformity are considered more central to social morality than the qualities of participation. Devotion to one's country, or the significance of this notion, declines in all social classes and in all age groups, especially among the young. The only civic quality that is actually hegemonic is participation in voting; trade union militancy or partisan activity is always least important. Perhaps the only individuals who would rank political morality as most important would be the group of approximately 7 per cent of the students in lycée debates surveyed by Madeleine Grawitz. For them, civic morality implies an acceptance of a system which is 'unjust', 'reactionary', 'patriarchal' and 'bourgeois'. In so far as they interpret civic morality as a product of the dominant ideology, only anti-civisme would be moral from their perspective. By contrast, for the influential and virtuous majority, the good citizen must inquire about the affairs of her country, respect its laws and carefully attend to the education of her children. This relative contempt for political virtues bears out the recommendations made twenty years ago by Michel Crozier for the encouragement of effective citizens' participation:[3] a sufficient decentralization of authority; the existence of independent sources of authority, allowing minorities to escape coercion by the majority; and an education and selection system which places less emphasis on competitive examinations.

Whether or not one approves of these insights, there is no doubt that citizenship implies that society and government can be intelligible. Intelligibility does not entail transparency or consent: citizenship does not abolish class struggle. This struggle is structured in terms of a system of communication between parties which originate in different conceptions of the public interest. There is, nevertheless, agreement that the 'public interest' does exist and that the parties have the right to participate in its elaboration and in the obligation of submission to society's laws.

None of this is obvious: society could very well be understood as totally opaque, or as a social war, and citizenship could be regarded as nothing but the diabolical weapon of the dominant for the disciplining of the dominated in battles which are not their own. (The workers' movement has at times taken this position, which recalls the ambiguous attitude of socialists towards the Dreyfus affair and their hesitations regarding anti-fascism during the interwar period.) There are still many other conceptions of citizenship. The sociology of citizenship appears at least to be in agreement on the necessity of cultural unification for the promotion of this conception of the world.[4] This is not only the product of a movement of ideas, but of transformations in the material existence of societies: political centralization, increasing divisions of labour, occupational mobility, development of technical knowledge, and extraction of the social surplus not through directly political means, but through the play of a market which exceeds the limits of the primary communities.

Community and Political Community

Both cultural unification, and the specific form of that unification, are important. It is true that citizenship implies a 'sense of community' in the terms of Marshall, 'the sentiment of belonging directly to a community, based on a loyalty *vis-à-vis* a civilization which is truly common to all ... a loyalty of free persons endowed with rights and protected by a common law'.[5] Rousseau states that the citizen gives to the nation a part of his *amour-propre*. But if this bond implies a certain spiritual interiorization of the social structure (which is either 'relational' and therefore 'convivial', or always 'stratified' and therefore non-egalitarian) and truly merits the qualifier 'communitarian', this community is only remotely analogous to the *Gemeinschaft* of Tönnies or the *esprit de corps* of Ibn Khaldoun. There are three differences: the group is smaller in the 'traditional community', the division of labour therein is simpler and above all more stable, and the bonds of solidarity do not have the same foundation.

Modern citizenship is truly the social element of a group and therefore an engagement *vis-à-vis* a group, but this 'group' is an abstraction without an immediate and concrete signification (like that of a primary group of a group of interests). The terms of other citizenships, 'familial', 'associational', 'partisan', 'trade union' and 'entrepreneurial', are not only metaphorical, but also empty the conception of citizenship of its meaning. They suppress the connotation of citizenship as an element which is proper to a modern political community. The latter reorganizes individuals and groups which are not immediately linked by a mutual dependence, but have as their only shared characteristic the same juridical attributes and, in principle, access to the same cultural resources for the exercise of these attributes. The modern political community organizes a division of political labour, between the citizens and governors, without reference to the organization of primary groups and the division of social labour. The 'public' affairs are not those of people who know each other or of people who are in the same 'camp', but instead, 'the terrains of action and interaction where the collective needs of individuals who do not know each other converge, are recognized, organized and administered'.[6]

Citizenship therefore establishes a double relation in terms of interests. On the one hand, it is derived from interests: those individuals who consider their interests as properly served through citizenship are recognized as the best citizens, and those who possess the most 'capital' (material, cultural or technological) are recognized as the most competent. But, on the other hand, citizenship is also a resource which permits more of the socially disempowered to acquire a greater political competence and to defend their interests more effectively. It is in this latter sense that Marshall views citizenship as a weapon in the class struggle which facilitates the politicization of social protest, the conquest of the public space by interests which have been excluded, and, at the same time, the dynamic education in the rules of the game in this space. Everyone who is in a position of social power knows that in face-to-face conflictual relations, an encounter with a fellow citizen is more agreeable than an encounter with a stranger (the argument for 'civic solidarity' does sometimes win out over others). Citizenship is a useful weapon in this sense, but those in positions of social power also know that if a fellow citizen has greater resources for negotiation such that she can extract concessions, citizenship can also turn against them.

One of the consequences which follows from this situation, and which is not always recognized, is that citizenship only exists if there is a social space between the public and private spheres. If society is conceived as a confrontation between particular interests or as the product of the political activity of the state, the possibility of citizenship is excluded. Citizenship depends on two simultaneous developments: the autonomous mobilization of interests, which is an expression of a limited social pluralism, and the communal participation in the activities of the political centre, which is an expression of a widespread and stable devotion to the symbols of the community. There is an intermediary sphere between private matters and the affairs of the state which is, perhaps, the most strategic. This is the sphere of altruistic participation in voluntary associations; although the latter are not directly political in character, they are, nevertheless, 'reservoirs of citizenship'.

Nationality and Citizenship

The majority of modern states establish a link between citizenship and nationality.[7] Whether this association is regarded as the product of biology or the effect of a contract (such as, for example, the 'civic oath' in French revolutionary legislation through which a nation is chosen and its rules are accepted), and whether it signifies a bond with a nation which is conceived as an ensemble of multiple interests, or submission to a uniform standard, nationality is considered as a necessary, if not suffi-cient, condition for the exercise of citizenship. By extension, national sentiment has been traditionally associated with 'civisme'. If public opinion, at least in France, places less importance on this link, not one government in a single country appears to have renounced it. Double nationality is always perceived as a specific and exceptional case. Citizenship, nationality and cultural community are superimposed.

Conversely, it is also not legitimate to claim political rights for cultural communities which are differentiated by their language or their ethnicity. Access to political rights does not result in the disappearance of non-national cultural symbols, but in their reduction to 'folkloric' symbols which are in themselves insufficient as a foundation for legiti-mate political bonds. Entities which extend beyond national alignments, such as the groupings in universalist ideology or transnational class discourse, are also not legitimate political bodies. In the collective consciousness, or at least in that of the intellectual producers of the dominant symbols, conflicts and inequalities are usually understood in functional terms (manual workers versus non-manual workers, wage-earners versus the bosses), morphologically (lower revenues versus higher revenues), or ideologically (right versus left), but not in terms of ascribed status (minority language versus dominant language, women versus men, for example).

If colonial conflicts, in which the issue is precisely the constitution of the new nation-state, are excepted, all important ideologies use universal metaphors to describe the relations between the dominant and the dominated within each state. Citizenship levels out and depoliticizes cultural differences. The democratic version of the nation represents the political as a mechanism for the confrontation and communication between the 'parties'. Party members can change their political identity by eventually abandoning their party. It is always possible to transfer one's loyalty from one party to another; only citizenship's national loyalty is not transferable. Naturalization is an entirely different process from changing one's vote.

In this conception, citizenship depends on three elements, moving from the more 'material' to the more 'symbolic': (1) a division of labour which ensures sufficient economic growth, such that relative satisfaction of social expectations of greater incomes and increased equality is secured; (2) geographical and occupational mobility, which is facilitated by an understanding between different cultural groups, and which is both accepted by the new entrants (into a new business, region, profession, etc.), and tolerated by those in established positions; (3) symbols of collective identification which are accepted by those who are 'still at the door'. These symbols must permit the latter group of newcomers to aspire to and attain the realization of the first two conditions, and to pay the 'cost of access' to the community. The cost of access for the first generation is generally their ostracism from those who are already settled in the community: workers are stereotyped as 'dirty' and 'drunkards', Corsicans as 'violent' and 'lazy', etc. The fundamental instrument of citizenship is the existence of a cultural and academic industry,[8] which not only successfully establishes the idea that political homogenization is a useful tool for both the 'outsiders' and the subordinated, but also realizes, to a certain extent, this idea. If an excluded group does not benefit from any one of these three elements, and if it also possesses a strong cultural tradition, a new nationalism and a new citizenship might develop, resulting in the creation of their own state and their own cultural industry.[9]

Cultural Pluralism

These processes work well as long as the modern society in the original nation-states achieves economic growth and sufficiently meets the symbolic demands of its citizens, and the new nations provide more or less the same achievements for their own citizens. The problem is evidently somewhat more complicated when the situation is inverted; there is a strong possibility that the cultural industry could increasingly fail to perform its homogenizing function. Certain regional groups in the older nations could decide retrospectively that they have paid too much in terms of the cost of access to citizenship because they believe that citizenship now offers them little in return.

The case of immigrant workers is even more complex. Their arrival, an effect of the failures of the economy and the cultural industry in the new states, has suddenly increased with decolonization. The relative difference between this and other waves of immigration is that these immigrants want to share in the distribution of the nation's material goods, but they are hardly interested at all in identifying with the political values of the same community.

The material motives appear to be the most important, even if they are always combined with others. In the division of labour, the majority of immigrants who do find work only have access to employment which does not require their passage through the cultural industry. They increasingly hope that their children will enjoy greater success because this passage is, in their children's case, mandatory. Their aspirations, however, are blocked in so far as the children do not succeed, or in so far as the education system itself, apart from the problem of cultural confrontation, is caught up in an identity crisis of its own. (This identity crisis corresponds to the crisis of 'mis-production', the idea that the academic product is sound and that it can in turn provide for the satisfaction of social expectations for the 'disadvantaged'.) The immigrants are obviously not represented among the elements of the national cultural industry, the civil servants, judges, police, engineers, etc., with intellectuals and artists as the only exceptions. Also, it is probably the opinion of immigrant intellectuals, especially African intellectuals, that the non-intellectuals scarcely view the intellectuals as their representatives.

The bonds with either their primary groups, clientele, religious groups or original nationality — even if the immigrant does not exercise her original citizenship — are therefore considered more real and more significant in their understanding of their class or marginality. None of these factors contributes to the harmonization and communication between different cultural groups.

The model of the community represented by the European nation-states is therefore no longer an attractive one. It signifies, perhaps, an unnecessary luxury, but, more importantly, it signifies imperialism (or, for the regionalists, the 'Parisian colonialism', which is, in truth, French colonialism) rather than liberty—equality—fraternity.

Cultural pluralism develops on these foundations. This is, then, a model for the construction of political identities based on sub- or trans-national elements: language, ethnicity, region, religion and race. It is linked with a type of organization of the social in which society is viewed as a mosaic of compartmentalized solidarities, and the system of justice must pursue the distribution of equal parts of the national wealth to each cultural segment. This situation is a modern one. The traditional empires confronted apparently similar problems, which they successfully dealt with for centuries, but only to the extent that authority was not legitimated through representation but through an external authority (God, the cosmos, a group endowed with special attributes which set them apart), or to the extent that this authority demanded a minimal loyalty from peripheral groups, and let them pursue economic self-sufficiency. This traditional model was broken with the gradual process of modernization and capitalization which accompanied the formation of the nation-state. Actual pluralism is 'post-national'. It separates the construction and maintenance of peripheral solidarities from the acceptance of the rules of administration and identification with the symbols of the central authority. The central authority must do something in return for the peripheral groups in so far as a self-subsistent existence is no longer possible. The claim that citizenship and nationality are not linked together is based on the paradoxical and yet rigorously logical character of these requirements.[10]

One or Many Political Communities?

One of the problems in the ethics of citizenship is the determination of the citizen's obligation towards the state: is her primary obligation towards the government or towards the society as a pact of association?[11] This determination is complicated by cultural pluralism to the extent that a society appears to take the form of many societies, each with its own political community. The stages of this transformation could be described in the following manner.

Education becomes more pluralist in terms of religious values, opinions, languages and cultural differences. Language instruction is no longer limited to a single language of communication and no longer ensures professional integration. Either the education system becomes increasingly less sufficient for the minorities even as they demand its diversification (the case of the Lebanese Shi'ites demonstrates that it is the most disadvantaged who are the victims of an education system which is dispersed across different communities); or it remains a truly 'national' one and becomes a place for consumption and marketing, in which the student no longer invests a sense of loyalty; or it fully adapts to the ethnic-social mosaic and becomes a terrain for the political mobilization of particular groups.

The system of political representation can change. Representation in the terms of democratic pluralism is based in part on a system of competing parties wherein interests are always negotiable and non-absolute. The 'new movements' which are likely to develop would be founded, by contrast, on a sense of identity which is absolute because it is prescribed (race and ethnicity, but also sex, age and sexual practices), rather than a position in the social contract (in the labour market, for example). These movements will not demand representation to improve their contractual position but to establish their autonomy on a meta-phorical terrain in which identity is non-negotiable. The most activist movements will demand that the state assists them in constituting their internal sovereignty whereupon the state would abandon its regulatory function. The right to difference will recede with this collective narcissism and the refusal of interaction.

The levels of citizenship multiply, and this in turn creates a vertical expansion. De Tocqueville, like Durkheim, claimed that these different levels (local, regional, professional, associative, etc.), in conferring on individuals greater powers for the realization of their objectives, and in giving a concrete form to relations of cooperation and reciprocity, permit these individuals both to escape anonymity and to develop an improved consciousness of their civic obligations. However, it is also possible that this process arrives at a different result, namely the affirmation of right without obligation. Obligation could be continually referred to a higher level. The combination of resistance against the construction of a nuclear plant or a mosque in one's own community with acceptance of, or even a demand for, a national nuclear energy plan and religious freedom is an entirely natural attitude.[12] Perhaps the new development in this respect is the weakening of regulations and arbitrations. For example, the deprived can be defended in an irresolvable manner in which the normative limits to individuals needs are denied and no distinction is made between social needs defined in terms of security, well-being or moral freedom. At the same time, the complete interpenetration of the public and private spheres,[13] which transforms an infinite number of problems into the 'state's affairs' (for example, spanking children is forbidden by law in Sweden), could promote the coexistence of a 'negative citizenship', wherein each individual demands more guarantees for her private needs, with the utilization by private communities of public means in the defence of their own interests. The distance between the legitimate defence of a specialized practice, and the pursuit of reparations by a deprived collectivity, defined in terms of a neighbourhood or an ethnic group, is not that great. The fact that public authority sometimes serves particular interests is not new, but what is perhaps more original is that these interests claim to be legitimate public authorities. 'Plogoff—Kaboul same fight' reads the graffiti on the walls of a village which is resisting against the construction of a nuclear power plant. But this depiction of these three stages is of course nothing but a caricature which has absolutely no relation with any actually existing individuals ...

The Explosion of Communication

Most of the western countries are experiencing a major expansion in communication. The explosion of language which has been produced in this expansion greatly exceeds the language training that is necessary for the modern worker. The consequence for the intelligibility of society which is closely associated with citizenship, or, on the terms of Jürgen Habermas, the consequence for competence in political communication, is that the grounding of the rational conviction of the citizen is no longer given.[14] In French opinion polls, the majority of the respondents stated that the 'affairs of the state' (in 1971) or 'politics' (in 1977) are decidedly complicated and that their complexity indicates the competence of political specialists first and foremost (72 per cent in 1971, 58 per cent in 1977; the state is more feared than politics ...) Would the results from this self-evaluation have been different in 1940 or in 1950? Our findings in this respect are reduced to the construction of impressions based on other information.

The explosion in communications produces two ambiguous effects.

In the expansion of communications, the development of horizontal communities, covering a specified territory, embracing a large field of problems, and, in principle, addressing all the concerns of the inhabitants, is at first emphasized over the development of local communities and vertical communities (in which the individual is defined in terms of one privileged aspect of his existence, such as the corporation, the professional association, the masonic lodge, the caste).[15] It could be argued that this process is presently being inverted. In their globalization, communications produce a double effect: international affairs become close at hand, but the sense of nation becomes less intelligible to the extent that the nation appears less self-sufficient and therefore more dependent in international terms. It becomes increasingly difficult for the state to explain, convincingly, its political position (economic, agricultural, social or strategic) since it appears alternatively as autonomous ('if the state has a political stance, it is only because this particular political tendency has developed on its own') and dependent ('if the state's political approach does not work, this is because of international constraints').

This situation can lead to the stimulation of national citizenship if the individual arrives at the conclusion that the government is not the sole owner of political truth, and if the reverence for the political experts, who are supposed to possess the solution to political conflicts, declines. However, it can also have the opposite effect. It can suppress global information and emphasize instead relations which are differentiated in terms of individual preferences or professional interests (the worlds of rock music, financial information, the community of biologists, of Judaism, of Islam or of Médecins sans Frontières). Vertical communities are thereby constructed, which is in itself perfectly legitimate, but in this case without communication between them. Concerns about the centralized control of communications and production for the community as a whole are quite proper and reasonable, but concerns about the possibility of the coexistence of multiple micro-communities are also justified.

Among the intellectual elites, the explosion of communications has produced a systematic critique of the media producers who create images which contain nothing but the discourse of authority. 'The spectacle is the uninterrupted discourse which the present order holds with itself, its eulogistic monologue. It is the autoportrait of authority at the time of its totalitarian management of the conditions of existence.'[16] Since then, there has been no more information, only simulacra; no more reality, nothing but representations (given by authority). As an extreme consequence of this critique, ideas are disconnected from all communi-cable and verifiable reality, and acquire a life of their own, protected from all rational refutation. 'The petrol crisis is an alibi for the power of the monopolies'; 'information on Iran is a manifestation of a hateful incomprehension of Islam'; 'information on the Soviet Union is funda-mentally an anti-communist discourse', etc. The critique of the simulacra ends in the transformation of all information which is not coded and made meaningful in an ideological system into irrelevance. There is, therefore, nothing but a constant flow of self-referential simulacra without a single instance of communication or judgement, except the judgement which declares the 'good' (but for whom?). The intelligibility of society is no longer destroyed by a lack but by an excess: each individual has their own system which can be deployed at will to demystify the simulacra and distinguish between them and other discourses. The critique of the media and the spectacle produces a succession of complacent exhibitions of criticism, which are themselves nothing but spectacles. Citizenship is diluted in the nonsense.

Pluralist Citizenship

In classical political theory, the conception of citizenship which is based on the conformity to laws in exchange for the protection of the social order is traditionally opposed to the conception of citizenship which is based on permanent and regular participation in political activities.[17] The first conception, expressed for example by Jean Bodin, insists on the private dimension, while the second, originally developed by Aristotle, insists on the public dimension. Benjamin Constant made this distinc-tion the key to the opposition between the modern conception of freedom (private and bourgeois within the great states) and the ancient conception of freedom (public in the small city-states) and rightly links this distinction to the fundamental transformations in the organization

of production.[18] He recognizes that in the modern world, the first
conception ultimately leads to the privatization and domination of the
citizen by the forces of commerce, while the second ultimately results in
the manipulation of the citizen by political and ideological professionals.
In contemporary terms, the logical conclusions of these conceptions are,
in the first case, the creation of a nomocratic state governed by the rule
of law, but, above all, the law of the market and the individual interest of
the rational actor, and, in the second, the creation of a telocratic state,
which pursues the project of social transformation in the name of the
law of history or the interest of the 'masses'. The first type of state
abandons society to its own devices as long as the law, the social order,
morality, the police and the army are well respected. The second type
annexes society in modelling its organization on that of political and
administrative bureaucracies.

Modern citizenship rests on two mechanisms: representation, upon
which Constant insists, and the corporation (in the terms of Hegel, the
professional and social groups which form 'the ethical root of the state,
the one planted in civil society').[19] In other words, citizenship is a
profoundly pluralist mechanism and offers little satisfaction for those
who seek unity in all aspects of life. Representation, in structural terms, is
always a betrayal of that which we desire, or believe we desire, and therefore constitutes an act of dispossession for the citizen. The corporations
permit the multiple manifestations of interests which are structurally in
conflict with one another and disturb the majestic rationality which the
philosophers of the nomocratic and telocratic states believe to be in the
real.[20] However, it is in this mediocre zone that the citizen engages in her
activities, which undoubtedly explains why a dose of civic virtue is
indispensable therein for the linking of interests to the political
community.

Pluralist citizenship is besieged by four problems:

The crisis of the cultural industry of the nation-state which en-
counters difficulties in the attainment of a minimum of relative equality
in the distribution of cultural and material goods and in the satisfaction
of social expectation.

The difficulty, in French political culture, of instilling confidence in
the social organizations' (or 'socio-publics'') ability to take charge of
social needs; each one is linked to a contractual management which is
detached from the guardianship of the state on the condition that those
who undertake this management benefit from the public prerogatives or

public resources. A poor form of the 'benevolent', this manager has no place between the civil servant, the militant, the contract worker and the marginal.

The communication between the different cultural groups: in the moment that the French demonstrated in 1977 an increasing cultural indifferentiation, they affirmed the right to difference and that which we have named cultural pluralism. How can citizenship be combined with the coexistence of different cultural groups which only communicate between themselves with the deafness of resentment?

The questions of symbols of identification (with what exactly, with the community or with communities?) is perhaps the most delicate. Uneven cleavages may be known throughout the whole of society, bearing on cultural differences, familial values, eating habits, living standards, partisan or ideological identities, the transcendent or profane 'ultimate values', the meanings of the identity of the political community.

A conception of citizenship which would accommodate all social cleavages simultaneously has not yet been elaborated. Better (or worse) still, the citizenship of the democratic nation-state seems to solicit the smoothing out of the primary cleavages and the suppression of the most recent.[21] What happens when the development of cultural pluralism, like the attitudes in public opinion, seems to manifest a weakening (relative weakening: the British Crown is still well established, but what do the Antilleans or Pakistanis in London or Manchester think of it?) of the great unifying symbols? Can a government reactivate these great symbols to defend its industry against 'foreign capital' and de-activate them to allow 'foreigners' to become 'citizens' at the same time? Obviously, there remains the identification with the 'international solidarity of workers' against the 'cosmopolitanism of capital', but this conception of the world has not yet constituted a single political community nor a single citizen.

Translated by Anna Marie Smith

Notes

1. T.H. Marshall, *Citizenship and Social Class*, Cambridge University Press, Cambridge 1950.

2. For example, *Actualités: Documents (études d'opinion), Les Français et l'état*, Premier

ministre, Comité interministériel pour l'information, April 1971. Alain Duhamel, 'Le consensus français', in SOFRES, *L'Opinion française en 1977*, Presses de la Fondation nationale des sciences politiques, Paris 1978, pp. 87–117. Madeleine Grawitz, *Elèves et enseignants face à l'instruction civique*, Bordas, Paris 1980.

3. Michel Crozier, 'Le citoyen', in Club Jean Moulin, *L'État et le citoyen*, Le Seuil, Paris 1961.

4. Morris Janowitz, 'Observations on the Sociology of Citizenship: Obligations and Rights', *Social Forces*, September 1980, pp. 1–24.

5. On this point, see also François Bourricaud, 'A quelles conditions les sociéties post-industrielles sont-elles governables?', in Jean-Louis Seurin, *La Démocratie pluraliste*, Economica, Paris 1980, especially pp. 162ff.

6. James Rosenau, 'Vers une nouvelle instruction civique', in Seurin, *La Démocratie pluraliste*, p. 271. That the meeting of these needs could be possible, that is, that in the end public matters could be resolved without the exclusion of a group, is evidently the stake of pluralist democracy.

7. The USSR is an exception, especially in its early history. It should also be emphasized that the 'multinational state' is closer in this regard to the conception of 'empire' than to the conception of the 'nation-state'.

8. This term, cultural industry, does not refer here to the transformation in the commodities produced through artistic labour, but simply to the production of education and information services on a large scale by specialized organizations which are different from the small primary groups. For example, Pierre Bourdieu speaks in this sense of a 'cultural industry which is oriented towards the production ... of instruments for linguistic correction'. *Ce que parler veut dire*, Fayard, Paris 1982, p. 51.

9. I am reorganizing and simplifying the ideas of Ernst Gellner, 'Nationalism', *Theory and Society*, November 1981, pp. 753–76. The poverty of French sociological literature on nationalism and citizenship is regrettable.

10. See the interesting debates in the colloquium held on 5 and 6 December 1981, *Les Droits politiques des immigrés*, *Études*, 15, rue Monsieur, 75007 Paris.

11. Michael Walzer, *Obligations: Essays on disobedience, war and citizenship*, Harvard University Press, Cambridge 1970; George Armstrong Kelly, 'Who Needs a Theory of Citizenship?', *Daedalus*, 1979, pp. 32–4.

12. Translator's note: In Britain, the combination of the demand for the construction of more major roads with the demand for the preservation of the countryside has been called the 'not-in-my-backyard' syndrome.

13. Although I can only make a passing reference to this problems here, I have attempted to formulate some general analyses in 'Pourquoi élire un President?', *Projet*, February 1981.

14. J. Habermas, *Raison et legitimité*, Payot, Paris 1978.

15. Karl Deutsch, *Nationalism and Social Communication*, MIT Press, Massachusetts 1966. The terms 'horizontal' and 'vertical' communities are taken from Rosenau, 'Vers une nouvelle instruction civique', p. 272.

16. Guy Debord, *La Société du spectacle*, Champ Libre, Paris 1971. See the strong criticisms of Alain Finkeilkraut, *L'Avenir d'une négation*, Le Seuil, Paris pp. 72ff.

17. Walzer, *Obligations*, pp. 203–25.

18. Benjamin Constant, 'De la liberté des anciens comparée à celle des modernes' (1819), in *De la liberté chez les modernes*, Le Livre de poche, Paris, pp. 491–515.

19. F. Hegel, *Principes de la philosophie du droit*, translated by André Kaan (*Philosophy of Right*, translated by T.M. Knox), paragraph 255.

20. In the curious paragraph 289, Hegel lets it be understood that the corporations can be directed by mediocre leaders, but that this has little importance to the extent that the affairs which they manage are secondary. These 'trivial' matters offer a sense of 'self-satisfaction and vanity' to their participants. Such a pleasant existence is no longer possible.

21. The contemporary sociologist who has expressed these ideas most vigorously is Edward Shils, *Center and periphery: Essays in macro-sociology*, University of Chicago Press, Chicago 1975.

2

Outline of a Theory of Citizenship

Bryan Turner

Citizenship as Participation

With the development of a world economic recession and the emergence of monetaristic politics, the threat to the welfare state has become a central topic of social science debate in the 1980s. This attack on the principles of public welfare is directly associated with the emergence of the New Right and the dominance of Thatcherism in British politics, but the parameters of this issue are in fact global. From a sociological perspective, these changes in political orientation and the creation of monetarist perspectives in social policy may, however, be treated as symptoms of a fundamental change in the politics of industrial societies, namely the break-up of corporatism and the collapse of the reformist consensus which dominated the post-war period of social reconstruction. The break-up of the corporatist consensus may be furthermore linked to radical reorganizations on global capitalism which some authors now regard as an entirely new stage in the development of world capitalism, leading to the disorganization of capitalism, or to the end of organized capitalism.

These structural reorganizations in world capitalism and the demise of government commitment to welfare expansion have had profound implications for social science research and teaching, producing a greater emphasis on interdisciplinary and applied research as a defence of the welfare state. While radical sociologists in the 1960s were often influenced by the critical work of Louis Althusser (1971), for whom the provision of welfare and the existence of health-care institutions were merely facets of the ideological state apparatus, in the crisis of the 1980s, critical theorists have returned to the questions of distributive justice, individual rights and notions of equality as the basis for social recon-struction and social reform. While the notion of abstract human rights (possibly in association with some commitment to natural law) no longer commands widespread intellectual support, it is clear that the institution of definite 'rights' is an essential feature in the protection of public space as an arena of legitimate debate. The secular institution of rights cannot, therefore, be separated from the question of democracy; and the infra-structure of democracy is a fundamental, if limited, restraint on the employment of coercive force. It is 'the democratic apparatus, which prevents the agencies of power, law and knowledge from fusing into a single leading organ' (Lefort 1988: 29).

In this outline of a theory of citizenship, it is argued that the current attempt to defend the principles of welfare in fact requires a far deeper sociological, historical and philosophical enquiry into the character of social membership and political participation, namely an enquiry into the extent and characteristics of modern social citizenship. This enquiry should have the theoretical goal of attempting to achieve a synthesis in the levels of analysis between the individual citizen, the organization of social rights and the institutional context of democracy. This renewed interest in the issue of social participation and citizenship rights has, in turn, resulted, at the theoretical level, in a revival of interest in the works of T. H. Marshall (1963, 1965, 1981) which provides an important point of departure for any debate about the contemporary complexities of the relationship between citizenship entitlements and the economic struc-ture of capitalist society.

Marshall's Account of Citizenship

In the United States Marshall was particularly influential on the work of T. Parsons, R. Bendix and S.M. Lipset, but his sociology of citizenship is perhaps only now being adequately recognized and discussed in Britain. In America Marshall's work was developed as a framework for the analysis of ethnic problems and race relations, whereas in Britain Marshall's work originally developed and flourished in the context of post-war social reconstruction and as a social justification for an ex-tension of state provision in the area of national welfare.

While Marshall's analysis of citizenship is well known, it will be valuable here to outline briefly the three dimensions of citizenship which he considered in his original work. Marshall, whose intellectual roots were in the liberal tradition of James Mill and J.S. Mill, elaborated a specifically social version of the individualistic ideas of English liberalism. One theoretical and moral weakness of the liberal tradition was its failure to address directly the problem of social inequality in relationship to individual freedoms. At the heart of Marshall's account of citizenship lies the contradiction between the formal political equality of the franchise and the persistence of extensive social and economic inequality, ultimately rooted in the character of the capitalist marketplace and the existence of private property. Marshall proposed the extension of citizenship as the principal political means for resolving, or at least containing, those contradictions.

The initial idea for his theory of citizenship was developed in 'Citizenship and social class' in 1949 (Marshall 1963). It was further developed in *Social Policy* (Marshall 1965), where he addressed the question of the evolution of welfare policies in Britain between approximately 1890 and 1945 as a specific example of the growth of social rights. However, his famous contribution to the analysis of social policy contained no explicit statement of his theory of social citizenship. Finally, he proposed a theory of capitalist society as a 'hyphenated society' in *The Right to Welfare and Other Essays* (Marshall 1981) in which there are inevitable tensions between a capitalist economy, a welfare state and the requirements of the modern state. Marshall was thus primarily concerned with the social-welfare history of Britain between the eighteenth and twentieth centuries in terms of the growth of citizenship as expressed in three dimensions, namely, the civil, the political and the social.

Marshall argued that in the eighteenth century there had been a significant development of civil rights which were mainly targeted at the legal status and civil rights of individuals; and these rights were to be defended through a system of formal law courts. Civil rights were concerned with such basic issues as the freedom of speech, rights to a fair trial and equal access to the legal system. Secondly, Marshall noted an important growth in political rights in the nineteenth century as an outcome of working-class struggle for political equality in terms of greater access to the parliamentary process. In this area, political citizenship required the development of electoral rights and wider access to political institutions for the articulation of interests. In the British case, this involved the emergence of political rights which were associated with the secret ballot box, the creation of new political parties and the expansion of the franchise. Finally, he drew attention in the twentieth century to the expansion of social rights which were the basis of claims to welfare and which established entitlements to social security in periods of unemployment, sickness and distress. Thus, corresponding to the three basic arenas of social rights (the civil, political and the social), we find three central institutions of contemporary society (the law courts, parliament and the welfare system). Marshall's final theorization of this issue conceptualized capitalism as a dynamic system in which the constant clash between citizenship and social class determined the character of political and social life. These tensions were summarized in his notion of the hyphenated society, that is a social system in which there were perpetual tensions between the need for economic profit-ability, the taxation requirements of the modern state and the rights of citizens to welfare provision.

While Marshall's theory proved influential in the development of American social theory in the area of race relations and in the develop-ment of British sociology in the analysis of the welfare system, Marshall has been continuously criticized for certain (alleged) problems in his theoretical analysis of rights. For example, Anthony Giddens (1982) has criticized Marshall for developing an evolutionary perspective on the historical emergence of citizenship in which social rights appear to be the effect of a broad and imminent development within society. Marshall was also criticized for failing to consider the wider social context within which welfare policy developed in Britain, particularly in war-time and post-war reconstruction. Giddens also noted that citizenship rights are not a unified, homogeneous set of social arrangements. The liberal rights, which were the outcome of bourgeois struggles, cannot be compared with the claims to welfare which were developed by socialism and other forms of working-class action. Whereas liberal rights to the parlia-mentary process tend to confirm and reaffirm the social and political dominance of private property over labour, welfare rights are, at least in principle, a potential challenge to the very functioning of capitalism as an economic system. Therefore, there is no necessary similarity between liberal bourgeois rights in the nineteenth century and socialist demands for equality in the twentieth century. There is furthermore no necessary parallel or even development of different rights. For example, while civil rights may be developed in capitalism, political citizenship may often be denied.

Marshall was also criticized for perceiving the historical emergence of citizenship as an irreversible process within contemporary society, whereas the experience of the last fifteen years, following the oil crisis of 1973, shows that welfare-state rights are clearly reversible and not to be taken for granted. On these grounds Marshall has also been criticized by writers who regard Marshall's underlying value system as essentially complacent and conservative. Marshall was also challenged for failing to perceive that additional social rights might be developed in the area of culture, where citizenship could be regarded as a claim upon a national cultural system, and these cultural claims might be further associated with the educational revolution of the twentieth century with the emergence of mass education and the university system of the post-war period. While the argument that the university system expressed the cultural expansion of citizenship has become associated with Talcott Parsons, in fact the link between democracy and higher education was also fundamental to the American pragmatist tradition which was grounded in Dewey's view of mind.

Although there are clearly problems in Marshall's theory, I suggest that Marshall has often been criticized on the wrong grounds, and at least some criticisms of Marshall are based upon a misunderstanding of the original texts. Marshall was, for example, clearly aware of the broad social and military context within which welfare rights have developed, because he saw war-time conditions in Britain as providing favourable circumstances for the successful claim for welfare rights and provisions. Furthermore, it is not clear that Marshall's theory in fact requires an evolutionary perspective, assuming the irreversibility of claims against the state; Marshall saw the contingent importance of war-time circumstances on the development of social policy. It is clear however that political rights are of a very different order from economic rights, since in many respects the development of citizenship in capitalist societies stopped, as it were, at the factory gates. Democracy did not develop fully into economic democracy, although experiences between societies (in terms of workers' participation and control) are clearly variable. Giddens is clearly wrong to suggest that Marshall treated civil and social rights as equivalent, or as having the same integrative functions. Marshall specifically argued that, whereas individualistic civil rights directly corresponded to 'the individualistic phase of capitalism', the social rights of trade unionism were 'even more anomalous, because they did not seek or obtain incorporation' (Marshall 1963: 103). There was, however, an unresolved issue at the centre of Marshall's theory, namely that it is not clear whether social rights are in a relation of tension, opposition or contradiction to the economic basis of capitalist societies.

Although these criticisms are important, I would like to identify some rather different criticisms of Marshall in order to suggest a more elaborate version of his original scheme. Any theory of citizenship must also produce a theory of the state, and this aspect of Marshall's work was the most underdeveloped. In Marshall's scheme it is implicitly the state which provides the principal element in the maintenance and development of social rights, being the political instrument through which various political movements seek some redress of their circumstances through the legitimization of their claims against society. Furthermore, Marshall failed to develop an economic sociology which would provide some explanation of how the resources which are necessary for welfare are to be generated and subsequently redistributed by the state to claimants in terms of health provision and general welfare institutions. In considering these aspects of Marshall's theory, it is important to put a particular emphasis on the notion of social struggles as the central motor of the drive for citizenship. Marshall failed to emphasize the idea that historically the growth of social citizenship has been typically the outcome of violence or threats of violence, bringing the state into the social arena as a stabilizer of the social system. Although a number of writers on citizenship have drawn attention to the function of mass wars in promoting successful claims to democratic participation, it is necessary to have a broader notion of 'struggle' as a critical aspect of the historic growth of citizenship. This emphasis provides the context within which we can begin to see the real importance of new social movements for social change. However, Barbalet (1988: 103) has correctly pointed out that the institutionalization of social rights also requires new political, legal and administrative practices which may have been only indirectly related to these social movements.

We can further elaborate the Marshall scheme by adopting a notion from Parsons (1966), namely that the development of citizenship involves a transition from societies based upon ascriptive criteria to societies based upon achievement criteria, a transition which also involves a shift from particularistic to universalistic values. Thus the emergence of the modern citizen requires the constitution of an abstract political subject no longer formally confined by the particularities of birth, ethnicity or gender. Parsons, following Max Weber's work on the city (1966), thought that Christianity had made possible the separation of the political and social, while also developing a notion of social relations which were independent of ethnicity and which treated faith, or abstract consciousness, as the ultimate source of community in modern societies (Parsons 1963). It is possible to regard the differentiation of the political and the social as the Parsonian version of the classical separation of the state from civil society (Berger 1986: 75).

We can suggest therefore that the historical development of citizenship requires certain universalistic notions of the subject, the erosion of particularistic kinship systems in favour of an urban environment which can probably only flourish in the context, initially, of the autonomous city. Citizenship is, as it were, pushed along by the development of social conflicts and social struggles within such a political and cultural arena, as social groups compete with each other over access to resources. Such a theory of citizenship also requires a notion of the state as that institution which is caught in the contradictions between property rights and political freedoms. Finally, the possibilities of citizenship in contemporary societies are, or have been, enhanced by the problems of war-time conditions in which subordinate groups can make more effective claims against the state. This emphasis on the importance of mass war as a primary factor in social change is an important criticism of the conventional 'society-centred' perspective of both classical sociology and Marxism.

Although the welfare system was clearly expanded in Britain in the post-war period of reformism and reconstruction, there has been both a political attack on the welfare state and considerable institutional demolition of welfare institutions with the rise of Thatcherism and the spread of global recession since 1973. The causes of these changes are yet to be fully analysed, but the decline of the welfare system may be associated with the historical decline of the organized working-class and class-based communities. The spatial reorganization of working-class communities under conditions of disorganized capitalism also makes the articulation of interests far more problematic, and these changes are also associated with the erosion of neo-corporatism and the class de-alignment of traditional political alliances with the restructuring of capitalism and the emergence of new social movements. With the growth of global capitalism, the state is no longer able to mediate between private property owners and the working class, because its economic autonomy is constrained by international agreements and institutions such that 'local' political decisions by the state may have very adverse consequences for the value of its currency within the international money markets. The problem with Marshall's theory is that it is not longer relevant to a period of disorganized capitalism. The British state, in fact, has very little scope for manoeuvre: while capital operates on a global scale, labour tends to operate within a local national market, articulating its interests in terms of a national interest group. Marshall's theory assumed some form of nation-state autonomy in which governments were relatively immune from pressures within the world-system of capitalist nations.

Marshall's theory was initially focused on the British case, but a general theory of citizenship, as the crucial feature of modern political life, has to take a comparative and historical perspective on the question of citizenship rights, because the character of citizenship varies systematically between different societies. The emergence of citizenship is a feature of the very different and specific histories of democratic politics in western societies, but a genuinely historical analysis of citizenship would be concerned with, not only the Greek and Roman legacy, but with problematic comparisons between western and non-western traditions.

Ruling Class Strategies?

A particularly important and systematic criticism of Marshall's theory of citizenship has been developed by Michael Mann (1987), who attacks the ethnocentric specificity and evolutionism of the Marshallian perspective. The problem is that, while Marshall's scheme may fit the English example, it is historically and comparatively inappropriate for other societies. It may be the case that England is the exception rather than the rule. Mann (1987: 340) notes that Marshall's argument is entirely about Great Britain. There is not a single mention of any other country. Did Marshall regard Britain as typical of the capitalist West as a whole? In fact, it would be more accurate to say that the Marshallian version of the theory of citizenship is entirely about England, since he takes for granted the socio-political unity of Great Britain (Turner 1986b: 46). The question of citizenship within the British state cannot be analysed historically without reference to the erosion of the cultural and political autonomy of the Celtic fringe. As Anthony Smith (1986) argues, the creation of citizenship within the Gesellschaft-like political space of the modern state may well require the subordination, or even eradication, of Gemeinschaft-like membership within an ethnic primary group (or Ethnie).

However, Mann's comment on the Anglophile character of Marshall's theory is merely the pretext for a more important exercise, namely the development of a comparative framework for the historical elaboration of five strategies of citizenship (liberal, reformist, authoritarian monarchist, fascist and authoritarian socialist). Having divided the regimes of pre-industrial Europe into two ideal-types (absolute monarchies and constitutional regimes), Mann proceeds to inquire into how the traditional regimes developed strategies to cope politically first with the bourgeoisie and secondly with the urban working class during the period of industrial capitalist development.

Britain provides the principal example of a liberal strategy. The state retained a liberal character and the working class was successfully incorporated through the welfare state which 'meshes into, rather than replaces, private market and insurance schemes' (Mann 1987: 343). Under the impact of trade union struggle and class conflict in the nineteenth century, Britain eventually moved from a liberal to a reformist solution. The United States and Switzerland are also examples of a liberal strategy, but social citizenship remained under-developed in both. However, their buoyant economies have permitted their citizens to insure themselves against personal hardship. By contrast, in France, Spain, Italy and Scandinavia, the development of citizenship was bitterly disputed by monarchical and clerical reactionaries, and the absolutist legacy remained (with the exception of France) largely unchallenged, until the modern period.

Germany, Austria, Russia and Japan provide examples of an authoritarian monarchist strategy. While these absolutist regimes initially resisted the citizenship claims of both bourgeoisie and proletariat, they were eventually forced to modernize their polities. Wilhelmine Germany enjoyed the most successful strategy of political and economic development, which resulted in the bourgeoisie, and to some extent the proletariat, being 'negatively incorporated' into the system via a superficial development of political citizenship. The Soviet Union and Nazi Germany provide Mann with two illustrations of authoritarian socialist and fascist strategies. Although neither system provided comprehensive civil and political rights, there was a significant development of social citizenship. In Germany, policies of full employment and public works programmes were combined with another objective: rearmament. In the Soviet Union, a programme of social citizenship for all existed alongside substantial social inequalities in the shadow economy and the black market. Both systems, while proclaiming powerful legitimating ideologies, had to depend on an extensive apparatus of violence and repression.

However, while German fascism was very unstable, the Soviet system was more successful in domesticating its labour force by converting the trade unions into 'a-political welfare state organizations' (Mann 1987: 350).

Mann's treatment of citizenship represents, not only a major theoretical advance over the Marshallian paradigm, but also an important contribution to our understanding of the historical processes of citizenship formation. However, Mann's theory appears to be weak on three crucial issues, and this debate with Mann's ruling-strategy thesis then provides the context in which I wish further to elaborate an alternative to, or at least a modification of, Mann's theory.

The first criticism is that, because Mann perceives the origin of citizenship as a strategy of *class* relationships in which the state has a major role to play in creating social stability, he fails to consider the questions of aboriginality, ethnicity and nationalism in the formation of modern citizenship. As I have already noted following Smith (1986), the creation of citizenship within the political boundaries of the modern nation-state has typically involved or required the subordination or incorporation of ethnic minorities and/or aboriginals. This incorporation may be achieved by the relatively painless process of the cultural melting pot, or it may be brought about by more violent means. Citizenship in societies like Canada, New Zealand and Australia has, as its dark underside, the 'modernization' of aboriginal communities. The debate about citizenship in the United States cannot take place without an analysis of the historical impact of the black South on American civil society, and yet Mann curiously ignores the issue of racial orders. Any further development of Mann's account of citizenship would have to examine social stratification in terms which are not class-reductionist, and his laudable attempt to provide a historical treatment of different types of ruling class strategies should be extended to include an analysis of the white-settler societies.

My second critical observation is that, while Mann (1987: 340) warns us that 'tradition matters', he completely neglects the impact of organized Christianity and Christian culture on the structuring of private/public spaces, and how the typically negative evaluation of the political in mainstream Christian theology continues to place an individualistic brake on the expansion of active political citizenship. I have argued elsewhere (Turner 1986b: 16) that both Christianity and Islam contributed to the development of citizenship by providing a universalistic discourse of political space (the City of God and the Household of Islam) which challenged ethnicity and kinship as the primordial ties of the societal community. However, Christianity also produced an important limitation on the emergence of an active view of the citizen as a carrier of rights. Christianity has emerged in the modern period as a radical threat to authoritarian or reactionary regimes (Poland, Soviet Union, South Africa or some Latin American states) in only exceptional circumstances, and specifically where alternative means of legitimate protest have been destroyed. In these circumstances, Christian theology often requires considerable revision and redirection.

The Protestant Reformation provided an ideology of rebellion against Catholic hegemony and papal authority, and, partly through the development of vernacular versions of the Bible, established a cultural basis for the eruption of the nation-state. However, once in power, the Protestant churches were forced to turn to the local nation-state or to regional authorities for secular (that is, military) support of the faith. In theory, of course, the reformed churches regarded the state as a necessary evil, but in practice they came, not only to depend on secular political support, but also provided an ideology of 'godly rule'. The churches required, however reluctantly, state power for the subordination of antinomianism, and in return they offered a theory of passive, obedient citizenship. In his *Institution de la Religion chrétienne*, Calvin was at pains to emphasize the Christian obligation to obey the laws of the land and to respect government, since the aim of the state was to create peace and stability during our miserable, but happily brief, sojourn on earth (Calvin 1939: 197ff). The effect of Protestant doctrine was to create a private sphere (of devotional religious practice, the subjectivity of the individual conscience, the privatized confessional and familial practices) in which the moral education of the individual was to be achieved, and a public world of the state and the market place, which was the realm of necessity. While religion through the institutionalized means of grace monitored the interior subjectivity of the individual, the state through the institutionalized means of violence regulated public space. This division did not provide an environment which was congenial to the full development of a view of the citizen as an active and responsible member of the public arena. Mann's revision of the Marshallian version of liberal citizenship does not have a perspective on these religio-cultural variations in the constitution of political space.

Of course, the churches were not merely the vehicles for Christian cultural beliefs towards the political: they materially influenced the ways in which public space was shared. For example, Colin Crouch (1986) has provided an important comparative framework for understanding the interaction between state and religion in the formation of European states. He distinguishes between: (1) secular liberalism versus Catholic corporatism (in the French Republic); (2) hegemonic Catholic corporatism (Portugal and Spain in which as a result the liberal tradition was very marginal); (3) Protestant neutrality (Denmark, Norway, Sweden); (4) consociationism (The Netherlands, Switzerland and Belgium) in which the public affairs of civil society are organized separately for and by the different communities. Crouch argues that these traditional patterns for 'sharing public space' had long-term implications for modern politics. Thus,

> It is important to distinguish this organic, Catholic fascism from the secular Nazism of Germany. This was made dramatically clear by Austrian history following the *Anschluss*, when the whole edifice of *Austrofaschismus* and its corporatism was abolished and replaced by the Nazi system, based on the *Führerprinzip* rather than corporatism. But the abiding, specifically Austrian tradition remained corporatist and space-sharing. (Crouch 1986: 186).

Again, any understanding of the issue of citizenship in a society like Israel would have to depend on an historical account of the settlement between religion and politics during the period of state formation.

My final (and possibly most important) criticism of Mann concerns the notion of a 'ruling-class strategy'. Mann can only conceive of citizenship being handed down from above (for example, by the state) such that rights are passive. Thus, citizenship is a strategy which brings about some degree of amelioration of social conflict and which is therefore a major contribution to social integration. Such a view of citizenship from above precludes, or restricts, any analysis of citizenship from below as a consequence of social struggles over resources. Because Mann concentrates on strategies from above, he cannot adequately appreciate the revolutionary implications of the oppositional character of rights. Is it possible that Mann regards the demands of millenarian Fifth Monarchy Men, incendiarist peasants, revolutionary republicans of the French Revolution, or radical Chartists as always capable of being successfully assimilated into the system by the calming oils of citizenship? I find Engels's view in *Anti-Dühring* more historically plausible:

> in the same way bourgeois demands for equality were accompanied by proletarian demands for equality. From the moment when the bourgeois

demand for the abolition of class *privileges* was put forward alongside it appeared the proletarian demand for the abolition of *classes themselves* — at first in religious form, leaning towards primitive Christianity, and later drawing support from the bourgeois equalitarian theories themselves. (Engels 1959: 146–7)

There is an important distinction here. In ideal-typical terms, and as a heuristic device for the development of theory, we can either regard rights as privileges handed down from above in return for pragmatic cooperation (Mann's thesis), or we can regard rights as the outcome of radical struggle by subordinate groups for benefits (Engels's thesis). There are in fact two related difficulties. The first is Mann's negation of rights from below, and the second is that, because the only important categories in Mann's theory are ultimately the Marxist categories of class, capitalism as a mode of production, the state and geopolitics, he cannot deal theoretically with the peace movement, feminism, Solidarity, the Green Movement, animal liberation or struggles for children's rights as genuine or important contributions to historical change — at least such movements do not figure in his account. While the cooperation of these movements rather than the satisfaction of their demands may be a common outcome, this is not always, or inevitably, the outcome. Furthermore, failure to satisfy demands within the welfare state creates conditions for new social movements which then become dependent on the state for the satisfaction of needs. Mann's analytical framework appears to preclude any such consideration of the impact of new social movements on the expansion of citizenship from below.

By combining these two aspects of citizenship (the private/public division, and the above/below distinction), we can develop a heuristic typology of four political contexts for the institutionalization or creation of citizenship rights:

Citizenship

Below	Above	
Revolutionary contexts	Passive democracy	Public Space
Liberal pluralism	Plebiscitary authoritarianism	Private Space

Revolutionary citizenship combines demands from below with an emphasis on the public arena, regarding the private world of the individual with suspicion. However revolutionary struggles for democratic rights often end in forms of public terror. Where revolutionary citizenship collapses into totalitarianism, *l'imaginaire social* (the social imaginary) results in the idea of 'People-as-One, the idea of society as such, bearing the knowledge of itself, transparent and homogeneous' (Lefort 1986: 305). In liberal pluralism, while interest group formation typically leads to movements for rights from below, the revolutionary thrust of social protest may be contained by a continuing emphasis on the rights of the individual for privatized dissent. The classical liberal view of politics insisted on diversity and freedom of *private* opinion against the threat of uniformity of belief. Hence, J.S. Mill in his essay 'On Liberty' in 1859 expressed the fear that the spread of mass opinion would mean that Europe was 'decidedly advancing towards the Chinese ideal of making all people alike' (Mill 1962: 130).

These forms of democratic citizenship may be contrasted with citizenship rights from above in which the citizen is a mere subject rather than an active bearer of effective claims against society via the state. Passive democracy recognizes the legitimate function of representative institutions, the courts and a welfare state system, but there is no established tradition of struggles for citizenship rights. For the reasons which are outlined in Mann's argument, citizenship remains a strategy for the regulation and institutionalization of class conflicts by public or governmental agencies rather than a set of practices which articulate popular demands for participation. Finally, we can identify an authoritarian form of democracy from above in which the state manages public space, inviting the citizens periodically to select a leader, who is then no longer responsible on a daily basis to the electorate. Private life emerges as a sanctuary from state regulation and, in the Germany described by Max Weber and Carl Schmitt, the private offered one possible, if fragile, shelter from the *obrigkeitliche Willkur* (arbitrariness of the authorities). This politico-cultural complex was the historical case of leader-democracy (*Führerdemokratie*).

This typology is regarded here as a mechanism for transcending the limitations of Marshall's theory of citizenship. Although Marshall distinguished between various types of citizenship rights (civil, political and social), he did not develop any view of active or passive citizenship. While agreeing with Mann's argument that we need a comparative perspective on citizenship in different historical contexts, Mann's thesis is limited by

the (largely implicit) Marxist paradigm in which citizenship is merely a
strategy of dominant towards subordinate classes. Hence Mann does not
consider social movements, which are not necessarily or directly tied to
class, as social forces, which contribute to the expansion of social rights.
In order to elaborate this alternative typology, I shall proceed by an
examination of the etymological and cultural roots of the concept of
citizenship in order to emphasize the argument that citizenship does not
have a unitary character.

From Denizens to Citizens

Historically the concept of citizenship is bound up with the development
of the city-state in the classical world of Rome and Greece. In the ancient
world, the city-state was a public arena for rational, free men which
functioned as a collective insurance against external threats, and internal
dispute. In classical Greek and Roman societies, the dominant classes
depended extensively upon slave labour for both direct production and
domestic services. Thus, the dominant class was an urban population of
free, legally constituted, citizens who nevertheless depended on the
exploitation of large agrarian estates by slave labour. Since these slaves
were often acquired by military conquest, every free-born citizen was
threatened by the possibility of servitude and loss of status. Because the
full rights of citizenship were conferred upon members of the *polis* who
had a right to speak and to govern, there was an ideological need to
explain and to legitimize the subordinate status of women, adult slaves
and children; the homosexual subordination of young men was therefore
an acute legal and philosophical problem. The problems of justifying on
rational grounds the existence of slavery came to dominate much of the
central issues of classical philosophy.

Of course, the class structure of the ancient world was far more
complex than a simple division between slave and non-slave. In early
republican Rome, the major social division was between the patricians
and the plebians; the patrician class was constituted by large landowners
who had the rights to function politically and to hold office, playing a
major role in the formation and direction of the army. The plebian class
was composed primarily of landless tenants, who were forced to work
patrician property and were excluded from entry into political life.
Through the operation of credit relations, a plebian debtor would often
be forced into the status of a debt-slave. As the Roman Empire developed,

these divisions in society became more precisely determined and defined, creating an enduring division between the lower classes (the *humiliores*) and the privileged class (the *honestiores*). Within this social context, the notion of citizenship rights had very circumscribed significance, being the status of (rational) property owners who had certain public duties and responsibilities within the city-state.

It would be wrong of course to imagine that the notion of citizenship remained historically static. There was, for example, a definite decline in the moral weight and importance of political commitment to the *polis* after its initial Socratic formulation. The Cynics and the Epicureans tended to give greater importance to the idea of individual autonomy and moral development rather than to the more collective virtues of Aristotelian philosophy. It was the Stoics who reformulated a notion of civic obligation. Thus Marcus Aurelius (121–80 AD) argued that our membership of (and therefore our citizenship in) a common political community was a necessary outcome of the fact that human beings *qua* humans have a common rational faculty, but his idea of political involvement represented a 'weary loyalty' (Sabine 1963: 174) towards his status in society. Eventually the Stoical values of discipline, frugality and industry reflected the changing political reality of the Roman Empire, whose size, social differentiation and bureaucratic complexity no longer corresponded to the moral idea of the *polis* as an ethical association. While Cicero (106–43 BC) had attempted to translate the ancient Greek conceptions of civic virtue and public obligation to the *polis* into a new rhetoric which would be adequate to the changing conditions of Roman society, in the world of later Roman absolutism, philosophers like Seneca (4 BC–65 AD) could at best offer comfort to the citizen and in his *De Clementia* beg rulers like Nero to rule with mercy. The citizen-legion which had been the basis, not only of Roman military power, but an essential basis of social solidarity had broken down. Thus, 'in place of the value of citizenship there is a common equality shared by all sorts and conditions of men; and in place of the state as a positive agency of human perfection there is a coercive power that struggles ineffectually to make an earthly life tolerable' (Sabine 1963: 179–80).

The problem in late Roman antiquity was how to combine an abstract notion of universal citizenship with strong political commitment, that is how to overcome political disengagement by citizenship (Wolin 1961: 77–8). These tensions in the classical world between the heavenly city of rational beings and the earthly city of self-interested men, and between the moral development of the individual and the need for political duty in the public sphere became in large measure also part of the Christian legacy within which political life was ethically dubious.

The term for citizen was derived in classical times from *civitas*, giving rise in Roman times to the notion of a *civitatus*. This etymological origin provided eventually the French term *citoyen* from *cité*, namely an ensemble of citizens enjoying limited rights within a city context. Thus in French we find in the twelfth century the notion of *citeaine* and eventually in the thirteenth century the notion of *comcitien*. A *citoyen* was the 'habitant d'une cité, d'une ville, d'un pays libre; qui aime son pays' (Nodier 1866: 145). A citizen was 'brave, honnête'. It is interesting to note that in the *Social Contract* of 1762, J.-J. Rousseau complained that it was a common mistake to confuse 'townsman' with 'citizen'. He asserted that 'houses make a town, but citizens make a city' (Rousseau 1973: 175). In English, the notion of a citizen can be detected in the medieval concept of *citizen*, but at least in the sixteenth century this term was interchangeable with the notion denizen (*deinsein*). This limited notion of the citizen as simply the inhabitant of a city was both extensive and continuous. Bailey's *Dictionary* says tersely that a citizen is 'a Freeman of a City' (1757). Brown's *Dictionary of the Holy Bible* gives us more fully 'one that has the freedom of trade and other privileges belonging to a city' (1851: 241). It was thus common to regard the inhabitants of a city as citizens, while outsiders beyond the city walls were 'subjects'.

The notion of the city and the historical evolution of autonomous cities played a critical role in the development of philosophical thought about freedom, individuality and civility. Weber thought this constellation was unique to the West: 'only in the Occident is found the concept of citizen (*civis Romanus, citoyen, bourgeois*) because only in the Occident again are there cities in the specific sense' (Weber 1966: 233).

The issue of citizenship was consequently an important issue in his view of the unique character of Western rationalism. These terms were also closely related to ideas about civility and civilization. To leave the countryside in order to enter the city was typically connected with the process of civilization; to become urban was to 'citizenize' the person. The city emerged as a topic in social philosophy with very contradictory meanings. Whereas Voltaire thought that the city was the core of individual freedoms which challenged the false hierarchies of traditional rural society, by the beginning of the nineteenth century the city came to be more frequently seen as the great centre of social corruption and moral decadence. In German social thought, there emerged in the nineteenth century a strong nostalgia for country life and rural practices. This

romantic nostalgia crystallized around the concepts of *Gemeinschaft* and
Gesellschaft in the work of Ferdinand Tönnies (1887), although Tönnies
himself did not share necessarily this conservative commitment to the
'organic' community. However the whole problem of the melancholy
return to nature and the development of bourgeois inwardness (*Inner-
lichkeit*) and loneliness (*Einsamkeit*) has to be located much earlier in
eighteenth-century romanticism. In Germany the radical humanists
generated an ideal vision of the Greek city-state as a major alternative to
the urban society which was developing alongside capitalism. Thus
Schiller, Fichte and Hölderlin merged the features of the Greek *polis* with
those of the medieval town to create an image of burgher culture as an
alternative to the emerging industrial cities of Germany. We can therefore identify a rather significant distinction between the emerging
concept of citizenship in Germany and the more revolutionary idea of
citizenship which had developed in France out of the French Revolution.

In the German philosophical tradition, the notion of social rights and
citizenship was closely connected with the development of the idea of
civil society (*die bürgliche Gesellschaft*). Within the German conception of
civil society, a citizen was any individual who had left the family context
in order to enter the public arena which was dominated by economic
competition and was contrasted with the state as that institution which
was the historical embodiment of reason. In this German tradition the
idea of the citizen was therefore necessarily tied to the idea of the burger,
and civil society was in a sense merely burgerdom. In German this
concept of burgerdom goes back to the fifteenth and sixteenth century,
when the notion of burgership embraced the inhabitants of a burgh who
enjoyed certain privileges and immunities. The *Bürgertum* (bourgeoisie)
was a product of the city who, through training and education, achieved
a civilized mastery of emotions; the result was a new status group, the
Bildungsbürgertum (Martin 1969: 138–45).

In social German philosophy, Hegel's concept of civil society was
adopted from the Scottish Enlightenment in which writers like Adam
Ferguson in *An Essay on the History of Civil Society* (1767) and John Millar
in *Observations Concerning the Distinction of Ranks in Society* (1771) had
attempted to provide a systematic view of the social development of
human societies towards more complex systems. Both Ferguson and
Millar were concerned to understand the development of a sharp
contrast between the 'rude' society of the Highlands and the civilized and
sophisticated world of the urban civilization of Edinburgh and Glasgow.
For Ferguson, it was the ownership of private property which produced

the crucial division between savagery and barbarism, but he feared that the egoism of commercial civilization could destroy the bonds of civil society. In the work of Hegel, civil society was that terrain lying between the family and the political relations of the state, where the state resolved the struggles and contradictions of conflicting interests providing a higher and more universal expression of the particularities of society. Against Hegel, Marx and Engels (1965) in *The German Ideology* of 1845 came to see civil society as the real 'theatre of all history' such that the state became merely an epiphenomenon of more basic social processes. For Marx the citizen of bourgeois theory was merely an abstract subject which disguised the real conflicts lying in the basic structures of society. Therefore, Marx in the debate on the 'Jewish Question' saw the political emancipation of the Jewish community as a rather superficial and partial historical development in the absence of a genuine reorganization of the socio-economic structure of society as such.

While Marx was highly critical of the abstract notion of bourgeois rights and civil society, the notion of civil society survived in critical theory through the writing of Antonio Gramsci (1971), who formulated the interconnections between the state, society and economy in terms of a set of contrasts between consent and coercion, private and public life. For Gramsci, civil society was not simply the domain of individual wills but a system of institutions and organization which had the potential for developing freedom in a system of consent; Gramsci came to believe that the state could play an important part in developing this self-regulation of civil society.

In Germany the absence of a successful radical bourgeois revolution and the development of capitalism from above, via Bismarckian legislation, created a social context in which the conditions for the development of a full and dynamic notion of citizenship were limited, giving rise therefore to the rather restricted conceptions of burghership as the main carrier of rights. The absence of a successful bourgeois-liberal revolution and the continuing political dominance of the Junker class created an underdeveloped civil or public realm. This political structure was reinforced and legitimized by Lutheranism, which sanctified the state as both the representative of the *Volksgemeinschaft* and as the guardian of the privatized individual. The private realm of the individual and the family assumed enormous ethical and educational significance over and against the public.

As the state emerged as the moral guardian of the people, it is easy to see how the state acquired extensive social prestige and powers over civil society. Because Lutheranism failed to offer a normative basis for dissent, the bourgeoisie were, by the end of the nineteenth century, committed to an ideology which supported the state in a context where parliamentary authority was clearly lacking. Sovereignty rested in the law and the state, not in elected assemblies. The result was that 'Nineteenth-century German Liberalism implicitly accepted the subordination of the individual to the moral expectations of the *Volk*, while Gustav Schmoller, for example, was lavish in praise of the unification and rationalization of control by bureaucratization' (Lee 1988: 34). In the political life of twentieth-century Germany, the impact of the First World War, military defeat and the weakness of the Weimar Republic created an environment in which totalitarian solutions were canvassed. Carl Schmitt's view that it was not the responsibility of the state to enter into consensual agreements with an electorate, but to take bold and firm actions against its enemies was a natural consequence of these developments. To be free, from the point of view of the individual citizen, was to serve the state.

A Typology of Citizenship

These comparisons between different histories of citizenship in Europe suggest a model of citizenship development in terms of two dimensions. The first dimension is the passive—active contrast depending on whether citizenship grew from above or below.[1] In the German tradition, citizenship stands in a passive relationship to the state because it is primarily an effect of state action. It is important to note that this distinction is in fact fundamental to the western tradition and can be located in medieval political philosophy, where there were two opposed views of citizenship. In the descending view, the king is all-powerful and the subject is the recipient of privileges. In the ascending view, a free man was a citizen, an active bearer of rights. In the northern city-states of Italy, the Roman law facilitated the adoption of a populist notion of citizenship; the result was that the *populo* came to be regarded as an aggregate of citizens who possessed some degree of autonomous sovereignty. The second dimension is the tension between a private realm of the individual and the family in relationship to the public arena of political action. In the German case, an emphasis on the private (the family, religion, and individual ethical development) was combined with a view of the state as the only source of public authority. This typology allows us to contrast Germany with other historical trajectories.

The contrast between the English and the German traditions of political participation would appear to be very considerable. It was Weber of course who drew attention to the historically important contrast between constitutional law in the Roman continental system and the English judge-made law within the common law tradition. Weber argued that continental constitutionalism provided better safeguards for the individual, but he underestimated the importance of the common law tradition in providing precisely a *common* basis for rights. The struggle against the absolutist state in England had lead to the execution of the king, an expansion of parliamentary authority, the defence of the English common law tradition and the assertion of individual religious rights. Of course, it has long been held that the English tradition of individual rights in fact supported an unequal and rigid class structure. Effective social rights resided in individual rights to property, thereby excluding the majority of the population from real social and political participation. The absence of a land army and the state's dependence on a navy, the early demilitarization of the English aristocracy and the incorporation of the urban merchants into the elite contributed to English gradualism. After the demobilization of the new model army, two royal guard units were retained for primarily ceremonial duties. The British army was not modernized until the late nineteenth century. The monarch could no longer intimidate parliament. A more important point is that the constitutional settlement of 1688 created the British citizen as the British subject, that is a legal personality whose indelible social rights are constituted by a monarch sitting in parliament. The notion of citizen-as-subject indicates clearly the relatively extensive notion of social rights but also the passive character of British civil institutions. The defeat of absolutism in the settlement of 1688 left behind a core of institutions (the Crown, the Church, the House of Lords and traditional attitudes about the family and private life) which continued to dominate British life until the destructive force of the First and Second World Wars brought British culture eventually and reluctantly into the modern world.

By contrast with both the English and German cases, the French conception of citizenship was the consequence of a long historical struggle to break the legal and political monopoly of a court society within a social system which was rigidly divided in terms of estates. The very violence of this social transformation resulted in a highly articulate conception of active citizenship in the revolutionary struggles of the eighteenth century. The old myth that the king represented, combined and integrated the multiplicity of orders, groups and estates had become transparent during the political conflicts of the eighteenth century. Revolutionary political theories, acting against the absolutist conception of sovereignty, followed Rousseau in conceptualizing society as a collection of individuals whose existence would be represented through the general will in popular parliamentary institutions. What bound Frenchmen together into a common nation was again the concept of citizenship. Frenchmen had ceased to be merely subjects of the sovereign and had become instead common citizens of a national entity. There are therefore two parallel movements whereby a state is transformed into a nation at the same time that subjects are transformed into citizens. The differences between the French and English revolutionary traditions may be summarized in two contrasted views of citizenship by Rousseau and Burke. For Rousseau in *The Social Contract* the viability of citizenship required the destruction of all particular intervening institutions which separated the citizen from the state. By contrast, Burke in *Reflections on the Revolution in France* in 1790 argued that the essence of citizenship was the continuity of local groups, particular institutions and regional associations between the sovereign power of the general will and the individual. For Burke an organized civil society must have hierarchy, order, regulation and constraint; its hierarchical character precluded the very possibility of 'the rights of man'.

Finally, the American case represents another variation on the history of western citizenship. The American example shared with the French a strong rejection of centralized power, adopting also the discourse of the rights of man and privileges of independent citizens. The Boston Tea Party was a symbolically significant expression of the idea 'no taxation without representation'. The radical nature of the 'democratic revolution' in America struck observers like Alexis de Tocqueville with great force; he came to regard America as the first macro-experiment in democracy in modern history. For de Tocqueville, the democratic foundation of the nation was explained by the absence of aristocracy, the frontier, and the exclusion of an established church. Although there was a radical tradition of citizenship expressed in the idea of an independent militia, American democracy nevertheless continued to exist alongside a divisive racist and exploitative South. In addition America's welfare state was late to develop and provided very inadequate forms of social citizenship and participation for the majority of the population. This weak tradition of citizenship in welfare terms has been explained by the very strength of American individualism, and by the checks and balances of the federal system; American citizenship was expressed in terms of localism versus centralism, thereby limiting the development of a genuinely national programme of welfare rights. To some extent, the dominance of individualism and the value of personal success have meant that the 'public arena' is typically understood in terms of individual involvement in local voluntary associations. Americans 'have difficulty relating this ideal image to the large-scale forces and institutions shaping their lives' (Bellah et al. 1985: 199). The political is seen as morally suspect. This cultural analysis of American individualism would not therefore contradict Mann's analysis. On the contrary, they may be regarded as complementary. In America, the articulation of sectional interests through democratic institutions constrains the emergence of class-based politics.

The point of this historical sketch has been partly to provide a critique of the monolithic and unified conception of citizenship in Marshall and partly to offer a sociological model of citizenship along two axes, namely public and private definitions of moral activity in terms of the creation of a public space of political activity, and active and passive forms of citizenship in terms of whether the citizen is conceptualized as merely a subject of an absolute authority or as an active political agent.

We can now indicate how this ideal-typical construction might be applied to specific cases:

Citizenship

Below	Above	
Revolutionary French tradition	Passive English case	+
American liberalism	German fascism	−

public space

In France, a revolutionary conception of active citizenship was combined with an attack on the private space of the family, religion and privacy. In a passive democracy, citizenship is handed down from above and the citizen appears as a mere subject (the English case under the seventeenth-century settlement). In a liberal democratic solution, positive democracy emphasizes participation, but this is often contained by a continuing emphasis on privacy and the sacredness of individual opinion. In plebiscitary democracy, the individual citizen is submerged in the sacredness of the state which permits minimal participation in terms of the election of leaders, while again family life is given priority in the arena of personal ethical development. While revolutionary democracy may collapse into totalitarianism, plebiscitary democracy degenerates into fascism. In totalitarian democracy, the 'state, in pushing egalitarianism to the extreme, closes off the private sphere from influencing the course of political affairs' (Prager 1985: 187)

The Geopolitics of Citizenship

Following the work of Barrington Moore (1966), the different routes towards modern polities have distinctive consequences for the character of citizenship. Historically, the presence of a successful bourgeois revolution in the development of politically modern systems was a significant ingredient in establishing parliamentary democracy and its associated civil rights. The revolutionary conflicts against aristocratic privilege in the Glorious Revolution of 1688 and the French Revolution of 1789 have been important in the establishment of the notions of sovereignty and citizenship, representation and social contract, and in the development of the concept of public opinion as significant in the shaping of political life. If a successful revolutionary conflict against aristocratic powers is at least one aspect of the historical emergence of democratic citizenship, then the failure of a liberal bourgeois struggle (as in Germany in 1848) provides one aspect of the peculiarly bureaucratic, authoritarian character of political life in Germany under the aristocratic dominance of the Junkers.

While Moore's primary orientation to the issue of the origins of democracy involved the historical relationship between lords and peasants in the development of modern societies, recent approaches to democracy (and by implication citizenship) have been more concerned with the implications of geopolitics for long-term constitutional change. Thus contemporary democratic politics owes a great deal to the military victories of the 'Anglo-Saxon' powers, but in the future, because of nuclear armaments, 'the war-assisted pattern of change' (Mann 1987: 352) will not be an option. However, if we examine a much longer period of western history, then we can also see that in early modern Europe the pattern of constitutionalism (parliamentary assemblies, city-state immunities, village councils, and so forth) represented an important foundation for later democratic movements. However, societies which were threatened by massive international military assaults were often converted from constitutionalism to military-bureaucratic absolutism. Brian Downing (1988) has shown how the different military histories of Brandenburg-Prussia, England, Sweden and The Netherlands were important in the survival or destruction of early forms of constitutionalism.

Thus, Downing is able to criticize Moore on two grounds, namely his failure to acknowledge early developments in democratic participation and the role of warfare in creating conditions of authoritarian rule. Downing's thesis does however confirm the importance of gradualism in English democratic history (in combination with the role of common law, demilitarization and island isolation) as the basis for (passive) citizenship. These historical accounts of the geopolitics of citizenship are compatible with the typology which has been developed in this argument, because the notion of democracy from above or from below is simply one version of Moore's perspective on the rise of modern democracies. In addition, mass warfare has, in the modern period, created conditions whereby there can be political mobilization to claim rights or to seek the satisfaction of rights through state mediation (Turner 1986b: 67–78).

The principal addition to these comparative studies of the history of citizenship in this article is the argument that the ways in which public space is culturally organized (in relation to notions of individualism, privatism and the ethical status of the domestic) also has important implications for whether the private is seen as an area of deprivation or an arena of moral fulfilment. In classical societies, the private was definitely a space of necessity and privation, whereas in modern societies with an emphasis on achievement orientation in public competition for material success, the private is seen as the space of personal leisure and enhancement. If we regard the historical emergence of the public as in fact the emergence of the political, then the structural relationship between the private and the public, and their cultural meanings, is an essential component in any understanding of the relationships between totalitarianism and democracy. The transfer of sovereignty from the body of the king to the body politic of citizens is thus a major turning point in the history of western democracies, because it indicates a major expansion of political space, indeed the creation of political spaces.

The revolutionary conflicts of the seventeenth and eighteenth centuries gave rise to an expanded notion of political participation and membership. The development of the concept of the political citizen was an important adjunct to the historical development of the nation–state as the principal political unit of contemporary political life. The failure of absolutism and the survival of constitutionalism created a niche for the gradual development of parliamentary rights and political participation. Marshall's work was important therefore in providing a theoretical perspective on a broader and deeper conception of social membership as expressed through the idea of a welfare state being itself the embodiment of certain social rights and claims. Citizenship became a form of entitlement.

Conclusion: The Globalization of Citizenship

While the notion of citizenship continues to provide a normative basis for the defence of the welfare state, certain crucial changes in the organization of global systems have rendered some aspects of the notion of citizenship redundant and obsolete. The contemporary world is structured by two contradictory social processes. On the one hand, there are powerful pressures towards regional autonomy and localism and, on the other, there is a stronger notion of globalism and global political responsibilities. The concept of citizenship is therefore still in a process of change and development. We do not possess the conceptual apparatus to express the idea of global membership, and in this context a specifically national identity appears anachronistic. Indeed the uncertainty of the global context may produce strong political reactions asserting the normative authority of the local and the national over the global and international.

The analysis of citizenship has in recent years become a pressing theoretical issue, given the problems which face the welfare state in a period of economic recession. However, the problem of citizenship is in fact not confined merely to a question of the normative basis of welfare provision; its province is global. It includes, on the one hand, the international consequences of perestroika and glasnost in the Soviet Union, and, on the other, the implications of medical technology for the definition of what will count as a human subject/citizen. While Marshall's aim in formulating a theory of citizenship was by contrast rather modest in its focus (to understand the tensions in Britain between capitalism and social rights), his statement of the issues has proved to be extremely fruitful in sociology and political science.

The limitations of Marshall's approach, however, are equally obvious.

His framework is now widely regarded as evolutionary, analytically vague and ethnocentric. Mann's treatment of citizenship in a comparative and historical context as a 'ruling class strategy' indicates a number of important directions by which the Marshallian framework might be expanded, elaborated and finally transcended. My commentary here on different types of citizenship could be regarded as compatible, therefore, with the spirit of Mann's critique in the sense that only a historical sociology of citizenship can take us out of the Anglophile orbit of the Marshallian view. It has also been argued that Mann's thesis fails to deal with revolutionary conceptions of citizenship, with cultural variations in the definition of public space, and with the problem of status as opposed to class in the formation of citizenship. For example, Mann appears to regard gender, age and race as variables which are irrelevant in the historical emergence of citizenship. Since Mann (1986: 222) has declared status to be 'that most vacuous of sociological terms', this absence is hardly surprising, and yet it can be argued that status is an essential concept for the analysis of modern problems of citizenship (Turner 1988).

In this article I have been concerned with two dimensions which I believe are missing in Mann's attempt to go beyond Marshall, namely the private/public division in western cultures, and the issue of passive and active versions of citizenship. However, any further development of the theory of citizenship will have to deal more fundamentally with societies in which the struggle over citizenship necessarily involves problems of national identity and state formation in a context of multiculturalism and ethnic pluralism. The societies on which this article has largely concentrated — France, Germany, England, the Netherlands and colonial America — were *relatively* homogeneous in ethnic terms during their period of national formation. With the exception of North America, these societies had no internal problem of aboriginality. The question of citizenship was less complicated therefore by questions of ethnic minorities, ethnic pluralism and cultural melting pots; it is partly for this reason that Mann's neglect of ethnicity is not an issue in the societies which he has chosen for debate, but ethnic migration has been critical (indeed crucial) in other contexts such as in South Africa, the Middle East, Australia and New Zealand (Turner 1986b: 64–84). We may in conclusion indicate two possible lines of theoretical development of the (western) notion of citizenship. The first would be the conditions under which citizenship can be formed in societies which are, as it were, constituted by the problems of ethnic complexity (such as Brazil), and the

second would be an analysis of the problems which face the development of global citizenship as the political counter-part of the world
economy.

Notes

A version of this article was first given as a public lecture to the West European
Studies Programme, University of Pittsburgh in 1989. I am grateful to the participants
for their commentary. I would also like to thank the anonymous reviewers of this
article for *Sociology* for their recommendations. My original interest in the whole issue
of citizenship was fostered by Dr Karen Lane's unpublished thesis *Broadcasting
Democracy and Localism*, University of Adelaide 1988. This research was originally
undertaken while I was an Alexander von Humboldt Fellow at Bielefield University,
West Germany 1987–88.

1. The active and passive notion of citizenship can be identified in medieval legal
and political philosophy where it was the product of two contrasted views of sovereign
power, namely whether the king was seen as *primus inter pares* or whether the king was
regarded as the separate and exclusive source of legitimate power. These two views
therefore pinpointed an essential and permanent conflict within a feudal system
between centralized and decentralized power, which involved a struggle over the
monopolization of the means of violence (Giddens 1985: 53–60). In this article,
however, the idea of citizenship from above through the state or from below via more
localized, participatory, civil institutions is derived from Lash and Urry (1987: 4–16).
Within this framework, just as one can speak about the historical organization of
capitalism as a socioeconomic system as a whole from above (for example, Germany) or
from below (such as Britain), so one might analyse the historical structuring of politics
(through the formation of citizenship) within the same paradigm. This particular
perspective on citizenship is also dependent on Claus Offe's analysis of capitalism in
terms of the tensions between economic and political functions (Offe 1985), but this
article, at least by implication, is also an attempt to translate the historical sociology of
Barrington Moore (1966) into a political sociology of citizenship. Finally, my treatment of the private/public dimension has been influenced by Charles Maier's *Changing
Boundaries of the Political* (1988).

References

Althusser, L., *Lenin and Philosophy and other Essays*, New Left Books, London 1971.
Barbalet, J.M., *Citizenship*, Open University Press, Milton Keynes 1988.
Bellah, R., Madsen, F., Sullivan, W.M., Swidler, A. and Tipton, S.M., *Habits of the Heart,
    individualism and commitment in American Life*, Harper & Row, New York 1985.
Berger, P.L., *The Capitalist Revolution*, Basic Books, New York 1986.
Brown, J., *A Dictionary of the Holy Bible*, Blackie, Glasgow 1851.

Calvin, J., *Institution de la Religion Chrétienne*, Volume 4, Sociéte les Belles Lettres, Paris 1939.

Crouch, C., 'Sharing Public Space: states and organized interests in Western Europe', in Hall, A., ed. *States in History*, Basis Blackwell, Oxford 1986.

Downing, B.M., 'Constitutionalism, Warfare and Political Change in Early Modern Europe', *Theory and Society* 17, 1988, pp. 1—56.

Engels, F., *Anti-Dühring*, Foreign Publishing House, Moscow 1959.

Giddens, A., *Profiles and Critiques in Social Theory*, Macmillan, London 1982.

Giddens, A., *The Nation-State and Violence, Volume Two: A Contemporary Critique of Historical Materialism*, Polity Press, Oxford 1985.

Gramsci, A., *Selections from the Prison Notebooks*, New Left Books, London 1971.

Lash, S. and Urry, J., *The End of Organized Capitalism*, Polity Press, Oxford 1987.

Lee, W.R., 'Economic Development and the State in Nineteenth-century Germany', *Economic History Review* 41, 1988, pp. 346—67.

Lefort, C., *The Political Forms of Modern Society*, Polity Press, Oxford 1986.

Lefort, C., *Democracy and Political Theory*, Polity Press, Oxford 1988.

Mann, M., *The Sources of Social Power, Volume 1. A history of power from the beginning to A.D. 1760*, Cambridge University Press, Cambridge 1986.

Maier C.S., ed., *Changing Boundaries of the Political, essays on the evolving balance between the state and society, public and private, in Europe*, Cambridge University Press, Cambridge 1988.

Mann, M. 'Ruling Class Strategies and Citizenship', *Sociology* 21, 1987, pp. 339—54.

Marshall, T.H., *Sociology at the Crossroads*, Heinemann Educational Books, London 1963.

Marshall, T.H., *Social Policy in the Twentieth Century*, Hutchinson, London 1965.

Marshall, T.H., *The Right to Welfare and Other Essays*, Heinemann Educational Books, London 1981.

Martin, A. von, 'Bürgertum', in Bernsdorf, W., ed., *Wörterbuch der Soziologie*, Ferdinand Enkeverlag, Stuttgart 1969.

Mill, J.S., *Utilitarianism, Liberty and Representative Government*, Dent, London 1962.

Moore, B., *Social Origins of Dictatorship and Democracy. Lord and Peasant in the Making of the Modern World*, Penguin Books, Harmondsworth 1966.

Nodier, C., *Dictionnaire Universel de la Langue française* (fifteenth edition), Pierre-Joseph Rey, Paris 1866.

Offe, C., *Disorganized Capitalism*, Polity Press, Oxford 1985.

Offe, C., 'Democracy against the Welfare State? Structural foundation of neo-conservative political opportunities', *Political Theory* X, 1987, pp. 501—37.

Parsons, T., 'Christianity and Modern Industrial Society', in E.A. Tiryakian, ed., *Sociological Theory, Values and Sociocultural Change, Essays in Honor of Pitrim A. Sorokin*, Free Press, New York 1963.

Parsons, T., *Societies, Evolutionary and Comparative Perspectives*, Prentice Hall, Englewood Cliffs 1966.

Parsons, T., *The System of Modern Societies*, Prentice Hall, Englewood Cliffs 1971.

Parsons, T. and Clark, K.B., eds, *The Negro American*, Houghton Mifflin, Boston 1966.

Prager, J., 'Totalitarian and Liberal Democracy: two types of modern political orders', in Alexander, J.C., ed. *Neofunctionalism*, Sage Publications, Beverly Hills 1985.

Rousseau, J.-J., *The Social Contract and Discourses*, Dent, London 1973.

Sabine, G.H., *A History of Political Theory*, Harrap, London 1963.

Smith, A.D., *The Ethnic Origins of Nations*, Basil Blackwell, Oxford 1986.

Tönnies, F., *Community and Association*, Michigan State University Press, Michigan [1887] 1957.

Turner, B.S., 'State, Civil Society and National Development: the Scottish problem', *Australian and New Zealand Journal of Sociology* 20, 1984, pp. 161–82.

Turner, B.S., *Equality*, Ellis Horwood, Chicester, and Tavistock, London 1986a.

Turner, B.S., *Citizenship and Capitalism: The Debate over Reformism*, Allen and Unwin, London 1986b.

Turner, B.S., *Status*, Open University Press, Milton Keynes 1988.

Weber, M., *The City*, Free Press, Glencoe, Illinois 1966.

Wolin, S.S., *Politics and Vision, continuity and innovation in western political thought*, Harrap, London 1961.

3

Context is All:
Feminism and Theories
of Citizenship

Mary Dietz

In Margaret Atwood's powerful novel *The Handmaid's Tale*,[1] the heroine Offred, a member of a new class of 'two-legged wombs' in a dystopian society, often thinks to herself, 'Context is all.' Offred reminds us of an important truth: at each moment of our lives our every thought, value and act — from the most mundane to the most lofty — takes its meaning and purpose from the wider political and social reality that constitutes and conditions us. In her newly reduced circumstances, Offred comes to see that matters beyond one's immediate purview make a great deal of difference with respect to living a more or less free and fully human life. But her realization comes too late.

Unlike Offred, feminists have long recognized as imperative the task of seeking out, defining and criticizing the complex reality that governs the ways we think, the values we hold, and the relationships we share, especially with regard to gender. If context is all, then feminism in its various guises is committed to uncovering what is all around us and to revealing the power relations that constitute the creatures we become. 'The personal is the political' is the credo of this critical practice.

The political and ideological context that most deeply conditions the American experience is liberalism and its attendant set of values, beliefs and practices. Without question, the liberal tradition can count many among its adherents, but it has its critics as well. Over the past decade in the United States, few critics of liberalism have been as persistent or as wide-ranging as the feminists. Certainly no others have been as committed to articulating alternatives to the liberal vision of gender, the family, the sexual division of labour and the relationship between the public and the private realm.[2]

In this chapter I shall focus on the aspect of the feminists' critique that concerns citizenship. First I will outline the dominant features of liberalisms's conception of citizenship, and then I will introduce two current feminist challenges to that conception. What I ultimately want to argue, however, is that although both of these challenges offer important insights, neither of them leads to a suitable alternative to the liberal view or a sufficiently compelling feminist political vision. In the third section I will make a preliminary sketch of what such a feminist vision of citizenship might be. In part, I would have it reconfirm the idea that 'equal access is not enough'.

I

The terrain of liberalism is vast, and its historical basis has over the past century been extensively surveyed in social, political and moral theory.[3] All I shall present here is the bare bones of the liberal conception of citizenship, but this skeletal construction may sufficiently set off the feminist critiques that follow. With this in mind and the caveat that all conceptions change through time, we can begin by considering the features that have more or less consistently distinguished the views of liberal political thinkers.

First, there is the notion that human beings are atomistic, rational agents whose existence and interests are ontologically prior to society.[4] In the liberal society one might say that context is not 'all'. It is nothing, for liberalism conceives of the needs and capacities of individuals as being independent of any immediate social or political condition.[5] What counts is that we understand human beings as rational individuals who have intrinsic worth.

A second tenet of liberal political thought is that society should ensure the freedom of all its members to realize their capabilities. This is the central ethical principle of the western liberal tradition. Perhaps the classic formulation is John Stuart Mill's observation that 'the only freedom which deserves the name, is that of pursuing our own good in our own way, so long as we do not attempt to deprive others of theirs, or impede their efforts to obtain it.'[6]

Closely associated with the principle of individual liberty is a third feature — an emphasis on human equality. Liberal theorists may differ in their formulations of this principle but not on its centrality. Locke, for example, held that 'reason is the common rule and measure that God has given to mankind' and therefore that all men must be considered created equal and thereby worthy of the same dignity and respect. Bentham argued (not always consistently) that the case for equality rests on the fact that all individuals have the same capacity for pleasure and hence that the happiness of society is maximized when everyone has the same amount of wealth or income. In his 'Liberal Legislation and Freedom of Contract', T.H. Green proclaimed that 'everyone has an interest in securing to everyone else the free use and enjoyment and disposal of his possessions, so long as that freedom on the part of one does not interfere with a like freedom on the part of others, because such freedom contributes to that equal development of the faculties of all which is the highest good of all.'[7] Since liberal theories usually begin with some version of the presumption of perfect equality among individual men, it is a relatively small step from this to the related argument that societal justice entrails equal suffrage, in which every single person should count, in Herbert Spencer's words, 'for as much as any other single individual in the community'.[8] As Allison Jagger writes, 'Liberalism's belief in the ultimate worth of the individual is expressed in political egalitarianism.'[9]

This egalitarianism takes the form of what theorists call 'negative liberty', which Sir Isaiah Berlin in his classic essay on freedom characterizes as 'the area within which a man can act unobstructed by others'.[10] It is the absence of obstacles to possible choices and activities. What is at stake in this liberal conception is neither the 'right' choice nor the 'good' action, but simply the freedom of the individual to choose his own values or ends without interference from others and consistent with a similar liberty for others. At the core of negative liberty, then, is a fourth feature of liberalism that speaks to the individual in his political guise as citizen: the conception of the individual as the 'bearer of formal rights' designed to protect him from the infringement or interference of others and to guarantee him the same opportunities or 'equal access' as others.

The concept of rights is of fundamental importance to the liberal political vision. In *A Theory of Justice*, John Rawls offers this classic formulation of the liberal view: 'Each person possesses an inviolability founded on justice that even the welfare of society as a whole cannot override.... The rights secured by justice are not subject to political bargaining or the calculus of social interests.'[11]

Not only does the concept of rights reinforce the underlying liberal principles of individual freedom and formal equality; it also sets up the distinction between 'private' and 'public' that informs so much of the liberal perspective on family and social institutions. Individual rights correspond to the notion of a private realm of freedom, separate and distinct from that of the public. Although liberal theorists disagree about the nature and degree of state intervention in the public realm — and even about what counts as 'public' — they nevertheless accept the idea that certain rights are inviolable and exist in a private realm where the state cannot legitimately interfere. For much of liberalism's past this private realm has subsumed, in Agnes Heller's phrase, 'the household of the emotions' — marriage, family, housework and childcare. In short, the liberal notion of 'the private' has included what has been called 'woman's sphere' as 'male property' and sought not only to preserve it from the interference of the public realm but also to keep those who 'belong' in that realm — women — from the life of the public.[12]

Another feature of liberalism tied to all of the above is the idea of the free individual as competitor. To understand it, we might recall liberalism's own context, its distinctive history and origin.[13] Liberalism emerged amid the final disintegration of, in Karl Marx's words, those 'motley feudal ties' — in the decline of aristocracy and the rise of a new order of merchants and entrepreneurs with a 'natural propensity', as Adam Smith wrote, 'to trade, truck, and barter'. The life of liberalism, in other words, began in capitalist market societies, and as Marx argued, it can only be fully comprehended in terms of the social and economic institutions that shaped it. For Max Weber, liberal political thought inherited the great transformation wrought by Protestantism and a new ethic of self and work soon to replace privilege, prescription and primacy of rank. As both Marx and Weber recognized, liberalism was the practical consciousness, or the theoretical legitimation, of the values and practices emanating from the newly emergent market society. Accordingly, liberalism lent support to the active pursuit of things beneficial to an economic system based on production for the sake of profit.

Among these 'things beneficial' is the notion of the rational man as a competitive individual who tends naturally to pursue his own interest and maximize his own gain. Although it would be mistaken to suggest that all liberal theorists conceive of human nature as being egoistic, most do argue that people tend naturally in this direction and must work to develop moral capacities to counter their basic selfish, acquisitive inclinations.[14] Thus, we can at least generally conclude that, for liberals, the motive force of human action is not to be found in any noble desires to achieve 'the good life' or 'the morally virtuous society' but rather in the inclination toward individual advancement or (in capitalist terms) the pursuit of profit according to the rules of the market.[15] Taken in this light, then, the liberal individual might be understood as the competitive entrepreneur, his civil society as an economic marketplace, and his ideal as the equal opportunity to engage, as Adam Smith wrote, in 'the race for wealth, and honors, and preferments'.

Vital in this race is the very issue that concerns us here – the equality of access to the race itself, to the market society. What liberty comes to mean in this context is a set of formal guarantees to the individual that he (and later she) may enjoy a fair start in Smith's 'race'. What citizenship comes to mean in this liberal guise is something like equal membership in an economic and social sphere, more or less regulated by government and more or less dedicated to the assumption that the 'market maketh man'.[16] To put this another way, under liberalism, citizenship becomes less a collective, political activity than an individual, economic activity – the right to pursue one's interests, without hindrance, in the marketplace. Likewise, democracy is tied more to representative government and the right to vote than to the idea of the collective, participatory activity of citizens in the public realm.

This vision of the citizen as the bearer of rights, democracy as the capitalist market society and politics as representative government is precisely what makes liberalism, despite its admirable and vital insistence on the values of individual freedom and equality, seem so politically barren to so many of its critics, past and present, conservative and radical. As far as feminism is concerned, perhaps Mary Shanley best sums up the problem liberalism poses when she writes:

> While liberal ideals have been efficacious in overturning restrictions on women as individuals, liberal theory does not provide the language or concepts to help us understand the various kinds of human interdependence which are part of the life of both families and polities, nor to articulate a feminist vision of 'the good life.' Feminists are thus in the awkward position of having to use rhetoric in dealing with the state that does not adequately describe their goals and that may undercut their efforts at establishing new modes of life.[17]

II

For good and obvious reasons, one might expect that a feminist critique of liberalism would best begin by uncovering the reality behind the idea of equal access. Not only is equal access a central tenet of liberal thought; it is also a driving part of our contemporary political discourse that is used both to attack and to defend special pleas for women's rights.

But a complementary approach may be in order as well. There is merit, I think, to the argument that to begin with the question of equal access is already to grant too much, to deal too many high cards to the liberal hand. Quite literally, 'access is not enough'. For once in the domain of 'equal access talk', we are tied into a whole network of liberal concepts — rights, interests, contracts, individualism, representative government, negative liberty. These open up some avenues of discourse but at the same time block off others. As Shanley implies, for feminists to sign on to these concepts may be to obscure rather than to illuminate a vision of politics, citizenship, and 'the good life' that is appropriate to feminist values and concerns.

By this I do not mean to suggest that feminists who proceed from the question of access are doing something unhelpful or unimportant. On the contrary, by using gender as a unit of analysis, feminist scholars have revealed the inegalitarianism behind the myth of equal opportunity and made us aware of how such presumptions deny the social reality of unequal treatment, sexual discrimination, cultural stereotypes and women's subordination both at home and in the marketplace. To the extent that this sort of gender analysis leads to positive political programmes — the extension of pregnancy leaves, affirmative action plans, childcare facilities, comparable-worth wages, sexual harassment laws, health care benefits — feminists give indispensable assistance to liberal practice.

However, we should not overlook the fact that this sort of analysis has boundaries that are determined by the concepts of liberalism and the questions they entail. So, for example, when power is perceived in terms of access to social, economic or political institutions, other possibilities (including the radical one that power has nothing to do with access to institutions at all) are left out. Or to take another example, if one establishes the enjoyment of rights or the pursuit of free trade as the criterion of citizenship, alternative conceptions like civic activity and participatory self-government are overlooked. Liberalism tends towards both an understanding of power as access and a conception of citizenship as civil liberty. What I want to emphasize is that neither of these formulations is adequate in and of itself or appropriate for a feminist political theory.

Of course, few feminist theorists would find these remarks startling or new. Indeed, much of recent feminist thought (liberal feminism notwithstanding) has been directed towards revealing the problems a liberal political theory poses for a vision of women's liberation and human emancipation. A variety of arguments and approaches has been articulated. Some have focused on the epistemological and ontological roots of liberalism, others on its implications for an ethical under-standing of personhood, still others on the assumptions that underlie its methodology.[18]

On the political side and with regard to the liberal theory of freedom, the role of the state, the public and the private, and capitalism and democracy, feminist critics seem to fall into two camps — the Marxists and what I will call the maternalists.[19] These two camps are of primary concern in this chapter because they address issues of 'the good life' and, more precisely, the nature of political community. A brief look at each should suffice to bring us up to date on the feminist alternatives to the liberal conception of the citizen — alternatives that are, as I shall go on to argue, not fully satisfactory counters to the liberal view, although they provide suggestive and thought-provoking contributions to the political debate.

First, the Marxists. Feminists working within the Marxist tradition seek to reveal the capitalist and patriarchal foundations of the liberal state as well as the oppression inherent in the sexual division of labor — or, as one thinker puts it, 'the consequences of women's dual contribu-tion to subsistence in capitalism'.[20] At stake in this economic critique, as another theorist argues, is the notion of the 'state's involvement in protecting patriarchy as a system of power, much in the same way it protects capitalism and racism ...'[21] In so far as they believe that the state participates in the oppression of women, Marxist feminists hold that the idea of the rights of citizenship granted by the state is a sham, a convenient ideological fiction that serves to obscure the underlying reality of a dominant male ruling class. Accordingly, so these theorists contend, the liberation of women will be possible only when the liberal state is overthrown and its capitalist and patriarchal structure dismantled. What will emerge is an end to the sexual division of labour and 'a feminist politics that moves beyond liberalism'.[22] What most Marxist feminists seem to mean by these politics is the egalitarian reordering of productive and reproductive labour and the achievement of truly liberating human relations, a society of 'propertyless producers of use values'.[23]

The strengths of this critique should be obvious. Marxist feminists would have us recognize that a system of economics and gender rooted in capitalist, male-dominant structures underlies much of liberal ideology, from the notion of independent, rational man to the conception of separate private and public realms, from the value of individualism to the equation of freedom with free trade. As such, the Marxist-feminist analysis reveals numerous inadequacies in the liberal feminist position, particularly in its mainstream view of women's work and its reliance on the law, the state, interest groups, and state-instituted reforms as the source of social justice, individual equality, and 'access'. The advantage of the Marxist-feminist approach is not only its critique of capitalism, which reveals the exploitative and socially constructed nature of women's work, but also its political critique, which challenges the liberal assumption that representative government is the sole sanctuary for politics and the legitimate arbiter of social change.

Nevertheless, even though the Marxist-feminist critique has much to offer from the standpoint of historical materialism, it has little to say on the subject of citizenship. As Sheldon Wolin has noted, 'Most Marxists are interested in the "masses" or the workers, but they dismiss citizenship as a bourgeois conceit, formal and empty ...'[24] Unfortunately, Marxist feminists are no exception to this generalization. *Citizenship* hardly appears in their vocabulary, much less any of the rest of its family of concepts: participation, action, democracy, community and political freedom.

To the extent that Marxist feminists discuss citizenship at all, they usually conflate it with labour, class struggle and socialist revolution, and with the advent of social change and certain economic conditions. In their view, true citizenship is realized with the collective ownership of the means of production and the end of oppression in the relations of reproduction. They associate both of these ideas with revolutionary action and the disappearance of the patriarchal state. In their approach to citizenship, Marxist feminists tend to reduce politics to revolutionary struggle, women to the category of 'reproducers', and freedom to the realization of economic and social equality and the overthrowing of natural necessity. Once freedom is achieved, they seem to say, politics ends or becomes little more than what Marx himself once termed 'the administration of things'.

Now no one would deny that economic equality and social justice empower people. A society that values and strives for them with both men and women in mind deserves admiration and respect. What I am suggesting is that because Marxist feminism stops here, its liberatory vision of how things will be 'after the revolution' is incomplete, for what emerges is a picture of economic, not political, freedom and a society of autonomous and fulfilled social beings, not a polity of citizens. As a result, a whole complex of vital political questions is sidestepped or ignored: What is political freedom? What does it mean to be a citizen? What does an expressly feminist political consciousness require? Or, to put the matter more bluntly, is there more to feminist politics than revolutionary struggle against the state?

The second camp of feminist theorists, the maternalists, would answer this last question with a resounding yes. They would have us reconsider both the liberal and the Marxist views of citizenship[25] and become committed to a conception of female political consciousness that is grounded in the virtues of woman's private sphere, primarily in mothering. Unlike the Marxist feminists, the maternal feminists hold that, as important as social justice is, it is not a sufficient condition for a truly liberatory feminist politics. Women must be addressed as mothers, not as 'reproducers', and as participants in the public realm, not just as members of the social and economic orders.

Like the Marxist feminists, however, the maternal feminists eschew the liberal notion of the citizen as an individual holder of rights protected by the state. For the maternalist, such a notion is at best morally empty and at worst morally subversive since it rests on a distinctly masculine conception of the person as an independent, self-interested, economic being. When one translates this notion into a broader conception of politics, the maternal feminist argues, one is left with a vision of citizens as competitive marketeers and jobholders for whom civic activity is, at most, membership in interest groups. Thus, the maternal feminist would deny precisely what the liberal would defend — an individualist rights-based, contractual conception of citizenship and a view of the public realm as one of competition. As one maternalist puts it:

> The problem — or one of the problems — with a politics that begins and ends with mobilizing resources, achieving maximum impacts, calculating prudentially, articulating interest group claims ... and so on, is not only its utter lack of imagination but its inability to engage in the reflective allegiance and committed loyalty of citizens. Oversimply, no substantive sense of civic virtue, no vision of political community that might serve as the groundwork of a life in common, is possible within a political life dominated by a self-interested, predatory, individualism.[26]

Maternal feminism is expressly designed to counter what it thinks are the arid and unimaginative qualities of the prevailing liberal view and, more emphatically, to present an alternative sense of civic virtue and citizenship. As a first step, it wants to establish the moral primacy of the family. Although this may seem to some a strange start for a feminist politics, the maternalists would have us rethink the rigid, liberal distinction of public and private realms and consider instead the 'private' as the locus for a possible public morality and as a model for the activity of citizenship itself. Or, to put this another way, maternal feminism criticizes 'statist' politics and individualist persons, and offers in their place the only other alternative it sees — a politics informed by the virtues of the private realm, and a personhood committed to relational capacities, love, and caring for others.

What makes this view expressly feminist (rather than, say, traditionally conservative) is its claim that women's experience as mothers in the private realm endows them with a special capacity and a 'moral imperative' for countering both the male liberal individualist world-view and its masculinist notion of citizenship. Jean Bethke Elshtain describes mothering as a 'complicated, rich, ambivalent, vexing, joyous activity' that upholds the principle that 'the reality of a single human child [must] be kept before the mind's eye.'[27] For her, the implications mothering holds for citizenship are clear: 'Were maternal thinking to be taken as the base for feminist consciousness, a wedge for examining an increasingly overcontrolled public world would open immediately.'[28]

Not only would maternal thinking chasten the 'arrogant' (i.e. male) public; it would also provide the basis for a whole new conception of power, citizenship and the public realm. The citizen that emerges is a loving being who, in Elshtain's words, is 'devoted to the protection of vulnerable human life' and seeks to make the virtues of mothering the 'template' for a new, more humane public world.

Much of the maternalist argument takes its inspiration from, or finds support in, the psychoanalytic object-relations theory of Nancy Chodorow and the moral development theory of Carol Gilligan.[29] These scholars argue that striking contrasts exist between men and women and can be understood in terms of certain experiential differences in the early stages of their development. At the crux of Chodorow and Gilligan's findings is the implication that women's morality is tied to a more mature and humane set of moral values than men's.[30] Gilligan identifies a female 'ethic of care' that differs from the male 'ethic of justice'. The ethic of care revolves more around responsibility and relationships than rights, and more around the needs of particular situations than the application of general rules of conduct. Maternal feminists seize upon this psychological 'binary opposition' and, in effect, politicize it. In their work, 'the male voice' is that of the liberal individualist who stands in opposition to the female, whose voice is that of the compassionate citizen as loving mother. For maternal feminists, as for feminist psychologists, there is no doubt about which side of the opposition is normatively superior and deserving of elevation, both as a basis for political consciousness and as an ethical way of being. The maternalists might say that the female morality of responsibility 'must extend its imperative to men', but they nevertheless grant a pride of place to women and to 'women's sphere', — the family — as the wellspring of this new 'mode of public discourse'.[31] They also maintain that public discourse and citizenship should be informed by the virtues of mothering — love, attentiveness, compassion, care and 'engrossment' — in short, by all the virtues the liberal, statist, public realm disdains.

What are we to make of this vision of feminist citizenship? There is, I think, much to be gained from the maternalist approach, especially if we consider it within the context of the liberal and Marxist-feminist views. First, the maternalists are almost alone among other 'feminisms' in their concern with the meaning of citizenship and political consciousness. Although we may disagree with their formulations, they deserve appreciation for making citizenship a matter of concern in a movement that (at least on its academic side) is too often caught up in the psychological, the literary, and the social rather than in problems of political theory that feminists must face. Second, the maternalists remind us of the inadequacy and limitations of a rights-based conception of the individual and a view of social justice as equal access. They would have us understand the dimensions of political morality in other ways and politics itself as potentially virtuous. Third, in an era when politics has on all sides become something like a swear word, the maternal feminists would have us rehumanize the way we think about political participation and recognize how, as interrelated 'selves', we can strive for a more humane, relational and shared community than our current political circumstances allow.

Despite these contributions, however, much is troubling about the maternalists' conception of citizenship. It has the same problems as do all theories that hold one side of an opposition to be superior to the other. For the maternalists, women are more moral than men because they are, or can be, or are raised by, mothers and because mothering itself is necessarily

and universally an affective, caring, loving activity. Leaving aside
what should be the obvious and problematic logical and sociological
character of these claims, suffice it to say that the maternalists stand in
danger of committing precisely the same mistake they find in the liberal
view. They threaten to turn historically distinctive women into a-
historical, universalized entities.[32]

Even more serious is the conviction of the maternalists that feminists
must choose between two worlds — the masculinist, competitive, statist
public and the maternal, loving, virtuous private. To choose the public
world, they argue, is to fall prey to both a politics and an ethic that
recapitulates the dehumanizing features of the liberal-capitalist state. To
choose the private world, however, is not only to reassert the value of a
'women's realm' but also to adopt a maternal ethic potentially appropriate for citizenship, a deeply moral alternative to the liberal, statist
one.[33]

When we look to mothering for a vision of feminist citizenship,
however, we look in the wrong place — or, in the language of the
maternalists, to the wrong 'world'. At the centre of the mothering
activity is not the distinctive political bond among equal citizens but the
intimate bond between mother and child. But the maternalist would
offer us no choice in the matter: we must turn to the 'intimate private'
because the 'statist public' is corrupt. This choice is a specious one,
however. Indeed, by equating the public with statist politics and the
private with the virtue of intimacy, maternalist feminism reveals itself to
be closer to the liberal view than we might at first suppose. Thus it is
open to much the same charge as liberalism: its conception of citizenship
is informed by a flawed conception of politics as impersonal, representative government. That liberalism is content to maintain such a conception and that maternalist feminism wants to replace it with a set of
prescriptions drawn from the private is not the real issue. The problem
for a feminist conception is that neither of the above will do, because
both leave us with a one-sided view of politics and therefore of citizenship. What we need is an entirely different conception. For the
remainder of this chapter, I will sketch out an alternative basis for a
feminist political vision, with a view to developing a more detailed
feminist vision in the future. I offer the following recommendations
more as a programmatic outline than as a comprehensive theory.

III

My basic point is a straightforward one: for a vision of citizenship, feminists should turn to the virtues, relations and practices that are expressly political and, more exactly, participatory and democratic. What this requires, among other things, is a willingness to perceive politics in a way neither liberals nor maternalists do: as a human activity that is not necessarily or historically reducible to representative government or 'the arrogant, male, public realm'. By accepting such judgements, the feminist stands in danger of missing a valuable alternative conception of politics that is historically concrete and very much a part of women's lives. That conception is perhaps best called the democratic one, and it takes politics to be the collective and participatory engagement of citizens in the determination of the affairs of their community. The community may be the neighbourhood, the city, the state, the region or the nation itself. What counts is that all matters relating to the community are undertaken as 'the people's affair'.[34]

From a slightly different angle, we might understand democracy as the form of politics that brings people together as citizens. Indeed, the power of democracy rests in its capacity to transform the individual as teacher, trader, corporate executive, child, sibling, worker, artist, friend, or mother into a special sort of political being, a citizen among other citizens. Thus, democracy offers us an identity that neither liberalism, with its propensity to view the citizen as an individual bearer of rights, nor maternalism, with its attentiveness to mothering, provides. Democracy gives us a conception of ourselves as 'speakers of words and doers of deeds' mutually participating in the public realm. To put this another way, the democratic vision does not legitimize the pursuit of every separate, individual interest or the transformation of private into public virtues. In so far as it derives its meaning from the collective and public engagement of peers, it sees citizens neither as wary strangers (as the liberal marketplace would have it) nor as 'loving intimates' (as the maternalist family imagines).

To return to my earlier point, democratic citizenship is a practice unlike any other; it has a distinctive set of relations, virtues, and principles all its own. Its relation is that of civic peers; its guiding virtue is mutual respect; its primary principle is the 'positive liberty' of democracy and self-government, not simply the 'negative liberty' of non-interference. To assume, then, that the relations that accompany the capitalist marketplace or the virtues that emerge from the intimate experience of mothering are the models for the practice of citizenship is to misperceive the distinctive characteristics of democratic political life and to misconstrue its special relations, virtues and principles.

The maternalists would have us believe that this democratic political condition would, in fact, flow from the 'insertion' of women's virtues as mothers into the public world. There is no reason to think that mothering necessarily induces commitment to democratic practices. Nor are there good grounds for arguing that a principle like 'care for vulnerable human life' (as noble as that principle is) by definition encompasses a defence of participatory citizenship. An enlightened despotism, a welfare-state, a single-party bureaucracy and a democratic republic may all respect mothers, protect children's lives and show compassion for the vulnerable.

The political issue for feminists must not be just whether children are protected (or any other desirable end achieved) but how and by whom those ends are determined. My point is this: as long as feminists focus only on questions of social and economic concern — questions about children, family, schools, work, wages, pornography, abortion, abuse — they will not articulate a truly political vision, nor will they address the problem of citizenship. Only when they stress that the pursuit of those social and economic concerns must be undertaken through active engagement as citizens in the public world and when they declare the activity of citizenship itself a value will feminists be able to claim a truly liberatory politics as their own.

I hope it is clear that what I am arguing for is the democratization of the polity, not interest-group or single-issue politics-as-usual. A feminist commitment to democratic citizenship should not be confused with either the liberal politics of pressure groups and representative government or the idea that after victory or defeat on an issue, the game is over and we can 'go home'. As one democratic theorist writes:

> The radical democrat does not agree ... that after solving [a] problem it will be safe to abandon the democratic struggle and disband the organizations.... The radical democrat does not believe that any institutional or social arrangement can give an automatic and permanent solution to the main question of political virtue, or can repeal what may be the only scientific law political science has ever produced: power corrupts.[35]

The key idea here is that citizenship must be conceived of as a continuous activity and a good in itself, not as a momentary engagement

(or a socialist revolution) with an eye to a final goal or a societal arrange-
ment. This does not mean, of course, that democratic citizens do not
pursue specific social and economic ends. Politics is about such things,
after all, and the debates and discussions of civic peers will necessarily
centre on issues of social, political and economic concern to the
community. But at the same time the democratic vision is, and feminist
citizenship must be, more than this. Perhaps it is best to say that this is a
vision fixed not on an end but rather inspired by a principle — freedom
— and by a political activity — positive liberty. That activity is a
demanding process that never ends, for it means engaging in public
debate and sharing responsibility for self-government. What I am
pressing for, in both theory and practice, is a feminist revitalization of
this activity.

The reader who has followed me this far is perhaps now wondering
whether I have not simply reduced feminist political consciousness to
democratic consciousness, leaving nothing in this vision of feminist
citizenship for feminism itself. In concluding these reflections, let me
suggest why I think the revitalization of democratic citizenship is an
especially appropriate task for feminists to undertake. Although the
argument can be made more generally, I will direct my remarks to
feminism in the United States.

Like Offred in *The Handmaid's Tale*, Americans live in reduced
circumstances, politically speaking. How we understand ourselves as
citizens has little to do with the democratic norms and values I have just
defended, and it is probably fair to say that most Americans do not think
of citizenship in this way at all. We seem hypnotized by a liberal conception of citizenship as rights, an unremitting consumerism that we
confuse with freedom, and a capitalist ethic that we take as our collective
identity.[36] Sheldon Wolin has noted that in the American political tradition there exist two 'bodies' within the historic 'body of the people' — a
collectivity informed by democratic practices on the one hand and a
collectivity informed by an anti-democratic political economy on the
other.[37] The latter is a 'liberal-capitalist citizenship' that has emerged
triumphant today. Truly democratic practices have nearly ceased to be a
part of politics in the United States. They exist only on the margins.
More disturbing still, I think, even the memory of these practices seems
to elude our collective imagination. As Hannah Arendt puts it, citizenship is the 'lost treasure' of American political life.

What I want to argue is that we may yet recover the treasure. We may
be able to breathe new life into the people's other 'body' — into our

democratic 'selves'. This prospect brings us back to feminism, which I think is a potential source for our political resuscitation. Feminism has been more than a social cause; it has been a political movement with distinctive attributes. Throughout its second wave in America, the movement has been informed by democratic organization and practice — by spontaneous gatherings and marches, diverse and multitudinous action groups, face-to-face assemblies, consensus decision-making, non-hierarchical power structures, open speech and debate.[38] That is, embodied within the immediate political past of feminism in this country are forms of freedom that are far more compatible with the 'democratic body' of the American experience than with the liberal-capitalist one.[39] These particular feminist forms are, potentially at least, compatible with the idea of collective, democratic citizenship on a wider scale.

I say 'potentially' because feminists must first transform their own democratic practices into a more comprehensive theory of citizenship before they can arrive at an alternative to the non-democratic liberal theory. Feminist political practice will not in some automatic way become an inspiration for a new citizenship. Instead, feminists must become self-conscious political thinkers — defenders of democracy — in a land of liberalism. To be sure, this task is neither easy nor short-term but it is possible for feminists to undertake it in earnest because the foundation is already set in the movement's own experiences, in its persistent attention to issues of power, structure, and democracy, and in the historical precedent of women acting as citizens in the United States.[40]

A warning is in order, however. What a feminist defence of democracy must at all costs avoid is the temptation of 'womanism'. To turn to 'women of the republic' and to feminist organization for inspiration in articulating democratic values is one thing; it is quite another to conclude that therein lies evidence of women's 'superior democratic nature' or of their 'more mature' political voice. A truly democratic defence of citizenship cannot afford to launch its appeal from a position of gender opposition and women's superiority. Such a premise would posit as a starting point precisely what a democratic attitude must deny — that one group of citizens' voices is generally better, more deserving of attention, more worthy of emulation, more moral, than another's. A feminist democrat cannot give way to this sort of temptation, lest democracy itself lose its meaning, and citizenship its special nature. With this in mind, feminists would be well advised to secure the political defence of their theory of democratic citizenship not only in their own territory but also in the diversity of other democratic territories historical and contemporary, male and female. We might include the townships and councils of revolutionary America, the populist National Farmers Alliance, the sit-down strikes of the 1930s, the civil rights movement, the soviets of the Russian Revolution, the French political clubs of 1789, the Spanish anarchist affinity groups, the KOR (Workers' Defence Committee) in Poland, the 'mothers of the disappeared ones' in Argentina, and so on. In short, the aim of this political feminism is to remember and bring to light the many examples of democratic practices already in existence and to use these examples as inspiration for a form of political life that would challenge the dominant liberal one.[41] What this aim requires is not only a feminist determination to avoid 'womanism' while remaining attentive to women but also a commitment to the activity of citizenship, which includes and requires the participation of men.

I began these reflections by agreeing with Offred that 'context is all'. I end on what I hope is a complementary and not an overly optimistic note. We are indeed conditioned by the contexts in which we live, but we are also the creators of our political and social constructions and we can change them if we are so determined. The recent history of democratic politics in this country has not been an altogether happy one, despite spontaneous movements and periodic successes. Rather than occasion despair, however, perhaps this realization can work to strengthen and renew our sense of urgency concerning our present condition and what is to be done.

First, however, the urgency must be felt, and the spirit necessary for revitalizing citizenship must be enlivened in the public realm. Democracy, in other words, awaits its 'prime movers'. My aim here has been to argue that one such mover might be feminism and to suggest why I think feminism is well suited to this demanding and difficult task that would benefit us all.

Notes

1. Margaret Atwood, *The Handmaid's Tale*, Simon & Schuster, New York 1986.
2. For some idea of the wide-ranging nature of the feminist critique of liberalism, see the following: Irene Diamond, ed., *Families, Politics, and Public Policy: A Feminist Dialogue on Women and the State*, Longman, New York 1983; Zillah Einstein, *The Radical*

Future of Liberal Feminism, Longman, New York 1981; Jean Bethke Elshtain, *Public Man, Private Woman,* Princeton University Press, Princeton 1981; Sandra Harding and Merrill Hintikka, *Discovering Reality: Feminist Perspectives on Epistemology, Metaphysics, Methodology, and the Philosophy of Science,* Reidel, Dordrecht 1983; Allison Jagger, *Feminist Politics and Human Nature,* Rowman and Allenheld, New York 1983; Juliet Mitchell and Ann Oakley, *The Rights and Wrongs of Women,* Penguin Books, Hardmondsworth 1976; Linda Nicholson, *Gender and History,* Columbia University Press, New York 1986; and Susan Moller Okin, *Women in Western Political Thought,* Princeton University Press, Princeton, NJ 1979. For a feminist critique of social contract theory, see Seyla Benhabib, 'The Generalized and Concrete Other: The Kohlberg—Gilligan Controversy and Feminist Theory', *Praxis International* 5 (4), 1986, pp. 402—24; Christine Di Stephano, 'Masculinity as Ideology in Political Theory: Hobbesian Man Considered', *Women's Studies International Forum* 6 (6), 1983; Carole Pateman, 'Women and Consent', *Political Theory* 8 (2), 1980, pp. 149—68; Carole Pateman and Teresa Brennan, 'Mere Auxiliaries to the Commonwealth: Women and the Origins of Liberalism', *Political Studies* 27 (2), 1979, pp. 183—200; and Mary Lyndon Shanley, 'Marriage Contract and Social Contract in Seventeenth-Century English Political Thought', *Western Political Quarterly* 32 (1), 1979, pp. 79—91. For a critique of the 'rational man', see Nancy Hartsock, *Money, Sex, and Power,* Longman, New York 1983; Genevieve Lloyd, *Man of Reason,* University of Minnesota Press, Minneapolis 1984; and Iris Marion Young, 'Impartiality and the Civic Public: Some Implications of Feminist Critiques of Moral and Political Theory', *Praxis International* 5 (4), 1986, pp. 381—401. On Locke, see Melissa Butler, 'Early Liberal Roots of Feminism: John Locke and the Attack on Patriarchy', *American Political Science Review* 72 (1), 1978, pp. 135—50; Lorenne M.G. Clark, 'Women and Locke: Who Owns the Apples in the Garden of Eden?' in Clark and Lynda Lange, eds, *The Sexism of Social and Political Theory,* University of Toronto Press, Toronto 1979; and Carole Pateman, 'Sublimation and Reification: Locke, Wolin, and the Liberal Democratic Conception of the Political', *Politics and Society* 5, 1975, pp. 441—67. On Mill, see Julia Annas, 'Mill and the Subjection of Women', *Philosophy* 52, 1977, pp. 179—94; Richard W. Krouse, 'Patriarchal Liberalism and Beyond: From John Stuart Mill to Harriet Taylor', in Jean Bethke Elshtain, ed., *The Family in Political Thought,* University of Massachusetts Press, Amherst 1982; and Jennifer Ring, 'Mill's *Subjection of Women*: The Methodological Limits of Liberal Feminism', *Review of Politics* 47 (1), 1985. On liberal moral theory, see Lawrence Blum, 'Kant and Hegel's Moral Paternalism: A Feminist Response', *Canadian Journal of Philosophy* 12, 1982, pp. 287—302.

3. For a sense of the historical and intellectual development of liberalism over the past three centuries, see the following (in chronological order): L.T. Hobhouse, *Liberalism,* London 1911; Guido De Ruggiero, *The History of European Liberalism,* Oxford University Press, Oxford 1927; Harold Laski, *The Rise of European Liberalism,* Allen & Unwin, London 1936; George J. Sabine, *A History of Political Theory,* Holt, New York 1937; Charles Howard McIlwain, *Constitutionalism and the Changing World,* Macmillan, New York 1939; John H. Hallowell, *The Decline of Liberalism as an Ideology,* University of California Press, Berkeley 1943; Thomas Maitland Marshall, *Citizenship and Social Class,* Cambridge University Press, Cambridge 1950; Michael Polanyi, *The Logic of Liberty,* University of Chicago Press, Chicago 1951; Louis Hartz, *The Liberal Tradition in America,* Harcourt Brace, New York 1955; R.D. Cumming, *Human Nature and History, A*

Study of the Development of Liberal Democracy, 2 vols, University of Chicago Press, Chicago 1969; C.B. MacPherson, *The Life and Times of Liberal Democracy*, Oxford University Press, Oxford 1977; Alan Macfarlane, *Origins of English Individualism*, Oxford University Press, Oxford 1978; Steven Seidman, *Liberalism and the Origins of European Social Theory*, University of California Press, Berkeley 1983; and John Gray, *Liberalism*, University of Minnesota Press, Minneapolis 1986.

4. Although Thomas Hobbes was not within the main (and broadly defined) tradition of liberal theory that includes but is not limited to Locke, Kant, Smith, Madison, Montesquieu, Bentham, Mill, T. H. Green, L. T. Hobhouse, Dewey, and, recently, Rawls, Dworkin and Nozick, he set the stage for the view of man that came to distinguish much of liberal thought. In *De Cive*, Hobbes wrote, 'let us ... consider men as if but even now sprung out of the earth, and suddenly, like mushrooms come to full maturity, without all kinds of engagement to each other.' 'Philosophical Rudiments Concerning Government and Society', in Sir W. Molesworth, ed., *The English Works of Thomas Hobbes*, Longman, London 1966, p. 102. This invocation to view man as an autonomous 'self' outside society is discernible, in varied forms, from Locke's state of nature to Rawls's 'veil of ignorance'. Contemporary critics of liberalism refer to this formulation as the 'unencumbered self'; see Michael Sandel, 'The Procedural Republic and the Unencumbered Self', *Political Theory*, 12 (1), 1984, pp. 81–96.

I will use the male referent in this discussion of liberalism for two reasons: first, it serves as a reminder of the exclusively male discourse used in traditional political theory, including that of the few theorists who are willing to concede that *he/him* means 'all'. Second, many feminist theorists have persuasively argued that the term *man* as used in liberal thought is not simply a linguistic device or a generic label but a symbol for a concept reflecting both masculine values and virtues and patriarchalist practices. See Brennan and Pateman, 'Mere Auxiliaries to the Commonwealth'.

5. As Brennan and Pateman point out in 'Mere Auxiliaries', the idea that the individual is by nature free – that is, outside the bonds of society, history and tradition – was bequeathed to liberalism by social contract theorists. The emergence of this idea in the seventeenth century not only marked 'a decisive break with the traditional view that people were "naturally" bound together in a hierarchy of inequality and subordination' but also established a conception of 'natural' individual freedom as the condition of individual isolation from others prior to the (artificial) creation of 'civil society'.

6. John Stuart Mill, 'On Liberty', in Max Lerner, ed., *The Essential Works of John Stuart Mill*, Bantam, New York 1961, p. 266.

7. T.H. Green, 'Liberal Legislation and Freedom of Contract', in John R. Rodman, ed., *The Political Theory of T.H. Green*, Crofts, New York 1964.

8. Quoted in Sheldon Wolin, *Politics and Vision*, Little, Brown, Boston 1963.

9. Jagger, *Feminist Politics*, p. 33.

10. Sir Isaiah Berlin, 'Two Concepts of Liberty', in *Four Essays on Liberty*, Oxford University Press, Oxford 1969, p. 122. Berlin goes on to note something that will be important to the argument I make in section III – that 'freedom [as negative liberty] is not, at any rate logically, connected with democracy or self-government.... The answer to the question "Who governs me?" is logically distinct from the question "How far does government interfere with me?"' (pp. 129–30). The latter question, as we shall see, is the one that is of primary concern for the liberal citizen; the former

must be of concern to the democratic citizen, and accordingly, to feminist political thought.

11. John Rawls, *A Theory of Justice*, Harvard University Press, Cambridge, MA 1971.

12. The denial of citizenship to women is, of course, a historical but not a contemporary feature of liberalism. Nevertheless, it is worth noting that at least in early liberal thought, the ethical principles that distinguish liberalism – individual freedom and social equality – were not in practice (and often not in theory) extended to women, but solely to 'rational men', whose 'rationality' was linked to the ownership of property.

13. Liberalism's context is actually a highly complex set of shifting social, political, and historical situations. We must not forget that in its earliest (seventeenth- and eighteenth-century) manifestations with the Levellers, the True Whigs, the Common-wealthmen and revolutionary 'patriots', the proclamation of individual rights and social equality were acts of rebellion against king and court. The domain of capitalist 'possessive individualism' developed in a separate but related set of practices. Thus liberalism's legacy is a radical as well as a capitalist one.

14. See Jagger, *Feminist Politics*, p. 31.

15. As C.B. MacPherson rightly points out in *The Life and Times of Liberal Democracy*, p. 2, one of the prevailing difficulties of liberalism is that it has tried to combine the idea of individual freedom as 'self-development' with the entrepreneurial notion of liberalism as the 'right of the stronger to do down the weaker by following market rules.' Despite attempts by J.S. Mill, Robert Nozick and others to reconcile market freedom with self-development freedom, a successful resolution has not yet been achieved. MacPherson argues that the two freedoms are profoundly inconsistent, but he also asserts that the liberal position 'need not be taken to depend forever on an acceptance of capitalist assumptions, although historically it has been so taken' (p. 2). That historical reality is the one I focus on here, and is what I think predominates in the liberal American view of citizenship. However, like MacPherson, I do not think liberalism is necessarily bound (conceptually or practically) to what he calls the 'capitalist market envelope'.

16. Ibid., p. 1.

17. Mary Lyndon Shanley, 'Afterword: Feminism and Families in a Liberal Polity', in Diamond, *Families, Politics, and Public Policy*, p. 360.

18. For example, see Jagger, *Feminist Politics*; Naomi Scheman, 'Individualism and the Objects of Psychology', in Harding and Hintikka, *Discovering Reality*; Jean Grimshaw, *Philosophy and Feminist Thinking*, University of Minnesota Press, Minneapolis 1986; Nicholson, *Gender and History*; and Young, 'Impartiality and the Civic Public'.

19. I intentionally leave radical feminism out of this discussion, not because it is insignificant or unimportant, but because it has, to date, not arrived at a consistent political position on the questions that concern us here. For a helpful critique of radical feminism's theoretical failings, see Jagger, *Feminist Politics*, pp. 286–90, and Joan Cocks, 'Wordless Emotions: Some Critical Reflections on Radical Feminism', *Politics and Society* 13 (1), 1984, pp. 27–57.

20. By delineating this category I do not mean to blur or erase the very real distinctions between various kinds of Marxist feminists or to obscure the importance of the 'patriarchy verus capitalism' debate. For a sense of the diversity of Marxist (or

socialist) feminism, see: Mariarose DallaCosta and Selma James, *Women and the Subversion of Community: A Woman's Place*, Falling Wall Press, Bristol 1981, Hartsock, *Money, Sex, and Power*; Zillah Eisenstein, *Capitalist Patriarchy and the Case for Socialist Feminism*, Monthly Review Press, New York 1978; Catherine A. Mackinnon, 'Feminism, Marxism, Method, and the State: An Agenda for Theory', in Nannerl O. Keohane, Michelle Rosaldo and Barbara Gelpi, eds, *Feminist Theory: A Critique of Ideology*, University of Chicago Press, Chicago 1981; Sheila Rowbotham, *Women, Resistance, and Revolution*, Vintage, New York 1974; and Lydia Sargent, ed., *Women and Revolution*, South End Press, Boston 1981. The quotations are from Hartsock, *Money, Sex, and Power*, p. 235.

21. Eisenstein, *The Radical Future of Liberal Politics*, p. 223.

22. Ibid., p. 222.

23. Hartsock, *Money, Sex, and Power*, p. 247.

24. Sheldon Wolin, chapter 12, this volume.

25. For various maternalist views see, among others, Jean Bethke Elshtain, 'Antigone's Daughters', *Democracy* 2 (2), 1982, pp. 46–59; Elshtain, 'Feminism, Family and Community', *Dissent* 29 (4), 1982, pp. 442–9; and Elshtain, 'Feminist Discourse and its Discontents: Language, Power, and Meaning', *Signs* 3 (7), 1982, pp. 603–21; also Sara Ruddick, 'Maternal Thinking', *Feminist Studies* 6 (2), 1980, pp. 342–67; Ruddick, 'Preservative Love and Military Destruction: Reflections on Mothering and Peace', in Joyce Treblicot, ed., *Mothering: Essays on Feminist Theory*, Littlefield Adams, Iotowa, NJ 1983; and Hartsock, *Money, Sex, and Power* (Hartsock incorporates both Marxist and maternalist perspectives in her 'feminist standpoint' theory).

26. Elshtain, 'Feminist Discourse', p. 617.

27. Elshtain, *Public Man, Private Woman*, p. 243, and Elshtain, 'Antigone's Daughters', p. 59.

28. Elshtain, 'Antigone's Daughters', p. 58.

29. See Nancy Chodorow, *The Reproduction of Mothering: Psychoanalysis and the Sociology of Gender*, University of California Press, Berkeley 1978, and Carol Gilligan, *In a Different Voice: Psychological Theory and Women's Development*, Harvard University Press, Cambridge 1982.

30. I qualify this with 'implication' because Gilligan is by no means consistent about whether the 'different voice' is exclusive to women or open to men. For an interesting critique, see Joan Tronto, 'Women's Morality: Beyond Gender Difference to a Theory of Care', in *Signs* 12 (4), 1987, pp. 644–63.

31. Elshtain, 'Feminist Discourse', p. 621.

32. For a complementary and elegant critique of binary opposition arguments, see Joan Scott, 'Gender: A Useful Category of Historical Analysis', *American Historical Review* 91 (2), 1986, pp. 1053–75.

33. For a more detailed critique, see Dietz, 'Citizenship with a Feminist Face: The Problem with Maternal Thinking', *Political Theory* 13 (1), 1985, pp. 19–35.

34. The alternative conception introduced here — of politics as participatory and citizenship as the active engagement of peers in the public realm — has been of considerable interest to political theorists and historians over the past twenty years and has developed in detail as an alternative to the liberal view. Feminists now need to consider the significance of this perspective in regard to their own political theories. Perhaps the leading contemporary exponent of politics as the active life of citizens is

Hannah Arendt, *The Human Condition*, University of Chicago Press, Chicago 1958 and *On Revolution*, Penguin Books, New York 1963. But alternatives to liberalism are also explored as 'civic republicanism' in the work of J. G. A. Pocock, *The Machiavellian Moment: Florentine Political Thought and the Atlantic Republican Tradition*, Princeton University Press, Princeton 1975, and in the recent 'communitarian turn' articulated by Michael Sandel in his critique of the tradition of thinkers from Kant to Rawls, *Liberalism and the Limits of Justice*, Cambridge University Press, Cambridge 1982. For other 'democratic' critiques of liberalism, see Benjamin Barber, *Strong Democracy: Participatory Politics for a New Age*, University of California Press, Berkeley 1984; Joshua Cohen and Joel Rogers, *On Democracy: Toward a Transformation of American Society*, Penguin, New York 1983; Russell Hanson, *The Democratic Imagination in America*, Princeton University Press, Princeton 1985; Lawrence Goodwyn, *Democratic Promise: The Populist Movement in America*, Oxford University Press, New York 1976; Carole Pateman, *Participation and Democratic Theory*, Cambridge University Press, Cambridge 1970; Michael Walzer, *Radical Principles*, Basic Books, New York 1980; and Sheldon Wolin, *Politics and Vision*, Little, Brown, Boston 1963. Also see the short-lived but useful journal *Democracy* (1981–83).

35. C. Douglas Lummis, 'The Radicalization of Democracy', *Democracy* 2 (4), 1982, pp. 9–16.

36. I would reiterate, however, that despite its historical propensity to collapse democracy into a capitalist economic ethic, liberalism is not without its own vital ethical principles (namely, individual freedom and equality) that democrats ignore to their peril. The task for 'ethical liberals', as MacPherson puts it in *The Life and Times of Liberal Democracy*, is to detach these principles from the 'market assumptions' of capitalism and integrate them into a truly democratic vision of participatory citizenship. By the same token, the task for participatory democrats is to preserve the principles of freedom and equality that are the special legacy of liberalism.

37. Sheldon Wolin, 'The Peoples' Two Bodies', *Democracy* 1 (1), 1981, pp. 9–24.

38. I do not intend to imply that feminism is the only democratic movement that has emerged in the recent American past or that it is the only one from which we can draw examples. There are others — the civil rights movement, the populist resurgence, the collective political gatherings occasioned by the farm crises of the 1980s, gay liberation, and so on. But in its organization and decentralized practices, the feminist movement has been the most consistently democratic, its liberal, interest-group side (NOW) notwithstanding.

39. The phrase 'forms of freedom' comes from Jane Mansbridge, 'Feminism and the Forms of Freedom', in Frank Fischer and Carmen Siriani, eds, *Critical Studies in Organization and Bureaucracy*, Temple University Press, Philadelphia 1984, pp. 472–86.

40. Some of the historical precedents I have in mind are developed in Linda Kerber's book, *Women of the Republic*, Norton, New York 1980, especially in chapter 3, 'The Meaning of Female Patriotism', in which she reconsiders the political activism of women in revolutionary America. Other activist precedents that contemporary feminists might recall and preserve are discussed in Sara M. Evans and Harry C. Boyte, *Free Spaces: The Sources of Democratic Change in America*, Harper & Row, New York 1986; these include the abolitionist movement, the suffrage movement, the Women's Christian Temperance Union, the settlement house movement, and the National

Women's Trade Union League, as well as contemporary forms of feminist organization and action.

41. My point here is not that the soviets of 1917 or the Polish KOR of 1978 can serve as models for participatory citizenship in late twentieth-century America, but rather that an alternative to liberal citizenship can take root only if it is distilled into a framework of conceptual notions. The historical moments I mention (and others) provide the experiential and practical reality for such a conceptual framework and thus merit incorporation into feminist democratic politics. Or, as Arendt writes in *On Revolution*, 'What saves the affairs of moral men from their inherent futility is nothing but the incessant talk about them, which in turn remains futile unless certain concepts, certain guideposts for future remembrance and even for sheer reference, arise out of it' (p. 20). The diverse practices mentioned above should be perceived as guideposts and references that might inspire a democratic spirit rather than as literal examples to be emulated in keeping with such a spirit.

PART II

4

The Civil Society Argument

Michael Walzer

I

My aim here is to defend a complex, imprecise and, at crucial points, uncertain account of society and politics. I have no hope of theoretical simplicity, not at this historical moment when so many stable oppositions of political and intellectual life have collapsed; but I also have no desire for simplicity, since a world that theory could fully grasp and neatly explain would not, I suspect, be a pleasant place. In the nature of things, then, my argument will not be elegant, and though I believe that arguments should march, the sentences following one another like soldiers on parade, the route of my march today will be twisting and roundabout. I shall begin with the idea of civil society, recently revived by Central and East European intellectuals, and go on to discuss the state, the economy and the nation, and then civil society and the state again. These are the crucial social formations that we inhabit, but we do not at this moment live comfortably in any of them. Nor is it possible to imagine, in accordance with one or another of the great simplifying theories, a way to choose among them — as if we were destined to find, one day, the best social formation. I mean to argue against choosing, but I shall also claim that it is from within civil society that this argument is best understood.

The words 'civil society' name the space of uncoerced human association and also the set of relational networks — formed for the sake of family, faith, interest and ideology — that fill this space. Central and East

European dissidence flourished within a highly restricted version of civil society, and the first task of the new democracies created by the dissidents, so we are told, is to rebuild the networks: unions, churches, political parties and movements, cooperatives, neighbourhoods, schools of thought, societies for promoting or preventing this and that. In the West, by contrast, we have lived in civil society for many years without knowing it. Or, better, since the Scottish Enlightenment, or since Hegel, the words have been known to the knowers of such things, but they have rarely served to focus anyone else's attention. Now writers in Hungary, Czechoslovakia and Poland invite us to think about how this social formation is secured and invigorated.

We have reasons of our own for accepting the invitation. Increasingly, associational life in the 'advanced' capitalist and social democratic countries seems at risk. Publicists and preachers warn us of a steady attenuation of everyday cooperation and civic friendship. And this time it is possible that they are not, as they usually are, foolishly alarmist. Our cities really are noisier and nastier than they once were. Familial solidarity, mutual assistance, political likemindedness – all these are less certain and less substantial than they once were. Other people, strangers on the street, seem less trustworthy than they once did. The Hobbesian account of society is more persuasive than it once was.

Perhaps this worrisome picture follows – in part, no more, but what else can a political theorist say? – from the fact that we have not thought enough about solidarity and trust or planned for their future. We have been thinking too much about social formations different from, in competition with, civil society. And so we have neglected the networks through which civility is produced and reproduced. Imagine that the following questions were posed, one or two centuries ago, to political theorists and moral philosophers: what is the preferred setting, the most supportive environment, for the good life? What sorts of institution should we work for? Nineteenth- and twentieth-century social thought provides four different, by now familiar, answers to these questions. Think of them as four rival ideologies, each with its own claim to completeness and correctness. Each of them is importantly wrong. Each of them neglects the necessary pluralism of any *civil* society. Each of them is predicated on an assumption I mean to attack: that such questions must receive a singular answer.

II

I shall begin, since this is for me the best-known ground, with two leftist answers. The first of the two holds that the preferred setting for the good life is the political community, the democratic state, within which we can be citizens: freely engaged, fully committed, decision-making members. And a citizen, on this view, is much the best thing to be. To live well is to be politically active, working with our fellow citizens, collectively determining our common destiny — not for the sake of this or that determination but for the work itself, in which our highest capacities as rational and moral agents find expression. We know ourselves best as persons who propose, debate and decide.

This argument goes back to the Greeks, but we are most likely to recognize its neoclassical versions. It is Rousseau's argument, or the standard leftist interpretation of Rousseau's argument. His under-standing of citizenship as moral agency is one of the key sources of democratic idealism. We can see it at work in liberals like John Stuart Mill, in whose writings it produced an unexpected defence of syndi-calism (what is today called 'workers' control') and, more generally, of social democracy. It appeared among nineteenth- and twentieth-century democratic radicals, often with a hard populist edge. It played a part in the reiterated demand for social inclusion by women, workers, blacks and new immigrants, all of whom based their claims on their capacity as agents. And this same neoclassical idea of citizenship resurfaced in the 1960s in New Left theories of participation, where it was, however, like many latter-day revivals, highly theoretical and without local resonance.

Today, perhaps in response to the political disasters of the late 1960s, 'communitarians' in the United States' struggle to give Rousseauian idealism a historical reference, looking back to the early American republic and calling for a renewal of civic virtue. They prescribe citizen-ship as an antidote to the fragmentation of contemporary society — for these theorists, like Rousseau, are disinclined to value the fragments. In their hands, republicanism is still a simplifying creed. If politics is our highest calling, then we are called away from every other activity (or, every other activity is redefined in political terms); our energies are directed towards policy formation and decision-making in the demo-cratic state.

I don't doubt that the active and engaged citizen is an attractive figure — even if some of the activists that we actually meet carrying placards and shouting slogans aren't all that attractive. The most penetrating

criticism of this first answer to the question about the good life is not
that the life isn't good but that it isn't the 'real life' of very many people
in the modern world. This is so in two senses. First, though the power of
the democratic state has grown enormously, partly (and rightly) in
response to the demands of engaged citizens, it cannot be said that the
state is fully in the hands of its citizens. And the larger it gets, the more it
takes over those smaller associations still subject to hands-on control.
The rule of the *demos* is in significant ways illusory; the participation of
ordinary men and women in the activities of the state (unless they are
state employees) is largely vicarious; even party militants are more likely
to argue and complain than actually to decide.

Second, despite the singlemindedness of republican ideology, politics
rarely engages the full attention of the citizens who are supposed to be its
chief protagonists. They have too many other things to worry about.
Above all, they have to earn a living. They are more deeply engaged in
the economy than in the political community. Republican theorists (like
Hannah Arendt) recognize this engagement only as a threat to civic
virtue. Economic activity belongs to the realm of necessity, they argue;
politics to the realm of freedom. Ideally, citizens should not have to
work; they should be served by machines, if not by slaves, so that they
can flock to the assemblies and argue with their fellows about affairs of
state. In practice, however, work, though it begins in necessity, takes on
value of its own — expressed in commitment to a career, pride in a job
well done, a sense of camaraderie in the workplace. All of these are
competitive with the values of citizenship.

III

The second leftist position on the preferred setting for the good life
involves a turning away from republican politics and a focus instead on
economic activity. We can think of this as the socialist answer to the
questions I began with; it can be found in Marx and also, though the
arguments are somewhat different, among the utopians he hoped to
supersede. For Marx, the preferred setting is the cooperative economy,
where we can all be producers — artists (Marx was a romantic), inventors
and craftsmen. (Assembly-line workers don't quite seem to fit.) This
again is much the best thing to be. The picture Marx paints is of creative
men and women making useful and beautiful objects, not for the sake of
this or that object but for the sake of creativity itself, the highest expres-

sion of our 'species-being' as *homo faber*, man-the-maker.

The state, in this view, ought to be managed in such a way as to set productivity free. It doesn't matter who the managers are so long as they are committed to this goal and rational in its pursuit. Their work is technically important but not substantively interesting. Once productivity is free, politics simply ceases to engage anyone's attention. Before that time, in the Marxist here and now, political conflict is taken to be the superstructural enactment of economic conflict, and democracy is valued mainly because it enables socialist movements and parties to organize for victory. The value is instrumental and historically specific. A democratic state is the preferred setting not for the good life but for the class struggle; the purpose of the struggle is to win, and victory brings an end to democratic instrumentality. There is no intrinsic value in democracy, no reason to think that politics has, for creatures like us, a permanent attractiveness. When we are all engaged in productive activity, social division and the conflicts it engenders will disappear, and the state, in the once-famous phrase, will wither away.

In fact, if this vision were ever realized, it is politics that would wither away. Some kind of administrative agency would still be necessary for economic coordination, and it is only a Marxist conceit to refuse to call this agency a state. 'Society regulates the general production', Marx wrote in *The German Ideology*, 'and thus makes it possible for me to do one thing today and another tomorrow ... just as I have a mind'. Since this regulation is non-political, the individual producer is freed from the burdens of citizenship. He attends instead to the things he makes and to the cooperative relationships he establishes. Exactly how he can work with other people and still do whatever he pleases is unclear to me and probably to most other readers of Marx. The texts suggest an extraordinary faith in the virtuosity of the regulators. No one, I think, quite shares this faith today, but something like it helps to explain the tendency of some leftists to see even the liberal and democratic state as an obstacle that has to be, in the worst of recent jargons, 'smashed'.

The seriousness of Marxist anti-politics is nicely illustrated by Marx's own dislike of syndicalism. What the syndicalists proposed was a neat amalgam of the first and second answers to the question about the good life: for them, the preferred setting was the worker-controlled factory, where men and women were simultaneously citizens and producers, making decisions and making things. Marx seems to have regarded the combination as impossible; factories could not be both democratic and productive. This is the point of Engels's little essay on authority, which I take to express Marx's view also. More generally, self-government on the job called into question the legitimacy of 'social regulation' or state planning, which alone, Marx thought, could enable individual workers to devote themselves, without distraction, to their work.

But this vision of the cooperative economy is set against an un-believable background — a non-political state, regulation without conflict, 'the administration of things'. In every actual experience of socialist politics, the state has moved rapidly into the foreground, and most socialists, in the West at least, have been driven to make their own amalgam of the first and second answers. They call themselves *democratic* socialists, focusing on the state as well as (in fact, much more than) on the economy and doubling the preferred settings for the good life. Since I believe that two are better than one, I take this to be progress. But before I try to suggest what further progress might look like, I need to describe two more ideological answers to the question about the good life, one of them capitalist, the other nationalist. For there is no reason to think that only leftists love singularity.

IV

The third answer holds that the preferred setting for the good life is the marketplace, where individual men and women, consumers rather than producers, choose among a maximum number of options. The auton-omous individual confronting his, and now her, possibilities — this is much the best thing to be. To live well is not to make political decisions or beautiful objects; it is to make personal choices. Not any particular choices, for no choice is substantively the best: it is the activity of choosing that makes for autonomy. And the market within which choices are made, like the socialist economy, largely dispenses with politics; it requires at most a minimal state — not 'social regulation', only the police.

Production, too, is free even if it isn't, as in the Marxist vision, freely creative. More important than the producers, however, are the entre-preneurs, heroes of autonomy, consumers of opportunity, who compete to supply whatever all the other consumers want or might be persuaded to want. Entrepreneurial activity tracks consumer preference. Though not without its own excitements, it is mostly instrumental: the aim of all entrepreneurs (and all producers) is to increase their market power, maximize their options. Competing with one another, they maximize everyone else's option too, filling the marketplace with desirable objects. The market is preferred (over the political community and the cooperative economy) because of its fullness. Freedom, in the capitalist view, is a function of plenitude. We can only choose when we have many choices.

It is also true, unhappily, that we can only make effective (rather than merely speculative or wistful) choices when we have resources to dispose of. But people come to the marketplace with radically unequal resources — some with virtually nothing at all. Not everyone can compete successfully in commodity production, and therefore not everyone has access to commodities. Autonomy turns out to be a high-risk value, which many men and women can only realize with help from their friends. The market, however, is not a good setting for mutual assistance, for I cannot help someone else without reducing (for the short term, at least) my own options. And I have no reason, as an autonomous individual, to accept any reductions of any sort for someone else's sake. My argument here is not that autonomy collapses into egotism, only that autonomy in the marketplace provides no support for social solidarity. Despite the successes of capitalist production, the good life of consumer choice is not universally available. Large numbers of people drop out of the market economy or live precariously on its margins.

Partly for this reason, capitalism, like socialism, is highly dependent on state action — not only to prevent theft and enforce contracts but also to regulate the economy and guarantee the minimal welfare of its participants. But these participants, in so far as they are market activists, are not active in the state: capitalism in its ideal form, like socialism again, does not make for citizenship. Or, its protagonists conceive of citizenship in economic terms, so that citizens are transformed into autonomous consumers, looking for the party or programme that most persuasively promises to strengthen their market position. They need the state, but have no moral relation to it, and they control its officials only as consumers control the producers of commodities, by buying or not buying what they make.

Since the market has no political boundaries, capitalist entrepreneurs also evade official control. They need the state but have no loyalty to it; the profit motive brings them into conflict with democratic regulation. So arms merchants sell the latest military technology to foreign powers and manufacturers move their factories overseas to escape safety codes or minimum wage laws. Multinational corporations stand outside (and to some extent against) every political community. They are known only by their brand names, which, unlike family names and country names, evoke preferences but not affections or solidarities.

V

The fourth answer to the question about the good life can be read as a response to market amorality and disloyalty, though it has, historically, other sources as well. According to the fourth answer, the preferred setting is the nation, within which we are loyal members, bound to one another by ties of blood and history. And a member, secure in his membership, literally part of an organic whole — this is much the best thing to be. To live well is to participate with other men and women in remembering, cultivating and passing on a national heritage. This is so, on the nationalist view, without reference to the specific content of the heritage, so long as it is one's own, a matter of birth, not choice. Every nationalist will, of course, find value in his own heritage, but the highest value is not in the finding but in the willing: the firm identification of the individual with a people and a history.

Nationalism has often been a leftist ideology, historically linked to democracy and even to socialism. But it is most characteristically an ideology of the right, for its understanding of membership is ascriptive; it requires no political choices and no activity beyond ritual affirmation. When nations find themselves ruled by foreigners, however, ritual affirmation is not enough. Then nationalism requires a more heroic loyalty: self-sacrifice in the struggle for national liberation. The capacity of the nation to elicit such sacrifices from its members is proof of the importance of this fourth answer. Individual members seek the good life by seeking autonomy not for themselves but for their people. Ideally, this attitude ought to survive the liberation struggle and provide a foundation for social solidarity and mutual assistance. Perhaps, to some extent, it does: certainly the welfare state has had its greatest successes in ethnically homogeneous countries. It is also true, however, that once liberation has been secured, nationalist men and women are commonly content with a vicarious rather than a practical participation in the community. There is nothing wrong with vicarious participation, on the nationalist view, since the good life is more a matter of identity than activity — faith, not works, so to speak, though both of these are understood in secular terms.

In the modern world, nations commonly seek statehood, for their autonomy will always be at risk if they lack sovereign power. But they don't seek states of any particular kind. No more do they seek economic arrangements of any particular kind. Unlike religious believers who are their close kin and (often) bitter rivals, nationalists are not bound by a body of authoritative law or a set of sacred texts. Beyond liberation, they have no programme, only a vague commitment to continue a history, to sustain a 'way of life'. Their own lives, I suppose, are emotionally intense, but in relation to society and economy this is a dangerously free-floating intensity. In time of trouble, it can readily be turned against other nations, particularly against the internal others: minorities, aliens, strangers. Democratic citizenship, worker solidarity, free enterprise and consumer autonomy — all these are less exclusive than nationalism but not always resistant to its power. The ease with which citizens, workers and consumers become fervent nationalists is a sign of the inadequacy of the first three answers to the question about the good life. The nature of nationalist fervour signals the inadequacy of the fourth.

VI

All these answers are wrong-headed because of their singularity. They miss the complexity of human society, the inevitable conflicts of commitment and loyalty. Hence I am uneasy with the idea that there might be a fifth and finally correct answer to the question about the good life. Still, there is a fifth answer, the newest one (it draws upon less central themes of nineteenth- and twentieth-century social thought), which holds that the good life can only be lived in civil society, the realm of fragmentation and struggle but also of concrete and authentic soli-darities, where we fulfil E. M. Forster's injunction 'only connect', and become sociable or communal men and women. And this is, of course, much the best thing to be. The picture here is of people freely associating and communicating with one another, forming and reforming groups of all sorts, not for the sake of any particular formation — family, tribe, nation, religion, commune, brotherhood or sisterhood, interest group or ideological movement — but for the sake of sociability itself. For we are by nature social, before we are political or economic, beings.

I would rather say that the civil society argument is a corrective to the four ideological accounts of the good life — part-denial, part-incorpora-tion — rather than a fifth to stand alongside them. It challenges their singularity, but it has no singularity of its own. The phrase 'social being' describes men and women who are citizens, producers, consumers, members of the nation and much else besides — and none of these by nature or because it is the best thing to be. The associational life of civil society is the actual ground where all versions of the good are worked out and tested ... and proven to be partial, incomplete, ultimately unsatisfying. It cannot be the case that living on this ground is good-in-itself; there isn't any other place to live. What is true is that the quality of our political and economic activity and of our national culture is intimately connected to the strength and vitality of our associations.

Ideally, civil society is a *setting of settings*: all are included, none is preferred. The argument is a liberal version of the four answers, accepting them all, insisting that each leave room for the others, therefore not finally accepting any of them. Liberalism appears here as an anti-ideology, and this is an attractive position in the contemporary world. I shall stress this attractiveness as I try to explain how civil society might actually incorporate and deny the four answers. Later on, however, I shall have to argue that this position too, so genial and benign, has its problems.

Let's begin with the political community and the cooperative economy, taken together. These two leftist versions of the good life systematically undervalued all associations except the demos and the working class. Their protagonists could imagine conflicts between political communities and between classes, but not within either; they aimed at the abolition or transcendence of particularism and all its divisions. Theorists of civil society, by contrast, have a more realistic view of communities and economies. They are more accommodating to conflict — that is, to political opposition and economic competition. Associational freedom serves for them to legitimate a set of market relations, though not necessarily the capitalist set. The market, when it is entangled in the network of associations, when the forms of ownership are pluralized, is without doubt the economic formation most consistent with the civil society argument. This same argument also serves to legitimate a kind of state, liberal and pluralist more than republican (not so radically dependent upon the virtue of its citizens). Indeed, a state of this sort, as we will see, is necessary if associations are to flourish.

Once incorporated into civil society, neither citizenship nor production can ever again be all-absorbing. They will have their votaries, but these people will not be models for the rest of us — or they will be partial models only, for some people at some time of their lives, not for other people, not at other times. This pluralist perspective follows in part, perhaps, from the lost romance of work, from our experience with the new productive technologies and the growth of the service economy. Service is more easily reconciled with a vision of man as a social animal than with *homo faber*. What can a hospital attendant or a school teacher or a marriage counsellor or a social worker or a television repairman or a government official be said to *make*? The contemporary economy does not offer many people a chance for creativity in the Marxist sense. Nor does Marx (or any socialist thinker of the central tradition) have much to say about those men and women whose economic activity consists entirely in helping other people. The helpmate, like the housewife, was never assimilated to the class of workers.

In similar fashion, politics in the contemporary democratic state does not offer many people a chance for Rousseauian self-determination. Citizenship, taken by itself, is today mostly a passive role: citizens are spectators who vote. Between elections, they are served, well or badly, by the civil service. They are not at all like those heroes of republican mythology, the citizens of ancient Athens meeting in assembly and (foolishly, as it turned out) deciding to invade Sicily. But in the associational networks of civil society, in unions, parties, movements, interest groups, and so on, these same people make many smaller decisions and shape to some degree the more distant determinations of state and economy. And in a more densely organized, more egalitarian civil society, they might do both these things to greater effect.

These socially engaged men and women — part-time union officers, movement activists, party regulars, consumer advocates, welfare volunteers, church members, family heads — stand outside the republic of citizens as it is commonly conceived. They are only intermittently virtuous; they are too caught up in particularity. They look, most of them, for many partial fulfilments, no longer for the one clinching fulfilment. On the ground of actuality (unless the state usurps the ground), citizenship shades off into a great diversity of (sometimes divisive) decision-making roles; and, similarly, production shades off into a multitude of (sometimes competitive) socially useful activities. It is, then, a mistake to set politics and work in opposition to one another. There is no ideal fulfilment and no essential human capacity. We require many settings so that we can live different kinds of good lives.

All this is not to say, however, that we need to accept the capitalist version of competition and division. Theorists who regard the market as the preferred setting for the good life aim to make it the actual setting for as many aspects of life as possible. Their singlemindedness takes the form of market imperialism; confronting the democratic state, they are advocates of privatization and *laissez-faire*. Their ideal is a society in which all goods and services are provided by entrepreneurs to consumers. That some entrepreneurs would fail and many consumers find themselves helpless in the marketplace — this is the price of individual autonomy. It is, obviously, a price we already pay: in all capitalist societies, the market makes for inequality. The more successful its imperialism, the greater the inequality. But were the market to be set firmly within civil society, politically constrained, open to communal as well as private initiatives, limits might be fixed on its unequal outcomes. The exact nature of the limits would depend on the strength and density of the associational networks (including, now, the political community).

The problem with inequality is not merely that some individuals are more capable, others less capable, of making their consumer preferences effective. It's not that some individuals live in fancier apartments than others, or drive better-made cars, or take vacations in more exotic places. These are conceivably the just rewards of market success. The problem is that inequality commonly translates into domination and radical deprivation. But the verb 'translates' here describes a socially mediated process, which is fostered or inhibited by the structure of its mediations. Dominated and deprived individuals are likely to be disorganized as well as impoverished, whereas poor people with strong families, churches, unions, political parties and ethnic alliances are not likely to be dominated or deprived for long. Nor need these people stand alone even in the marketplace. The capitalist answer assumes that the good life of entrepreneurial initiative and consumer choice is a life led most importantly by individuals. But civil society encompasses or can encompass a variety of market agents: family businesses, publicly owned or municipal companies, worker communes, consumer cooperatives, nonprofit organizations of many different sorts. All these function in the market though they have their origins outside. And just as the experience of democracy is expanded and enhanced by groups that are in but not of the state, so consumer choice is expanded and enhanced by groups that are in but not of the market.

It is only necessary to add that among the groups in but not of the state are market organizations, and among the groups in but not of the market are state organizations. All social forms are relativized by the civil society argument — and on the actual ground too. This also means that all social forms are contestable; moreover, contests can't be won by invoking one or another account of the preferred setting — as if it were enough to say that market organizations, in so far as they are efficient, do not have to be democratic or that state firms, in so far as they are democratically controlled, do not have to operate within the constraints of the market. The exact character of our associational life is something that has to be argued about, and it is in the course of these arguments that we also decide about the forms of democracy, the nature of work, the extent and effects of market inequalities, and much else.

The quality of nationalism is also determined within civil society, where national groups coexist and overlap with families and religious communities (two social formations largely neglected in modernist answers to the question about the good life) and where nationalism is expressed in schools and movements, organizations for mutual aid, cultural and historical societies. It is because groups like these are entangled with other groups, similar in kind but different in aim, that civil society holds out the hope of a domesticated nationalism. In states dominated by a single nation, the multiplicity of the groups pluralizes nationalist politics and culture; in states with more than one nation, the density of the networks prevents radical polarization.

Civil society as we know it has its origin in the struggle for religious freedom. Though often violent, the struggle held open the possibility of peace. 'The establishment of this one thing', John Locke wrote about toleration, 'would take away all ground of complaints and tumults upon account of conscience.' One can easily imagine groundless complaints and tumults, but Locke believed (and he was largely right) that tolerance would dull the edge of religious conflict. People would be less ready to take risks once the stakes were lowered. Civil society simply is that place where the stakes are lower, where, in principle, at least, coercion is used only to keep the peace and all associations are equal under the law. In the market, this formal equality often has no substance, but in the world of faith and identity, it is real enough. Though nations do not compete for members in the same way as religions (sometimes) do, the argument for granting them the associational freedom of civil society is similar. When they are free to celebrate their histories, remember their dead, and shape (in part) the education of their children, they are more likely to be harmless than when they are unfree. Locke may have put the claim too strongly when he wrote that 'There is only one thing which gathers people into seditious commotions, and that is oppression', but he was close enough to the truth to warrant the experiment of radical tolerance.

But if oppression is the cause of seditious commotion, what is the cause of oppression? I don't doubt that there is a materialist story to tell here, but I want to stress the central role played by ideological single-

mindedness: the intolerant universalism of (most) religions, the exclus-
ivity of (most) nations. The actual experience of civil society, when it can
be had, seems to work against these two. Indeed, it works so well, some
observers think, that neither religious faith nor national identity is likely
to survive for long in the network of free associations. But we really don't
know to what extent faith and identity depend upon coercion or
whether they can reproduce themselves under conditions of freedom. I
suspect that they both respond to such deep human needs that they will
outlast their current organizational forms. It seems, in any case, worth-
while to wait and see.

VII

But there is no escape from power and coercion, no possibility of
choosing, like the old anarchists, civil society alone. A few years ago, in a
book called *Anti-Politics*, the Hungarian dissident George Konrad
described a way of living alongside the totalitarian state but, so to speak,
with one's back turned towards it. He urged his fellow dissidents to reject
the very idea of seizing or sharing power and to devote their energies to
religious, cultural, economic and professional associations. Civil society
appears in his book as an alternative to the state, which he assumes to be
unchangeable and irredeemably hostile. His argument seemed right to
me when I first read his book. Looking back, after the collapse of the
communist regimes in Hungary and elsewhere, it is easy to see how
much it was a product of its time — and how short that time was! No
state can survive for long if it is wholly alienated from civil society. It
cannot outlast its own coercive machinery; it is lost, literally, without its
firepower. The production and reproduction of loyalty, civility, political
competence and trust in authority are never the work of the state alone,
and the effort to go it alone — one meaning of totalitarianism — is
doomed to failure.

The failure, however, has carried with it terrible costs, and so one can
understand the appeal of contemporary anti-politics. Even as Central
and East European dissidents take power, they remain, and should
remain, cautious and apprehensive about its uses. The totalitarian project
has left behind an abiding sense of bureaucratic brutality. Here was the
ultimate form of political singlemindedness, and though the 'democratic'
(and, for that matter, the 'communist') ideology on which it rested was
false, the intrusions even of a more genuine democracy are rendered

suspect by the memory. Post-totalitarian politicians and writers have, in addition, learned the older anti-politics of free enterprise — so that the *laissez-faire* market is defended in the East today as one of the necessary institutions of civil society, or, more strongly, as the dominant social formation. This second view takes on plausibility from the extraordinary havoc wrought by totalitarian economic planning. But it rests, exactly like political singlemindedness, on a failure to recognize the pluralism of associational life. The first view leads, often, to a more interesting and more genuinely liberal mistake: it suggests that pluralism is self-sufficient and self-sustaining.

This is, indeed, the experience of the dissidents; the state could not destroy their unions, churches, free universities, illegal markets, *samizdat* publications. None the less, I want to warn against the anti-political tendencies that commonly accompany the celebration of civil society. The network of associations incorporates, but it cannot dispense with the agencies of state power; neither can socialist cooperation or capitalist competition dispense with the state. That's why so many dissidents are ministers now. It is indeed true that the new social movements in the East and the West — concerned with ecology, feminism, the rights of immigrants and national minorities, workplace and product safety, and so on — do not aim, as the democratic and labour movements once aimed, at taking power. This represents an important change, in sensibility as much as in ideology, reflecting a new valuation of parts over wholes and a new willingness to settle for something less than total victory. But there can be no victory at all that does not involve some control over, or use of, the state apparatus. The collapse of totalitarianism is empowering for the members of civil society precisely because it renders the state accessible.

Here is the paradox of the civil society argument. Citizenship is one of many roles that members play, but the state itself is unlike all the other associations. It both frames civil society and occupies space within it. It fixes the boundary conditions and the basic rules of all associational activity (including political activity). It compels association members to think about a common good, beyond their own conceptions of the good life. Even the failed totalitarianism of, say, the Polish communist state had this much impact upon the Solidarity union: it determined that Solidarity was a Polish union, focused on economic arrangements and labour policy within the borders of Poland. A democratic state, which is continuous with the other associations, has at the same time a greater say about their quality and vitality. It serves, or it doesn't serve, the needs of the associational networks as these are worked out by men and women who are simultaneously members and citizens. I will give only a few obvious examples, drawn from American experience.

Families with working parents need state help in the form of publicly funded day-care and effective public schools. National minorities need help in organizing and sustaining their own educational programmes. Worker-owned companies and consumer cooperatives need state loans or loan guarantees; so (even more often) do capitalist entrepreneurs and firms. Philanthropy and mutual aid, churches and private universities, depend upon tax exemptions. Labour unions need legal recognition and guarantees against 'unfair labour practices'. Professional associations need state support for their licensing procedures. And across the entire range of association, individual men and women need to be protected against the power of officials, employers, experts, party bosses, factory super-visers, directors, priests, parents, patrons; and small and weak groups need to be protected against large and powerful ones. For civil society, left to itself, generates radically unequal power relationships, which only state power can challenge.

Civil society also challenges state power, most importantly when associations have resources or supporters abroad: world religions, pan-national movements, the new environmental groups, multinational corporations. We are likely to feel differently about these challenges, especially after we recognize the real but relative importance of the state. Multinational corporations, for example, need to be constrained, much like states with imperial ambitions; and the best constraint probably lies in collective security, that is, in alliances with other states that give economic regulation some international effect. The same mechanism may turn out to be useful to the new environmental groups. In the first case, the state pressures the corporation; in the second it responds to environmentalist pressure. The two cases suggest, again, that civil society requires political agency. And the state is an indispensable agent — even if the associational networks also, always, resist the organizing impulses of state bureaucrats.

Only a democratic state can create a democratic civil society; only a democratic civil society can sustain a democratic state. The civility that makes democratic politics possible can only be learned in the associa-tional networks; the roughly equal and widely dispersed capabilities that sustain the networks have to be fostered by the democratic state. Confronted with an overbearing state, citizens, who are also members, will struggle to make room for autonomous associations and market relationships (and also for local governments and decentralized bureaucracies). But the state can never be what it appears to be in liberal theory, a mere framework for civil society. It is also the instrument of the struggle, used to give a particular shape to the common life. Hence citizenship has a certain practical pre-eminence among all our actual and possible memberships. That's not to say that we must be citizens all the time, finding in politics, as Rousseau urged, the greater part of our happiness. Most of us will be happier elsewhere, involved only sometimes in affairs of state. But we must have a state open to our sometime involvement.

Nor need we be involved all the time in our associations. A democratic civil society is one controlled by its members, not through a single process of self-determination but through a large number of different and uncoordinated processes. These need not all be democratic, for we are likely to be members of many associations, and we will want some of them to be managed in our interests, but also in our absence. Civil society is sufficiently democratic when in some, at least, of its parts we are able to recognize ourselves as authoritative and responsible participants. States are tested by their capacity to sustain this kind of participation — which is very different from the heroic intensity of Rousseauian citizenship. And civil society is tested by its capacity to produce citizens whose interests, at least sometimes, reach further than themselves and their comrades, who look after the political community that fosters and protects the associational networks.

VIII

I mean to defend a perspective that might be called, awkwardly, 'critical associationalism'. I want to join, but I am somewhat uneasy with, the civil society argument. It cannot be said that nothing is lost when we give up the singlemindedness of democratic citizenship or socialist cooperation or individual autonomy or national identity. There was a kind of heroism in those projects — a concentration of energy, a clear sense of direction, an unblinking recognition of friends and enemies. To make one of them one's own was a serious commitment. The defence of civil society does not quite seem comparable. Associational engagement is conceivably as important a project as any of the others, but its greatest virtue lies in its inclusiveness, and inclusiveness does not make for heroism. 'Join the associations of your choice' is not a slogan to rally political militants. and yet that is what civil society requires: men and women actively engaged — in state, economy and nation, and also in churches, neighbourhoods and families, and in many other settings too. To reach this goal is not as easy as it sounds; many people, perhaps most people, live very loosely within the networks, a growing number of people seem to be radically disengaged — passive clients of the state, market drop-outs, resentful and posturing nationalists. And the civil society project doesn't confront an energizing hostility, as all the others do; its protagonists are more likely to meet sullen indifference, fear, despair, apathy, and withdrawal.

In Central and Eastern Europe, civil society is still a battle cry, for it requires a dismantling of the totalitarian state and it brings with it the exhilarating experience of associational independence. Among ourselves what is required is nothing so grand; nor does it lend itself to a singular description (but this is what lies ahead in the East too). The civil society project can only be described in terms of all the other projects, against their singularity. Hence my account here, which suggests the need (1) to decentralize the state, so that there are more opportunities for citizens to take responsibility for (some of) its activities; (2) to socialize the economy so that there is a greater diversity of market agents, communal as well as private; and (3) to pluralize and domesticate nationalism, on the religious model, so that there are different ways to realize and sustain historical identities.

None of this can be accomplished without using political power to redistribute resources and to underwrite and subsidize the most desirable associational activities. But political power alone cannot accomplish any of it. The kinds of 'action' discussed by theorists of the state need to be supplemented (not, however, replaced) by something radically different: more like union organizing than political mobilization, more like teaching in a school than arguing in the assembly, more like volunteering in a hospital than joining a political party, more like working in an ethnic alliance or a feminist support group than canvassing in an election, more like shaping a co-op budget than deciding on national fiscal policy. But can any of these local and small-scale activities ever carry with them the honour of citizenship? Sometimes, certainly, they are narrowly conceived, partial and particularist; they need political correction. The greater problem, however, is that they seem so ordinary. Living in civil society, one might think, is like speaking in prose.

But just as speaking in prose implies an understanding of syntax, so these forms of action (when they are pluralized) imply an understanding of civility. And that is not an understanding about which we can be entirely confident these days. There is something to be said for the neo-conservative argument that in the modern world we need to recapture the density of associational life and relearn the activities and understandings that go with it. And if this is the case, then a more strenuous argument is called for from the Left: we have to reconstruct that same density under new conditions of freedom and equality. It would appear to be an elementary requirement of social democracy that there exist a *society* of lively, engaged, and effective men and women — where the honour of 'action' belongs to the many and not to the few.

Against a background of growing disorganization — violence, homelessness, divorce, abandonment, alienation and addiction — a society of this sort looks more like a necessary achievement than a comfortable reality. In truth, however, it was never a comfortable reality, except for the few. Most men and women have been trapped in one or another subordinate relationship, where the 'civility' they learned was deferential rather than independent and active. That is why democratic citizenship, socialist production, free enterprise, and nationalism were all of them liberating projects. But none of them has yet produced a general, coherent or sustainable liberation. And their more singleminded adherents, who have exaggerated the effectiveness of the state or the market or the nation and neglected the networks, have probably contributed to the disorder of contemporary life. The projects have to be relativized and brought together, and the place to do that is in civil society, the setting of settings, where each can find the partial fulfilment that is all it deserves.

Civil society itself is sustained by groups much smaller than the *demos* or the working class or the mass of consumers or the nation. All these are necessarily pluralized as they are incorporated. They become part of the world of family, friends, comrades and colleagues, where people are connected to one another and made responsible for one another. Connected and responsible: without that, 'free and equal' is less attractive than we once thought it would be. I have no magic formula for making connections or strengthening the sense of responsibility. These are not aims that can be underwritten with historical guarantees or achieved through a single unified struggle. Civil society is a project of projects; it requires many organizing strategies and new forms of state action. It requires a new sensitivity for what is local, specific, contingent — and, above all, a new recognition (to paraphrase a famous sentence) that the good life is in the details.

5

On the Subject of Rights: Pluralism, Plurality and Political Identity

Kirstie McClure

Across a wide range of US journals in both women's studies and the social sciences, post-structuralist approaches to political inquiry are frequently criticized as inimical to an effective oppositional or trans-formative political practice. A reviewer of two recent treatments of the historical construction of the category 'women', for example, not only describes the work of those 'bitten by the virus of post-structuralist critical philosophy' as 'a shade ludicrous', but suggests as well that such thinkers 'have placed themselves outside the range of feminism'.[1] This chapter attempts to respond to this position. In particular, it speaks to the critical claim advanced by many feminist political theorists that the contemporary assertion of the status of 'subject' by historically sub-jugated or silenced identities of race, gender, ethnicity and sexuality renders politically suspect any interrogation of either the status of 'subject' or the language of rights.[2] The edge of that criticism might be summarily cast in the following terms: 'Just when marginal and oppressed groups are asserting their rights as political subjects is no time to deconstruct the categories. Indeed, to do so at present is to become complicitous with a neo-conservative agenda, an agenda which aims precisely to restrict both the scope of such rights claims and the potential power of those actively beginning to advance them.' Jane Flax put the point succinctly in confessing a deep suspicion 'of the motives of those who counsel such a move at the moment when women have just begun to remember their selves and claim an argentic subjectivity.'[3]

This is an accusation that deserves consideration, and one that demands some form of constructive theoretical and political response. Broadly speaking, the criticism suggests a necessary opposition between post-structuralism and political agency or, put somewhat differently, between the deconstruction of essential identities and the possibility of effective political action. Although the bulk of these remarks will focus on questions of rights, power and identity in Anglo-American pluralist discourse, I would like to open with a few more general observations about the assumptions conditioning the construction of that opposition itself. For the sake of brevity I must do so simply by assertion; but I hope the remainder of this chapter will offer at least a glimpse of some of the directions a more robust articulation might take.

I shall begin by suggesting that the claimed opposition between post-structuralism and political agency is itself produced by a series of intimately related, if unacknowledged, commitments. By way of a preface, then, to the question of pluralism, I shall characterize these and offer something in the way of alternative critical commitments in their place.

First, and perhaps most obviously, the claim clearly presupposes an identity between 'the subject of rights' and the unitary self-present subject of modernity. In predicating 'political efficacy' as an attribute of this subject, and this subject alone, a commitment is thereby made to a particular construct of rights-claiming activities as a formal expression of 'active citizenship' in the context of the modern democratic state. Second, and following from this, the criticism presumes that the contemporary rights-claiming activities on the part of subordinated, oppressed, 'peripheral,' or 'marginalized' others *necessarily* signifies the achievement and assertion of such subjectivity, as well as the expansion of the determinate content of the category. It implies, in other words, two things. It suggests, to begin with, that such activities — for example, on the part of the poor, women, blacks, ethnic minorities, lesbians and gay men — entail something of a passage *from* subjection *to* subjectivity, a passage, in the language of liberal political discourse, from subordination to effective citizenship. Further, though, it suggests that this passage signifies an historical broadening of who *counts* as such a subject, an expansion of who counts as a political agent or citizen beyond its modernist preserve as a fraternity bounded by the privileges of dominant race, class and sexual prerogatives.

Finally, and implicit in both of these commitments, the assertion of an opposition between post-structuralism and political agency takes as

given the institutions, both formal and informal, of the modern constitutional state as a privileged expression of political community, and
hence as the principle and necessarily privileged site of political action. If
politics can be characterized, in Michael Oakeshott's formidable terms,
as the activity of 'attending to the arrangements' of one's society, of
participating in the determination of its fate in time and its character as a
place, then surely an emphasis upon the rights of citizens as the modern
form of such activity presupposes the national state as the necessary arena
or site of its expression. In figuring the 'subject of rights' as the active
citizen in these terms, we presume both the potency and the efficacy of
the modern state as a singular and sovereign adjudicator and enforcer of
rights within a bounded and definite 'society'.

Taken together, these commitments suggest that the claimed opposition between post-structuralism and political agency is produced by a
double affirmation of the categories central to modern political theory
since the rise of a recognizably modern state form in seventeenth century
Europe. On the one hand, it affirms the sovereign subject as a privileged
political agent, not simply *in* itself as an ontologically privileged origin of
meaning, but *for* itself as a right-bearing citizen. On the other hand, and
simultaneously, it affirms the sovereign state as a primary site of political
struggle, as the principle and privileged location for the recognition,
validation and enforcement of rights claims on the part of those
sovereign subjects, understood as members of a particular 'society'. In
sum, the critical roots of the alleged opposition continue to circulate
within, and thus reproduce, the distinctively modern political problematic described by Foucault as the intimate relation and reciprocal tension
between subjectivity and subjection in the context of the modern state.[4]

I want to suggest, by contrast, the possibility that post-structuralist
contributions to political understanding may not dissolve so much as
reinscribe 'the subject of rights' and that, to the extent that this is so, they
may not exile so much as reconstitute questions of political identity and
agency, as well as questions about the character, scope and potential sites
of political action. This, perhaps, could be done by citing Foucault's
analysis of 'governmentality', but such a strategy is unlikely to be very
compelling to US critics of post-structuralism. Indeed, from their standpoint such a reiteration would be viewed as yet another instance of the
problem. I think, however, that there are ways of responding to the
criticism from the interior of what circulates as liberal political theory,
and more particularly through the resources provided by various discursive shifts in the development of its 'pluralist' wing since the turn of

the twentieth century. To begin to develop a framework for this strategy, I would offer the following as counter-claims or alternatives to the modernist commitments or presuppositions I just sketched.

First, rather than assume an identity between the modern subject and the 'subject of rights', we might begin by noting that the relation between the 'sovereign subject' of Enlightenment modernity and the 'subject of rights' as citizen of a national state is not necessary, but historically contingent. The language of rights indeed long precedes this particular articulation, and there is, I think, no *prima facie* case to be made that *a* 'subject of rights' cannot or will not survive the dissolution of its modernist incarnation. The 'subject of rights' in this modernist form itself has its histories, at least one significant instance of which, to take its Anglo-American development as an example, was the displacement of a range of diverse and contradictory localist and participatory constructs by centralized national and statist codifications of legal discourse.[5] Thus the modern form of the 'subject of rights' can itself be understood as an effect of the practical and discursive struggles of modern constitutionalism under very specific historical and geopolitical conditions. From the vantage point of contemporary feminism this is, to be sure, a decidedly checkered history. While this historical figuration of the 'subject of rights' as an autonomous 'individual' provided a successful historical counter to absolutist denials of participatory channels, it none the less excluded from the public realm all sectors of the population as were conventionally coded as 'dependent' or 'other' by the dominant cultural frame: women, children, labourers, aliens, the mad, and criminals, etc. In this, the historicity of the modern subject and that of western masculinity are, to be sure, intimately connected.[6] The political issue involved here, however, is more complex than the exclusion of these multiple 'others' from participatory rights; for the historical effectivity of modern constitutionalism is not contained within its inscription of bourgeois man as the model of the citizen. At the same time, and significantly for my present purposes, that history has more broadly constituted the national citizen as the paradigmatic figure of properly 'political' agency.

What I am suggesting most broadly is that the construction of the 'subject of rights' was, and by extension continues to be, a process consequent upon the articulation of particular and specific historical struggles, and the very pervasiveness, as well as porousness and contentiousness, of 'rights talk' in the late twentieth century in a variety of contexts suggests that these processes of construction are hardly at an end. If this is the case, to presume the modernist form of that subject as essential to politics in general, or to democratic politics in particular, is to avoid not only the politics of its historical constitution, but the possibility of its contemporary political transformation.

Secondly, if the 'subject of rights' is a contingent construct, we might question rather than presume its relation to contemporary assertions of rights on the terrain of 'differences', for these may themselves significantly transform or exceed the conventional figuration of that subject, especially as this has taken the formal character of individual citizenship in the modern state. In other words, such assertions (whether in the nineteenth century of class, or subsequently of race, gender, ethnicity, sexuality or, indeed, any combination of these) may signify something quite exceeding the entrance of such 'identities' into the status of unitary subject-as-citizen. And this excess may well imply the contingent re-inscription or transformation of specifically *political* identity and *political* subjectivity in a distinctly different register than has heretofore been the case. That such differences as race, gender, sexuality and ethnicity are, for example, articulated in terms that may imply potential solidarities not only within but beyond the domestic context or territorial confines of the national state is, I think, itself significant. This is not, I should add, to imply that formal citizenship is thereby rendered obsolete. It is, however, to suggest that it may well be better understood as but a part, rather than the sum or apex, of the political identity of social subjects.

Third, and perhaps most contentiously, we might challenge rather than assume the adequacy of the state as unique or privileged location of political address. To the extent that such contemporary assertions of what we might call the rights of 'otherness' *can* be understood as re-inscriptions, they may well call into question more than the statist affinities of the modern subject-as-citizen. They may interrogate the sovereign state itself, and this in two respects. On the one hand, such reinscriptions may problematize the state and its formal institutions, both as a privileged site and as a privileged object of political struggle. This is not to evoke the romantic revolutionary illusion that the state can be literally 'smashed' or dissolved by an act of will. Rather, it is to suggest that, to the extent that such differences do gesture towards trans- or non-national solidarities, the political sites upon which their rights claims are articulated cannot be neatly contained either within the juridical boundaries of national states or within the modernist identification of political agency with national citizenship. Further, however, such reinscriptions of 'the subject of rights' may call the state into question, as well, as a sovereign and necessarily privileged form of political association. They

may, to put the point somewhat differently, suggest a certain disarticula-
tion of the privilege accorded to the modern nation-state as the signal
expression and singular referent of what Benedict Anderson has referred
to as an 'imagined community'.[7]

These counter-constructs are admittedly dense, compacted in large
part by my own reduction or condensation of the claims to which they
are styled as alternatives. To unpack them a bit and elaborate what I take
to be some of their instances and implications, I shall turn to the more
specific context provided by the historical development and recent
resuscitation of pluralist discourse. In particular, I want to consider the
extent to which or conditions under which pluralist constructs,
including contemporary 'post-Marxist' pluralism informed by post-
structuralist critiques of identity, might gesture towards such a transformation or reinscription of the 'subject of rights' in liberal
constitutional orders. I speak here with particular reference to the
contemporary United States, where the claim to being a pluralist democracy is a central element of the dominant political culture; I make no
claims to extension or generalization beyond this, nor do I wish to assert
a necessary priority or uniqueness to this context.[8] Rather, I offer these
remarks in the way of an intervention, at once limited and strategic, in
both American pluralist discourse and feminist theory. And I do so with
a particular concern that the potentially radical implications of 'post-
modern pluralism' in its post-Marxist form not be lost in its reception on
this side of the Atlantic, whether that take the form of either rejection or
too hasty acceptance.

In the United States, for the third time this century, arguments for a
'pluralist politics' are beginning to command attention and debate, both
as a practical concern and as a theoretical term of art. Each of these
generations of pluralist argument, as is perhaps befitting the term,
encompasses a variety of perspectives and emphases — loose affinities
that appear as temporally localized kindred less in terms of a common
programme than by virtue of a common critical opposition to similarly
localized monolithic or unitary conceptions of the political domain.

Anglo-American pluralism initially arose around the turn of the
century and peaked over the decade following the First World War.
Connected on the terrain of practice to political agitation on a number
of fronts, and in Britain to that of the labour movement in particular, it
found its theoretical voice in the works of such Anglophone writers as
Ernest Barker, Harold Laski, Arthur Bentley and, although somewhat

ambiguously, Mary P. Follett.[9] Often drawing upon the philosophy of William James as well as the work of American and continental jurists, its political purchase was constituted in opposition to the unitary conceptions of state sovereignty forwarded by the Austinian school of jurisprudence as well as by Hegelian philosophy in the hands of such English Idealists as Bernard Bosanquet. It was framed, in short, as a critical counter to theoretical perspectives that affirmed the sovereign state as the centre of political life.

The second generation of pluralism, something of a more indigenous American growth, found expression in the 1950s and 1960s, in the work of such US social scientists as Robert Dahl and David Truman, among numerous others.[10] Framed in part as an 'empirical democratic theory' capable of explaining American politics, and invested as well in an effort to build a 'discipline' of political science within the American academy, it was posed in opposition to sociological theories of a 'power elite'. Unlike first-generation pluralists, whose intimate connections to political struggle generated a critical perspective on the state as such, the second generation donned the mantle of scientific observers, representing their findings as above the fray of political argument and taking as their project the theoretical articulation and empirical testing of hypotheses concerning the location of power in American political life. This, on their account, operated through a diffuse concatenation of autonomous and competing groups, rather than through the socio-economic sovereignty of a dominant elite whose interests determined the policy outcomes of American political institutions and processes.

At present, we are in the midst of a third generation of pluralist debate, one which, like its predecessors, includes a range of diverse perspectives. But while current arguments for cultural pluralism, as well as the pluralist democratic theory of Michael Walzer, continue to circulate largely within the general problematic established by the preceding pluralist generations, the recent theoretical work of Ernesto Laclau and Chantal Mouffe signals a potentially significant transformation of pluralist politics.[11] As one might expect, this most recent incarnation of pluralism bears certain affinities to its predecessors. Indeed, in this context, that is, on this side of the Atlantic, this is so much the case that the politically significant aspects of its post-modern deconstructive presentation are threatened by the very familiarity of the term, and perhaps in particular by the sedimentation of previous pluralist articulations into the 'common sense' of the dominant political discourse. Before speaking of the differences between this postmodern pluralism and its predecessors, however, I'd like first to suggest some of the general characteristics of all three pluralist generations. With this as a frame, perhaps the political implications of their points of differentiation can be seen more clearly.

All three pluralisms have been articulated in critical opposition to unitary, monolithic or totalizing conceptions of the political domain, particularly in so far as these presume some singularly sovereign or unique agency overseeing or determining political processes and/or social relations. That opposition, further, across all three instances, has insisted upon the irreducible plurality of the social, specifically as this finds expression in the plurality or multiplicity of social groups. For all three pluralist generations, however, the political valence of such groups is understood to have no necessary ontological grounding. They are not, in other words, a political expression of 'natural kinds' or essences, but appear rather as contingently constituted political entities: that is, they emerge through the dynamics of particular struggles arising within the realm of the social, and are elaborated as 'political' through a process of articulation.[12] Finally, and I think significantly, all three pluralisms view the social subject, or what I have here termed the 'subject of rights', as a site of multiple and intersecting group memberships or identities within that social plurality, only one, and by no means necessarily the most significant, of which is that of formal citizenship in the state.

Twentieth-century pluralist accounts of the political thus tend to begin, as it were, *in medias res*, in the middle of things, focusing upon the constellation and character of groups as they appear or emerge in a given present. Within pluralist discourses such groups are seen not as political 'essences', but are understood rather to generate their own peculiar relationship to the established political order of things. They are represented as self-defining and independent, in particular of the state — in the limited or bounded sense of not depending upon its sovereign recognition or licence for their existence. They are, in sum, understood to have no necessary relation to state power except in so far as they articulate such a relationship. To put the point in somewhat different terms, within pluralist constructs such groups have an 'objective' political character and identity with regard to political power, processes or institutions only in so far as they have articulated a 'subjective' political identity and character in these terms.

Despite this broad kinship, these three generations of pluralist argument also have significant political differences which I would like to characterize in terms of their respective constructions of the relationship between the plurality of the social and political struggle. These successive expressions can, I think, be fruitfully summarized, in turn, as 'resighting' the political, in the sense of *seeing* again; as 'reciting' the political, in the sense of *saying* again; and as 'resisting' the political, in the sense of *relocating* the potential sites of political agency and address.

For the first generation at the turn of the century, pluralism provided an opportunity for resighting or rediscovering the political in the midst of the social. In theoretical terms it offered a counter to philosophical monism, while on the plane of practice it affirmed the independence of group life from state determination. It forwarded instead the idea of 'distributive sovereignty', a move that, by seeing the plurality of the social in a variety of self-constituting groups, in effect levelled the state to the status of one group among many others and rendered it dependent upon them for loyalty and support. In this, the first wave of pluralism effected a significant displacement of the earlier liberal rhetoric of 'autonomy' from the individual to the group. At the same time, however, it disrupted the social atomism of earlier liberalism, for the pluralist social subject was reinscribed as a complex and multifaceted member of a variety of groups, rather than a unified and autonomous self. For early pluralists, in short, both the sovereign state and the sovereign subject were fictions, fictions which they replaced by what, on their account, was a more 'realistic' account of the fluidity and diversity of social experience and practice.

However, just as this pluralism continued the liberal rhetoric of autonomy in a new form, so too did it reinscribe the liberal distinction between public and private. And just as the 'sovereign individual' in earlier liberalism functioned as a principle of both inclusion and ex-clusion, so did the pluralist construct of autonomous groups redraw these lines by distinguishing between groups of a public/political and those of a private or non-political character. In particular, this pluralism drew upon political economy to argue for the distinctive public character of occupational groups, not as objects of regulation by a sovereign state, but as functional groups whose 'interests' were a signifi-cant element of the welfare of the nation as a whole. 'Occupational groups' in this period is, of course, a euphemism for or displacement of the language of class, and in this respect pluralism can be understood in much the same terms as Hofstadter describes the American Progressives, as a counter-reformation in the face of something far more radical.

But even a counter-reformation initiates certain forms of change, and the effort to recuperate certain aspects of liberal constitutionalism required its transformation. For pluralists like Laski and Barker especially, the multiplicity of groups and group identities not only called into question the 'autonomous' and 'sovereign' character of the state; it demanded as well a significant rethinking of both citizenship and representation. On this pluralist account, in particular, the traditional individualist principle of geographical numerical representation was inadequate to reflect the political significance of occupational group concerns and interests. As an alternative, they proposed to augment this with 'occupational representation' in a number of possible institutional forms, ranging from the notion of a 'social parliament', to formal electoral categories specific to labor, to special forms of interest representation through boards and commissions with specific points of influence built into the policy process.

Counter-reformation though it may have been, this pluralism transformed the figure of the 'subject of rights' into something quite other than the autonomous individual. Not least of all, it shifted the distinction between public and private in a way that removed labour struggles from the atomistically grounded private realm protection of 'liberty of contract' doctrine, and invested occupational identity with political privilege.[13] And while first-generation pluralism ultimately reconstituted the modernist dynamic between subjectivity and subjection, by recuperating the occupational fragment of its 'multiple subject' and directing the political edge of its identity towards participation in formal state institutions, it none the less simultaneously reconstituted the basis of its citizenship as well as the mode of its representation. In so doing, however, it reinscribed the 'subject of rights' as a creature whose *political* identity was no longer given by virtue of its 'individuality', but rather was contingently constituted, *within* the social, by its participation in group processes. And this, I think, initiated a shift in the interior of Anglo-American liberalism towards the construction of a social subject distant not only from Marxism's ontologically privileged class agency, but from liberalism's autonomous, rational individual as well.

If this first pluralist generation rediscovered politics in group processes and interactions, the second in significant respects *recited* or reiterated that frame in the context of the post-war United States. But here, where totalizing narratives of both left and right had little historical purchase, where political power was conventionally coded as located in '*a* government' rather than '*the* state', this recitation of the autonomy of group life necessarily put a rather different political spin on pluralism's original categories. Here, 'pluralism' was recited not as a middle ground between an absolutist fiction of state sovereignty and the 'objective' historical agency of an international proletariat, but in opposition to sociological accounts of a 'power elite', representing business or corporate interests, as the one group that subtly but surely dominated the American political agenda. Presuming 'government' to be simply the arena in which social groups engaged in political conflict, the American pluralist critique of sovereignty was thus shifted from the institutional context of the state onto the terrain of the social itself. As a consequence of that shift, even this pluralism, despite what most of its critics rightly regard as its ideological support for the status quo, once again re-formulated the relation between the plurality of the social and political struggle.[14] And in so doing it again reconstituted the pluralist social subject as a 'subject of rights' but one distanced yet further from the traditional liberal figure of the autonomous individual. Let me briefly mention a few aspects of this.

Unlike its predecessor, this pluralism was marked largely, especially in political science, by a strategic avoidance of political economy, focusing rather upon the contingent formation, organization and expression of group 'interests', around specific 'issues', particularly as these pressed demands upon governmental institutions through a variety of partici-patory channels.[15] The political meaning of this strategy is, however, equivocal. On the one hand, in the context of the Cold War, this may well have been driven by liberal resistance to sociological accounts of corporate dominance; such conclusions could only be embarrassing to the self-proclaimed paragon of the free world. On the other hand, however, the abandonment of political economy simultaneously deprived pluralist theory of the discourse that had, in its initial formulation, functioned as an external means of differentiating between 'private associations' and groups of public significance which required some form of representation or inclusion in the formulation of public policy. Absent from this exclusionary mechanism, the theoretical distinc-tion between public and private, between the plurality of the social in a general sense and the erstwhile 'properly political concerns' of the industrial political economy, is dissolved. In effect, within second-generation pluralism, the political character and significance of group identities and associational life *within* the social plurality becomes itself a matter of contingent articulation, no longer either delimited or guaran-teed by purely economic or 'occupations' considerations. Thus while behavioural pluralism offered a getaway car, so to speak, for corporate power, it simultaneously provided vehicles for the political articulation of group identities and interests previously relegated to the private realm.

The 'subject of rights' for this second generation of pluralism, like that of its predecessor, was a multiple subject, its identities constituted by its membership in a plurality of groups. Further, though, and precisely because such groups were presumed to be autonomous and their 'interests' contingently constituted, this new pluralist subject became itself a site of potential contradiction, of potentially conflicting identities, loyalties or 'interests'. For behavioural pluralism, in short, as the terrain of the social was contingently riven by 'cross-cutting cleavages', so was its social subject potentially fraught with contradictions to the extent that the articulated interests of the groups to which it belonged came into conflict.

It is, however, at the very point of thinking this possibility that second-generation pluralism reinscribed the modernist dynamic between subjectivity and subjection by reaffirming the investment of its multiple subject's *political* identity into formal avenues of participatory citizenship. Channelled through the institutional frameworks of electoral and policy processes, the political activities of its 'subject of rights' are forced into a decisionist model that takes state institutions and processes both as the necessary sites of political expression or agency and as the necessary objects of political influence. In this context, the pluralist subject's *political* identity is articulated through decisions expressing support or opposition to particular policy alternatives or issues touching its various filiations within the social plurality. Where the 'interests' of its various group identities or filiations conflict, however, this pluralism rewrites that subject as a rational preference orderer, weighing and evaluating the 'interests' of its multiple allegiances. The outcome of this process is cast as a choice, a decision specifying which of its identities, or what combination of its allegiances, it will express through such specific institutional channels as electoral politics, lobbying and pressure group activities, or political demonstrations. And needless to say, it is impossible to express contradiction through a vote or policy preference; and political demonstrations, to be credible, must speak in something approximating a unified voice.

But if, by this institutional channelling, the multiplicity of the pluralist subject is dissolved at the level of the citizen, it none the less re-emerges in a different form at the systemic level of state institutions themselves. The 'real' political interests of various groups within the social plurality become, for this pluralism, simply the outcome of the state's policy processes at any given point in time. As such they are always subject to revision and reformulation on the basis of contingent re-articulations of group interests, reframed and renegotiated through conflict with other groups, within the policy process as a continuous and institutionally bounded location of political struggle. In political practice over time, however, this pluralism's initial opening of political space has culminated in that curious combination of open expression and political closure that goes by the name of 'interest group liberalism'.[16]

The first two generations of pluralism, in sum, suggest partial transformations of the 'subject of rights'. More specifically, they have reinscribed that subject by opening successively broader spaces for the *political* expression of identities constructed *within* the plurality of the social, identities which by virtue of their very particularity are in excess of the autonomous self or unitary subject requisite to traditional liberal accounts of active citizenship. But both, albeit in different ways, re-cuperated and disciplined that excess into a collaborative relationship with the sovereign state: the first by using the discourse of political economy to distinguish between public and private group identities, and the second by funnelling the political claims of all groups through institutional channels into one or another form of addressing the state. And it is, I think, precisely such recuperation that contemporary post-structuralist 'pluralism' offers the possibility of resisting, not in the sense of opposition to the state as such, but rather as resistance to constructions of political identity and subjectivity that take state institutions as the principal sites, and state power as the primary object, of political struggle. It is to this possibility that I now turn.

Let me recall where I began, with the suspicion voiced by a number of feminist political theorists that the deconstruction of essential identities is antithetical to political agency. I hope that even this brief excursion through earlier pluralist frames has suggested that, with regard to the 'subject of rights', the trajectory of twentieth-century Anglo-American liberalism has been similar in significant respects to that of European post-structuralism, at least with regard to its disruption of the pre-sumption that the autonomous individual is a necessary requisite to political agency. Where the two differ most significantly, however, is where American pluralism stands most in need of its European cousin and where feminist criticism might find post-structuralist insights more politically constructive and theoretically productive than is often assumed. And this, I would suggest, is in the extent to which the latter, particularly in the work of Laclau and Mouffe, has focused theoretical

attention upon the construction of identities *within* the plurality of the
social, rather than looking only to their end-points as representations of
'group interests' in the house of mirrors that passes for the policy process
of the contemporary state. In particular, where their post-Marxist
pluralism is most distant from its American relation is in its insistence
that 'politics' is not simply the projection of group 'interests' onto the
screen of state policy, but indeed precedes this in the intricate processes
of articulation through which such identities, representations, and rights
claims are themselves contingently constructed.

To spell this out briefly, let me return to feminist criticism that post-
structuralism renders political agency impossible on the part of 'women'.
This, I think, makes sense only within the frame of a politics that
requires 'women' to be a bounded group, with identifiable and coherent
common 'interests', a frame which I have tried to suggest is itself bound
up with second-generation pluralism's state-centric construction of the
relation between the plurality of the social and political struggle. What
post-structuralism can do to this frame is less a dissolution than a
diffusion of its political import, specifically by redirecting attention to
the *process* rather than simply to the *outcome* of 'interest articulation'. And
in so doing, what it offers is the potential for 'resiting' or resituating
political agency and struggle within the plurality of the social itself. To
make the political valence of this resiting clear, however, especially for
feminists operating in the already presumptively pluralist context of US
interest group liberalism, something more must be said.

Here, I think, this post-Marxist pluralism might be brought into
fruitful conjuncture with recent feminist discussions of 'sexual
difference', and in particular with attempts to confront the inadequacy of
thinking this 'difference' as a universal sex opposition in the face of
differences between and within women and, by implication, between
and within men as well. De Lauretis, for example, speaks of 'the subject
of feminism' as a 'subject constituted in gender though not by sexual
difference alone, but rather across languages and cultural representations; a subject en-gendered in the experiencing of race and class, as well
as sexual, relations; a subject, therefore, not unified but rather multiple,
and no so much divided as contradicted.'[17] What is most provocative in
this formulation is its insistence, on the one hand, upon the materiality
of the discursive production of gender in social relations and subjectivity
and, on the other, upon its historically and culturally-specific imbrica-
tion with hierarchically articulated relations of race, class, ethnicity and
sexuality. No subject, in sum, is simply gendered; there are no 'women'

simpliciter, already constituted as a bounded political group with necessary common interests, already given as a political category. Instead, subjectivities are socially located, temporally specific and potentially riven within a series of other relational differences. And where social subjects are complexly constituted not only through categories of gender, but of race and sexuality, ethnicity and class, and perhaps of religion and nationality as well, a position of privilege within one frame may be simultaneously and contradictorily constructed within a position of oppression within another.

De Lauretis and numerous other feminist theorists, such as Donna Haraway, Sandra Harding and Elizabeth V. Spelman, have suggested that such multiple subjectivities imply a radical epistemological potential.[18] The question I would like to raise is the extent to which this might pose a radical political possibility as well, specifically with regard to its distance from the singular identity required of the citizen-subject of the modern state. Consider, for instance, its resonance with Laclau and Mouffe's description of the 'democratic revolution' as a series of successive displacements of the line of demarcation between public and private, extending from nineteenth-century workers' struggles to contemporary resistances of subjects constituted as the sexual and racial boundaries of dominant culture. We are, they suggest, confronted with a 'politicization far more radical' than ever before, because today's erasure of the boundaries between public and private is accomplished not through the incursion of public authority into a pre-existing private realm, but through a 'proliferation of new political spaces'.[19] Although spoken in very different theoretical languages, I wonder if both these formulations might not constitute a third reinscription of the 'subject of rights', a reinscription that implies neither an escape from the state as such, nor necessarily an abdication from political participation more conventionally understood, but rather a potential refusal of a unitary construct of citizenship as exhaustive of the political tasks of the present.

We might ask, for example, if their parallel politicization of such differences as race, class, gender, ethnicity and sexuality might signal not only a disjuncture within the modernist problematic of subjectivity and subjection but, consequently, and precisely through the multiplication of such excess identities, a potential unsettling of the statist elements of pluralist politics. The multiplicity and contradiction of this post-modern subject may, in other words, constitute a significant disruption of the logic of sovereignty, particularly as this has entailed the condensation and channelling of political agency into the activities of 'citizen-subjects' addressing rights claims to the state. 'What has been exploded', as Laclau and Mouffe suggest, 'is the idea and the reality itself of a unique space of the constitution of the political.'[20] The new 'political spaces' to which they refer point to the diffusion of political sites across the surface of the social itself, to the elaboration of 'the political' beyond its modernist enclosure within the territorially-bounded juridical institutions of the state into the far more fluid and shifting domain of cultural representations and social practices.

To reconceptualize the relation between the plurality of the social and political struggle in these terns seems to me to extend rather than dissolve the political agency of the pluralist social subject, and to do so in a number of respects. First, it sustains the capacity of that subject to make claims on behalf of any, or any combination, of its multiple dimensions, across the myriad instances of the social: in the family and on the street; in the workplace and the church; in economic transactions, sexual relations or educational institutions. Instead, in other words, of framing such claims as juridical demands upon the state, instead of directing them into law and social policy, this post-modern pluralism opens the possibility of a quotidian politics — a politics which extends the terrain of political contestation to the everyday enactment of social practices and the routine reiteration of cultural representations. To deny the uniqueness of the national state both as a site and as an object of political struggle, then, is not to eviscerate the potential for a transformative politics, but rather to resist its recuperation within the reductive and unifying mechanisms of interest group liberalism. And in this respect, it suggests the possibility of a politics that begins not with the object of constructing similarities to address rights claims to the state, but opens rather with the object of addressing such claims to each other, and to each 'other', whoever and wherever they may be.

As a consequence of this possibility, what might be termed a politics of direct address, the political character of the post-modern pluralist subject is expanded in a second and more complex sense as well. Not only is its agency affirmed by recasting 'the social' as a terrain of political contestation; it is extended further by insisting that its multiple identities are themselves not given as 'natural kinds' but contingently constructed and reconstructed through the reiteration of cultural codes and through participation in the social practices through which these codes are enacted in daily life. As Judith Butler has suggestively argued with regard to gender and sexuality, the recognition that such identities are constructed is by no means antithetical to agency, for such constructions provide 'the very terms in which agency is articulated and becomes culturally intelligible'.[21] 'Identity', on this account is not what one *is*, but what one *enacts*, and its political transformation entails neither an Archimedean point exterior to social constructions nor an ontological bedrock beneath them. Rather, it implies 'strategies of subversive repetition', the introduction of variation into the codes, performatively reconfiguring such constructions from their interior in social practice, and thereby shifting the very terms of cultural intelligibility.[22]

For the postmodern subject, however, such strategies are necessarily complicated, precisely because its multiplicity and contradictions have been constituted via historically and culturally specific politicizations of class, gender and race relations, of ethnic and sexual 'identities', as well as, most recently, able-bodiedness. What produces contradictions in the postmodern subject, in other words, are not 'natural' antitheses between the 'interests' of 'women', the 'differently abled', 'blacks', 'homosexuals' or 'Hispanics' and their respective 'others', but the division of its subjective allegiances between contingent constructions of the needs, as well as articulations of the 'rights', of each of these now politicized 'identities'. If, therefore, as de Lauretis argues, such a subject has been 'engendered in the experiencing of race and class, as well as sexual, relations', then the enactment of a subversive variation on the codes governing, say, its gender or sexuality might yet intensify its contradictions by reinforcing the codes constituting its race or class. The political question, if this is the case, cannot be contained within such singular reconfigurations, but extends to the possibility of negotiating the broader political resonances of their shape and form across, and in light of, the multiplicity of such differences. It is here, then, that the possibility of direct address politicizes these postmodern subjects yet further, by recognizing their agency in such contingent reconfigurations, however local or transitory they may be. In short, by recasting their production and reproduction of their own 'identities' as political investments, it constitutes their participation in culture itself as a political commitment.

To frame 'the social' as a site of political action, to take cultural codes as objects of political struggle, is not to invoke the lightness of being nor is it simply to replace the logic of sovereignty with the play of signifiers. Such extensions of agency into social practices and cultural representations carry with them the weight of responsibility, and the constant risk of being called to account. This is, to be sure, no panacea for the woes of either feminist policy theory or of 'pluralist' politics. It offers no resolution of the tensions and contradictions of 'identity' politics as an un-settled, unsettling, and contentious discursive field. It may however, suggest avenues for political and theoretical exploration that lead out of the conceptual *cul-de-sac* within which the modernist conflation of political agency with the citizen-subject of a sovereign state seems to circulate, for if it accomplishes nothing else it at least recognizes the state as a blunt instrument for cultural transformation.

Notes

Earlier versions of this chapter were presented at the Center for Cultural Studies, University of California/Santa Cruz; at the Gender and Politics Colloquium, Department of Government, Harvard University; and at the 1990 Western Political Science Association meeting. Participants at those events provided useful comments, and I am particularly grateful to Bonnie Honig and Christine di Stephano for their comments and criticism.

1. Karen Offen, 'The Use and Abuse of History', a review of Denise Riley's *Am I That Name?*, University of Minnesota Press, Minneapolis, MN 1988, and Joan Landes' *Women and the Public Sphere in the Age of the French Revolution*, Cornell University Press, Ithaca, NY 1988, in *The Women's Review of Books*, vol. VI, no. 7, April 1989.

2. See, for example, Nancy Hartsock, 'Rethinking Modernism: Minority vs. Majority Theories', *Cultural Critique* vol. 7, 1987, pp. 187–206; Jane Flax, 'Remembering Selves: Is the Repressed Gendered?', *Michigan Quarterly Review*, vol. 26, no. 1, 1987, pp. 92–110; Christine di Stefano, 'Dilemmas of Difference: Feminism, Modernity, and Postmodernism', *Women and Politics*, vol. 8, no. 3/4, 1988, pp. 1–24; and Nancy Hartsock, 'Foucault on Power: A Theory for Women?', in *The Gender of Power: A Symposium*, ed. Monique Leijenaar, Vakgroep Vrouwenstudies/Vena, Leiden 1987. The latter two of these, as well as a number of other essays addressing the question, are reprinted in the recent anthology edited by Linda Nicholson, *Feminism/Postmodernism*, Routledge, New York 1990.

3. Flax, 'Remembering Selves', p. 106.

4. 'The Subject and Power', in *Michel Foucault: Between Structuralism and Hermeneutics*, ed. Hubert Dreyfus and Paul Rabinow, University of Chicago Press, Chicago 1983.

5. See, for example, Howard Nenner's *by colour of law*, University of Chicago Press, Chicago 1977.

6. For a detailed account of this in the context of eighteenth-century French republicanism see Joan B. Landes, *Women in the Public Sphere in the Age of the French Revolution*, Cornell University Press, Ithaca, NY 1988.

7. *Imagined Communities*, Verso, London 1983.

8. In particular, I want to disclaim affinity with the standard American pluralist image of the 'stages of development', a construct that posits the United States as a model for the rest of the world.

9. Ernest Barker, 'The Discredited State', *Political Quarterly*, no. 5, February 1915; Harold Laski, *Studies in the Problem of Sovereignty*, Yale University Press, New Haven, CT 1917; *Authority in the Modern State*, Yale University Press, New Haven, CT 1919; *The Foundations of Sovereignty and Other Essays*, Harcourt, Brace and Co., New York 1921; Arthur Bentley, *The Process of Government*, University of Chicago Press, Chicago 1908; Mary P. Follett, *The New State*, Longmans, Green and Co., Boston 1918; and *Creative Experience*, Longmans, Green and Co. 1924.

10. Among the better known are Robert Dahl, *Who Governs?*, Yale University Press, New Haven, CT 1961; and *Pluralistic Democracy in the United States*, Rand McNally & Co., Chicago 1967; David Truman, *The Governmental Process*, Alfred A. Knopf, New York 1951; Edward C. Banfield, *Political Influence*, The Free Press, New York 1965; Charles E. Lindblom, *The Intelligence of Democracy*, The Free Press, New York 1965.

11. *Hegemony and Socialist Strategy*, Verso, London 1985. See also Chantal Mouffe, 'Hegemony and New Political Subjects: Toward a New Concept of Democracy', in Cary Nelson and Lawrence Grossberg, eds, *Marxism and the Interpretation of Culture*, University of Illinois Press, Urbana/Chicago, Illinois 1988. Ernesto Laclau's 'Politics and the Limits of Modernity' and Mouffe's 'Radical Democracy: Modern or Post-modern?' are included in Andrew Ross, ed., *Universal Abandon?*, University of Minnesota Press, Minneapolis, MN 1988, a book version of the journal *Social Text*, vol. 7, no. 3, Winter 1989.

12. Parenthetically, we might note here that this term 'articulation' is central to both second- and third-generation pluralist constructs. In the phrase 'interest articulation' it has served as a descriptive/empirical term for American social science since the immediate post-war period, while for Laclau and Mouffe it operates as a central theoretical concept as well.

13. For a very interesting account related to this in the American context, see Gary Peller, 'The Metaphysics of American Law', *California Law Review*, vol. 73, 1985.

14. For arguments emphasizing the 'conservative' character of post-war US pluralism, see E.E. Schattschneider, *The Semi-Sovereign People*, Holt, Rinehard and Winston, New York 1960; Robert Paul Wolff's essay, in Robert Paul Wolff, Barrington Moore Jr and Herbert Marcuse, *A Critique of Pure Tolerance*, Beacon Press, Boston 1965; William E. Conolly, ed., *The Bias of Pluralism*, Atherton Press, New York 1969; and Peter Bachrach and Morton S. Baratz, *Power and Poverty*, Oxford University Press, New York 1970, 'Decisions and Non-decisions', *American Political Science Review*, vol. 57, no. 3, September 1963, pp. 641–51, as well as 'Two Faces of Power', *American Political Science Review*, vol. 56, no. 4, December 1962, pp. 947–52.

15. In response to criticism, many of the initial contributors to this second generation pluralism themselves began to reconsider the implications of this avoidance. See for example, Robert Dahl's later focus in *Polyarchy*, Yale University Press, New Haven, CT 1971, as well as the second edition of his account of democracy in the United States (note 10 above) in which the term 'pluralism' is abandoned for 'polyarchy'. See also Charles Lindblom's subsequent *Politics and Markets*, Basic Books, New York 1977. Dahl's more recent works continue this shift, albeit with a curious return to the initial terminology, as in *Dilemmas of Pluralist Democracy*, Yale University Press, New Haven, CT. See also his *A Preface to Economic Democracy*, University of California Press, Berkeley, CA 1985.

16. The classic critical view here is that of Theodore J. Lowi, *The End of Liberalism*,

W.W. Norton & Co., New York 1969.

17. *Technologies of Gender*, Indiana University Press, Bloomington, IN 1988, p. 2.

18. See, for example, Sandra Harding, *The Science Question in Feminism*, Cornell University Press, Ithaca, NY 1986; Donna Haraway, 'Situated Knowledges: The Science Question in Feminism and the Privilege of Partial Perspectives', *Feminist Studies*, vol. 14, no. 3, Fall 1988, pp. 575–99. For a critical view of the issue see Mary E. Hawkesworth, 'Knowers, Knowing, Known: Feminist Theory and Claims to Truth', *Signs*, vol. 14, no. 3, Spring 1989, pp. 533–57. Well worth a reflective reading in this context is Elizabeth V. Spelman, *Inessential Woman*, Beacon Press, Boston 1988.

19. *Hegemony*, p. 181.

20. Ibid.

21. *Gender Trouble*, Routledge, New York and London 1989, p. 147.

22. Ibid.

The Paradoxes of Pluralism

Louise Marcil-Lacoste

Pluralism has had quite a calm history within systematic philosophy. One major reason for this is that the meaning, articulation and implications of thought about plurality – or, as philosophers used to say, the relations between the One and the Many – were consigned not just to metaphysics but to elementary metaphysics, not to say the domain of common sense. To demonstrate that there are several things or types of thing in the universe whose diversity or plurality is an illusion – that is the task that philosophy set itself. The universe was 'all of a piece', as William James (and Thomas Davidson) put it when speaking of Parmenides. Apparent diversity was but the manifestation of a single substance or single being in its various states or from various points of view.[1] Even if it was accepted that there were two types of thing in the universe – the world of the senses and the world of forms, mind and matter, phenomena and noumena – this in no way contradicted the general notion that plurality itself was an illusion. Dualism appeared above all, in the words of Roland Hall,[2] as a failed monism, or even a 'category mistake', as Gilbert Ryle maintained.[3]

Things stand quite differently, however, with the view that the beings who compose the world are multiple, individual and 'independent' (the expression derives from Rudolph Hermann Lotze, who seems to have been the first to use 'pluralism' in this sense),[4] that the realities which make up the richness of the world exceed what science is able to explore, or that the 'parts of experience' cannot be conceived on the basis of ultimate or irreducible categories, as William James held.[5] That is a non-mainstream metaphysics which appeared late in the history of philosophy. It was received as a kind of ontological abdication, so spectacular that the thesis was soon relegated to the status of a common-sense belief. Significantly, when Bertrand Russell rejected monism and converted to what he called 'absolute pluralism' — better known as logical atomism — he himself described the change as a return to common sense.[6] And in so far as there is a 'family resemblance' between postmodern deconstruction and classical pluralist ontology, the major reversal has borne not on the objects (universe or subject) in respect of which monism (or dualism) is rejected, but rather on the relationship between this rejection and common sense. Although common sense was until recently still aware of the discontinuity of things, it would appear to have become the site of a primary monism, which needs to be dislodged.

It was only late in the day, then, and outside the field of philosophy, that ethical and political theories of pluralism began to appear, initially without any great resonance. One thinks here mainly of early twentieth-century sociology where, amid the rush of associationist doctrines (corporatism, guild socialism, unionism, syndicalism), the term 'pluralism' seems to have first been introduced to designate the coexistence of beliefs in different areas of social life.[7] But we should not forget political science, which in 1908 saw the publication of Arthur F. Bentley's important work *The Process of Government*, the first, in Léon Dion's view, to have formulated the major themes of political pluralism as 'the first systematic revolt' after Marxism against 'the romanticism of Jean-Jacques Rousseau and individual liberalism'.[8]

In fact, we had to wait until the middle of the twentieth century for the major characteristics of pluralism to be expressed in the sense in which they are now used. In the work of the economist Joseph Schumpeter, for example, whose *Capitalism, Socialism and Democracy* appeared in 1942, democracy is a method stemming from an idea of politics in which any concept of general will is rejected in favour of self-regulation or self-administration of society through the competition of groups sharing the roles and privileges of the social domain. During the same period, as a prerequisite for cultural analysis, the theory of pluralism was gradually and ever more extensively applied to the anthropological field. Horace M. Kallen is usually thought of as the leading innovator in this respect — particularly his 1954 lectures at the Center for Human Relations of the University of Pennsylvania.

Although ethical and political theories of pluralism were born outside philosophy, and although philosophy took a long time to take their measure, this does not mean that the schemata of ontological thinking about relations between the one, the dual and the many were everywhere abandoned. Indeed, their resurgence is especially apparent in the ease with which discussions of pluralism proceed to pass superficial verdicts, as if it were a question of teaching that pluralism, monism and dualism do not have the same meaning. This resurgence — which involves a systematic depreciation of the many, as well as a difficulty in conceiving pluralism as anything other than a pure negation of either monism or dualism — can also be observed in the way in which contemporary judgements of pluralism have converged from an initially favourable attitude towards an eventual balance-sheet of failure.

The main lines of this judgement are that pluralism opposed political totalitarianism only to venerate one-dimensional man, the ever more amorphous, apathetic and anonymous mass; that it opposed the single party, two-party systems or the rule of the majority only to sanctify competition between interest groups; and that it opposed the state only to hallow the instrumentality of politics. Pluralism, it is therefore concluded, applies historically only to a period of transition, or even to a political tactic; at most, it is but a zero-sum game, a theory in which the critical scope of the recognition of plurality is systematically placed in check.

A Threefold Ambiguity

This leads us to the preliminary observation that the fascinating thing about pluralism is its ambiguity. First of all, there is an ambiguity of fact and norm: to move from saying that plurality exists to saying that it should be treated as a value is to pass illegitimately, as Hume would have put it, from an 'is' to an 'ought', from fact to prescription. In the case of plurality, the transition from the one to the other is all the more disturbing in that — as P. Nowell-Smith pointed out — a systematic misunderstanding is involved in reducing reflection about pluralism to the noting of diversity. The most important (and, for Nowell-Smith, the most interesting) arguments are always located at the crossroads between observations and moral injunctions that cannot as such be deduced from diversity.[9]

Pluralism also exhibits an ambiguity of the overfull and the empty. It evokes potential abundance, for to say of an environment that it is pluralist, or of a politics that it recognizes plurality, is to suggest an expansion or flowering of 'freedoms', a democratic embracing of characteristics, choices and values — individual, collective and group-centred — which are so rich that they defy enumeration or classification. But it also evokes emptiness, for to say of an environment that it is pluralist, or of a politics that it recognizes plurality, is to say nothing about the nature of the elements, relations and issues that constitute it as a totality. It is to offer a statement rather like Daniel Bell's view in 1960 — which strikes me as an optical illusion — that the 'End of Ideology' is upon us. The sub-title of Bell's book, by the way, eloquently refers to 'the exhaustion of political ideas' — exhaustion through a rhetoric that he then distinguished from utopia.[10]

The third ambiguity is in my view the most important and the most difficult to detect. One feature of pluralism is a capacity to combine, in an unexpected heuristic complicity, both critique and evasion. Pluralism involves critique by virtue of casting aside all 'isms' that gravitate around either monism or dualism. Whether the point has been to show that absolutism, totalitarianism, monolithism and dogmatism lack any foundation, or to refute the shortcuts whereby hierarchy is immediately introduced into dualist systems through the supremacy of one element over another, the critical fertility of the pluralist thesis has been amply demonstrated.

And yet there is also evasion, in so far as the double negation operating here suggests in turn a banalization of the issues generally at stake in these debates. Thus we can talk of evasion when the adoption of a pluralist thesis suggests that, in rejecting monism, the political sphere has no aim — not even the democratic search for consensus — other than the instrumental one of managing politics. Another evasion occurs when we are required to close our eyes to the issues covered by dualities which are, to say the least, problematic — those which used to be involved, for example, in the expression 'class struggle'. There are not two classes, it is said; at most, there is a multiplicity of groups and individuals numeri-cally reducible to a middle class. Similarly, there is supposed to be not one sex dominating the other nor even two sexes, but rather n sexes (in the formula used by Deleuze and Guattari) — a type of proposition that still makes one wonder about the kind of future relations that are envisaged between human beings.[11]

It should be stressed that this threefold ambiguity of pluralism involves far more than a simple confusion. Its systematic operation permits all manner of misunderstandings, from the infatuation of some to the irritation of others, in such a manner that the basic issue seems unresolved, as it seems theoretically impossible simply to cut one's losses. From a critical point of view, it therefore has to be asked whether the recognition of pluralism might designate something other than a zero-sum game, a systematic playing on its ambiguity.

In what follows, I shall focus on some conceptual obstacles that have to be cleared if pluralism is to be given a critical value uncoupled from evasion. My argument is that, despite appearances, pluralism is conceptualized within an epistemological and axiological monism which — and here is the paradox — makes it inseparable from its opposite, the lack, negation, scorning or obliteration of pluralities. I shall stress that, in and through pluralism, the denial of pluralities operates in two ways, which are both problematic. The first negates the *positive* value of those pluralities that we have in mind when we associate defence of pluralism with democratic extension of the principle of freedom. The second negates the *negative* value of those pluralities that we have in mind when we associate pluralism with the maintenance of inequalities.

The problem, then, concerns the paradox of a pluralism whose *internal* logic would seem to call for the production of its opposite, a lack or negation of pluralities. Here I shall draw on three examples of ways in which pluralism has been criticized from different theoretical (and ideological) locations. These three examples, however, all examine pluralism at the moment in which it presents *itself* not just as fact but as norm. In this respect, they cast a revealing light on the task that concerns us — namely, to pin down what it is in the *internal* logic of pluralism which makes the critique pertinent.

First Paradox: An Error of Generalization

According to the first line of critique, pluralism is so far from producing a relatively peaceful coexistence of values within historical ensembles that it actually introduces the rule of conflict as a moral, social and political imperative. To give the status of ultimate value to the plurality of individuals, groups and collectivities is not only to introduce disorder as a systemic rule. It is also, and above all, to abandon the quest for a principle of order or common good and to replace it with violence, legitimized in advance by a pluralized process of banalization. If this violence is said to be diminishing through polymorphism, this is due only to the cultivation of general apathy and is at most a temporary phenomenon.

The postulate of oneness underlying this first critique is, from the vantage point of pluralism, undoubtedly the easiest misconception to track down. By reducing the plurality of values to a kind of fray, it blinds itself to the fact that pluralism plays the plurality of values as an axiological trump card, making plurality itself a value. In a way, pluralism is like a moral-political laboratory which in principle shields the debate from any simplistic thinking (whose true name is dogmatism) and seeks to engage in ethical reflection at a site compatible with its object, the extreme complexity of values.

At the same time, this critique fails to grasp the extent to which the postulate of unanimity or uniformity, as a token of ethical and political rationality, itself transforms the plurality of values into conflict. For the rule of uniformity or unanimity puts a new face on the Kantian imperative: not 'act in such a way that the maxim of your action could be universal', but more specifically 'act in such a way that the maxim of your action could be imposed on all'. It is precisely this implicit schema of imposition which, from the viewpoint of pluralism, makes the ethical and political debate degenerate into violence. Passing over any thought of coexistence, it transforms plurality into divergence, divergence into incompatibility, and incompatibility into warfare not over values but over the monopoly to be forced upon them.

The critical identification of pluralism with conflict would however be without interest if there were nothing in pluralism that actually provoked it. But in so far as pluralism indicates an ensemble in which values do and must coexist, the rejection of dogmatism is far from sufficient to define the moment whereby the ethical laboratory fixes the assumption of the complexity of the axiological universe or, for example, the generalization of the rule of interests to ethics as a whole. At this level, it becomes impossible to surmount the ethical ambiguity of pluralism. It is exactly as if, by a common error of generalization, the critic and the pluralist found themselves in perfectly symmetrical relations, the former generalizing interest and the latter generalizing values.

It is missing the point, then, to invoke here the inextricable relations between interests and values, or to underline the carrying over of the monist postulate into the grammar of its usage. (The ethical monopoly certainly tends to characterize as 'interests', and most often as 'particular interests', any vision that is opposed to its own.) It misses the point because the false generalization here at issue has logically greater import in the case of the pluralist thesis than in that of the objection addressed to it. Here lies the paradox: pluralism does not seem to have allowed for a differential moral rule that bars it from treating on the same level and in the same way a plurality made up of values and interests. This is all the more remarkable, given the fact that the political version of contemporary pluralist theory has given rise to a new variant of Hobbesian egoism. This leads us into analysis of a second paradox.

Second Paradox: An Error of Predication

The theory of political pluralism, in substituting groups for individuals as its reference point, appears to generalize the interest principle to society as a whole by means of the notion of functional equilibrium. It is not, however, a question of glorifying conflict as a political rule – on the contrary, the theoretical wager is that the greater the field of legitimate coexistence, the smaller will be the field of structurally imposed violence. Functional group equilibrium is here defined as a way of policing, or even reducing, conflict through political pluralism. This policing of competition by the very fact of generalizing it here appears as a systemic phenomenon, a tendency whose importance was recognized by the first critique when it spoke of the 'banalization' of conflict. For pluralism, then, the self-regulation of society through functional group competition takes place when the activity of some (the so-called 'active minorities') and the apathy of others (the 'silent majority') inscribe decision and, above all, non-decision as the integrative rule of regulation.

It is thus in its operational mechanisms that the constitutive 'bias' of political pluralism becomes apparent.[12] Politics is to be reduced to the instrumentality of management, and democracy to a set of procedural rules – a reduction whose emergence was already being heralded by Schumpeter in 1942 as the ultimate reference. Through this functional 'bias' pluralism refers us to its opposite, ruling out any definition of society in terms of substantive normative choices about social, economic and political finalities. Given the plurality of values and the competition of interests, agreement or consensus are supposed to be impossible, if not undesirable. In short, it is assumed that plurality requires an 'agent-rationality process' rather than an 'option-rationality process', to use the distinction suggested by Michael Davis.[13]

Once it has accepted that unanimity or consensus is impossible and undesirable, this political conception of pluralism seeks to identify not *what* should be done but *who* has the authority to choose. In the name of the choice principle, it then introduces what David Easton has called 'authoritarian allocation of values' — above all, I would add, 'of social value'.[14] What we see taking shape, under cover of group self-regulation, is the well-known phenomenon of the power elite or democratic elitism, not to speak of Dahl's 'polyarchy'.[15] The sum of these regulations then serves to denote plurality or, more precisely, a deprecatory image of the crowd, and to give fresh justification to the age-old ontological thesis that Habermas has interpreted as 'the repression of plebeian public opinion'.[16]

As a general theory of politics, functional pluralism should not be understood in terms of axiological *laissez-faire*. As the Frankfurt School pointed out, it is rather defined by a ban on going beyond the instrumentality of politics, a refusal to develop substantive normative positions concerning social, economic and political finalities. Contemporary political pluralism thus practises 'repressive tolerance', whose structural weight and range were rightly stressed by Marcuse. Here we can see the kind of optical illusion that makes it possible to hail the emergence of political pluralism as the 'end of ideology'. In fact, it would be much more appropriate to speak, like Theodor U. Lowi, of the 'end of liberalism'.[17] But this still does not take us to the heart of the problem.

The drift of pluralism into its opposite through a flattening of assertions — whether individuals, groups or collectivities are at issue — derives in turn from a new form of epistemological and axiological monism which consists in indiscriminately applying to all the predicate 'pluralist'. The categorical imperative here says (to individuals, groups and collectives): 'Be pluralist; give your assertion the content, form and model of plurality.' Otherwise — from the point of view of the pluralist predicate — the individual will inevitably slide into dogmatism, the group into sectarianism, and the collectivity into totalitarianism, or imperialism. The paradox is that pluralism itself functions as an erosion or even a functional-moral disqualification of the pluralities that it claims to recognize, organize and manage.

Let us try to put the argument in a different way. It has often been noted that pluralism and monism are mutually antagonistic in that pluralism entails a rejection of authoritarianism, dogmatism, monolithism, and so on. What is forgotten, however, is that from the pluralist point of view any assertion of values threatens to be deemed dogmatic, as if there were no interstices between pluralism and relativism in the assertion of a norm for the coexistence of values.

I have already argued elsewhere that this drift of pluralism into its opposite stems from an error of predication or, to use Gilbert Ryle's term, an extraordinary 'category mistake'.[18] For, as a predicate, pluralism is and has to be the *formal* predicate of an ensemble through which it is designated as involving plurality. This implies that, whatever its meaning, pluralism cannot and should not be thought of as the actual, normative and substantive predicate of either an individual, a group or a collectivity when the individual, group or collectivity speaks in its own name, affirming certain values as its own.

In reality, pluralism cannot be the ethical predicate of an individual, for then it would be necessary to speak *oratio obliqua*.[19] The individual would have to try not only to incorporate all values in a single glance but above all to remain equidistant from all dogmas — that is, to be nowhere. The same reasoning also applies to groups: their affirmations, which are moreover not reducible to interests, could not coexist if the ground rule actually prohibited them. For just as the pluralist predicate requires of individuals that they should be nowhere, so it demands of groups that they should be as small, peaceful and apathetic as possible, it being understood that functional equilibrium is achieved through the integration of decision-making and non-decision-making processes.[20]

The pluralist predication error is harder to detect in the case of collectivities, for pluralism, as the predicate of an ensemble, would here seem to be quite applicable. But although pluralism is and can be the formal predicate of a collectivity taken as a whole — the one that defines it as involving plurality — it could not be the only predicate of that collectivity as such. In particular, it could not be the substantive predicate of a collectivity which affirms itself, for example, through broad consensus on fundamental issues.

It is then a mistake to believe that pluralism and consensus are antinomic concepts. What pluralism requires is the right to choose, the right to affirm and to affirm oneself. And this right applies to individuals and groups, as well as to collectivities taken as a whole, when the individuals, groups and collectivites engage in debate about values. Here we can follow the tracks roughly defined by John Dewey in 1927, in *The Public and its Problem*, where he attempted to refute the isolationist, monadic aspect of William James's style of pluralism. The notion of 'public' was then proposed as that which connects the individual and the social without setting an *a priori* limit on the role of the state. It emerges that pluralism demands a critical attitude to the imperative rule of consensus — not the abolition of consensus itself but rather of its compulsory, *a priori* character. In other words, pluralism requires that the quest for consensus should itself be made the object of critical enquiry, in order to separate out problems whose solution calls for common affirmation from those which demand the elaboration of alternatives and the coexistence of individual and group affirmations.

It follows that pluralism, as the *predicate of an ensemble*, cannot be applied indiscriminately to individuals, groups and collectivities. Otherwise it is all too easy to make of pluralism a zero-sum game, playing off individuals against groups, groups against the individual, the state against the one and the other, and the whole plurally *ad infinitum*. Furthermore, as a *formal* predicate of a social ensemble, pluralism cannot refer to a real ensemble open to an infinite number of possibles — unless the 'open society' is transformed into an abstract society (in Karl Popper's sense of the terms), thereby consummating the failure of pluralism as the failure of any affirmation.[21] It must be understood that pluralism, as the formal predicate of a real system, can only refer to an open system (as against a closed or totalitarian system) and to a semi–closed system (as against the infinite number of possibles evoked by the formalism of the predicate).

Third Paradox: An Error of Identification

The third paradox of pluralism, which largely follows from the first two but is not reducible to them, underlies the critique of pluralism that makes it a theory incompatible with an egalitarian vision of society. To a considerable extent this overlaps with the second critique, to the extent that a clear result of 'functional pluralism' is to deny both the inequalities flowing from the formal rules of the social game, and the structuring inequalities inscribed in these rules through the random paradigm of procedural equality. I will make one observation here. There is certainly a paradox in the evidence that, by proclaiming the right of all values to coexistence, pluralism is at once compelled to exclude the value of equality, unless this is reduced like all values to a functional datum, a procedural rule whose non-egalitarian implications need scarcely be demonstrated.

But there is a deeper paradox in this idea that pluralism and egalitarianism are necessarily incompatible — one which, if my analysis is correct, derives from an error of identification. What has to be discussed and questioned is the *a priori* notion that there is a necessary conceptual linkage between a unitary theory of society and an egalitarian design, and an equally necessary linkage — somehow enhanced by symmetrical inversion — between a pluralist theory of society and a non-egalitarian vision of society. According to this notion, then, unity and equality on the one hand, plurality and inequality on the other, form a conceptually inseparable binomial.

I have argued elsewhere that this antinomy, doubtless well founded historically, nevertheless involves unacceptable shortcuts when it refers to contemporary theories of pluralism as well as contemporary theories of equality.[22] The crucial and, in my view, most striking misunderstanding derives from what my research on theories of equality has shown about the blind spot of contemporary thought: namely, that it is extremely difficult to arrive at an adequate definition of equality, even within egalitarian theories, given that equality is not synonymous with identity.[23] In other words, despite appearances the idea that the quest for unity is at least problematic — an argument dear to pluralists who are anxious to avoid monism — is at the very heart of contemporary reflections about egalitarianism. Stanley Benn has rightly said of such reflections that they are better described as a set of objections to forms of inequality than as substantive, positive theories of equality itself — a point that cannot fail to recall the greater skill of pluralism in refuting monism and dualism than in positively conceptualizing plurality.

I shall focus here on the way in which the allegation of a necessary antinomy between pluralism and equality shifts the argument away from the critical potential of the negative function of pluralism. Here we have the identification of all differences as overdetermination of the banalization of pluralities. The pluralist, then, sees in the demand for equality only dangerous symptoms of imposed uniformity. And here we have a valorization of differences in which the diversity proclaimed by the pluralist is seen by the egalitarian as nothing but a conservation of inequalities.

In both cases, the result is certainly to conceptualize a rejection: of *unjust* difference for the egalitarian, of *imposed* uniformity for the pluralist. But in both cases, the problem left undeveloped is the axiological status to be accorded to differences which are themselves — and this is not a play on words — morally and socially different from one another. For there are differences which exist but should not exist — discrimination, for example. There are differences which do not but should exist — for example, what lies buried beneath oppression. There are also differences which more or less exist with a more or less real right to exist — for example, the lottery as the ultimate model of egalitarian interaction.

For the moment, however, theories of pluralism have produced more verdicts of failure about the impossibility of unity than differentiated thinking about difference. This difficulty in turn entails that the conceptual models of pluralism are inscribed in a meta-discourse whose result — it has not been sufficiently noted — is to cancel the effective plurality that it proclaims. By dint of their formalism, contemporary theories of pluralism are equipped to conceptualize coexistence, variety, diversity, heterogeneity, counter-values and even a lack of values. But they cannot conceptualize differences without banalizing them, without (as Henri Lefebvre wrote in *Le manifeste différentialiste*, 1970) moving from difference to both non-difference and indifference.

But the enquiry must not be broken off at this point. For, despite appearances, the contemporary thematization of equality powerfully and in unexpected ways intersects with the thematization of pluralism, reproducing in a kind of inverted form the failure verdict on unity. In the case of equality, however, this failure has less to do with the proven and recognized diversity of humans than with the vague, catch-all and ultimately inoffensive character of what is usually called 'general equality'. The end-point of this aporia, whose acme Rawls lays before us with his 'veil of ignorance', is to be found in the difference-negating doctrine nestling within the contemporary idea of 'equal consideration', sometimes also called 'procedural equality'. According to this notion of equality, the first condition for humans to be treated equally is that one should close one's eyes to what differentiates them. This is the well-known formula of general equality, which enjoins us to treat individuals *without regard* to their race, sex, beliefs, status, and so on. Once equal consideration is rounded off with a procedural rule, the principle then states that people should be treated equally *unless* some difference between them has been shown to be relevant — a notion all the more circular in that the fundamental idea of pluralism quite simply proclaims 'differences' on every side.

The neglected reverse of this story is the way in which negativities continually pile up. The pro-diversity thesis (pluralism) here manages to conceptualize only the formal coexistence of pluralities. The pro-unity thesis (egalitarianism) manages to conceptualize only its rejection of general equality having the attributes of identity. But beyond the mis-apprehensions, which in themselves clearly show the limits of that fascination for difference sustaining present-day blindness, the analysis displays a dangerous set of aporias. Unity, as conceived by the egalitarian theorist, is most often a vague and empty idea of something grouping together human beings. Plurality, as theorized by the pluralist, is most often the instrumental and empty idea of an ensemble whose coexistence is all the more thinkable in that it is composed of functionally inter-changeable entities.

The disastrous paralogism in this whole story is that present-day discourse about plurality and quality is no longer capable of producing anything other than disjunctions, parallelisms and non-sequiturs. Yet it is to the pluralists that the full logical force of the objection applies, for they contradict their own postulates whenever they claim to treat all differences on the same moral plane, whether they concern discrimina-tion, oppression, lagging development, injustice, luck, competition or 'freedoms'.

It is thus in the case of pluralism that the supposed non-sequitur between plurality and equality stems directly from an error of identifica-tion. For the reason why equality as a value poses a problem lies precisely in the basic critical idea that equality is not and should not be synony-mous with identity. Just as little can equality be reduced to the formalism that the 'club of equals' would like to impose on it. In the mouth of unequals, it is the name given to the search or equity in human relations, the search for justice in the distribution of goods. And in the mouth of unequals, this equity and this justice do not and cannot mean identity.

Let us conclude, then, that a normative asymmetry distinguishes the equality of equals from the equality of unequals. The former can impose formalism all the more readily in that it provides the best of alibis. The latter originates in another heuristics: is critical thinking about the differences between differences possible? Will a plural concept of justice eventually be conceivable with regard to pluralities?[24]

Let us put it in another way. To ask whether pluralism and equality can be compatible is to miss the urgency of the matter. For the unequal, equality will be plural or it will be nothing at all.[25] Through what dis-cursive paroxysm should the thought of plurality lead to obliteration of the underlying critical promises? We should be concise: time is pressing on us. The thought of plurality has confined its critical spirit in such an obsession with monism and dualism that it has made their negation into the incarnation of good, only to reproduce by inverted monism such non-differentiation in the ethical issues at stake that it has become blind to the way in which, by presenting itself as universal norm, it overturns its own postulates.

The urgency, then, is bound up with an epistemology and a differ-ential ethic of differences, those which doing away with evasion would release the critical potential of the pluralism we see acting in a zero-sum game. For alongside the much-heralded death of all 'isms' is a large-as-life thing which centuries of devaluing the many have not managed to annihilate. The thing resembles the sphinx who, however exhausted, utters a question, I was going to say a hope.[26]

> I'm not like you
> how should I call you
> so at last we may
> fairly
> place signals
> between us

Translated by Patrick Camiller

Notes

1. The term 'monism' is attributed to Christian Wolff (1679—1754) and 'dualism' to Thomas Hyde's *Philosophia Prima sive Ontologia*, 1729.

2. See the entry on 'monism' in P. Edwards, ed., *The Encyclopedia of Philosophy*, vols 5—6, p. 364.

3. Gilbert Ryle, *The Concept of Mind*, London 1949.

4. R.H. Lotze, *Metaphysik*, 1841. 'Independent' is used in the sense that beings are not the modes, accidents or phenomena of a single, absolute reality.

5. W. James, *The Varieties of Religious Experience*, 1902. See also the 'Postscript' to his *Pragmatism: A New Name for Some Old Ways of Thinking*, 1907, and the final chapter of *A Pluralistic Universe*, 1909. James describes as 'vicious intellectualism' the 'treating of a name as excluding from the fact named what the name's definition fails positively to include'.

6. See Bertrand Russell, 'The Philosophy of Logical Atomism', *The Monist*, vols 28 and 29, 1918/1919, reprinted in *Logic and Knowledge*, London 1956. Common-sense belief — which Russell sets out as his most fundamental — holds that 'there are many separate things'. In *The Scientific Outlook*, New York 1931, p. 98, he declared of all monism that it was mere 'rubbish', since the universe is 'all spots and jumps, without unity, without continuity, without coherence or orderliness or any of the other properties that governesses love'.

7. The main works in the period from 1895 to 1920 were those of J. Neville Figgs, Harold J. Laski, A.D. Lindsay and Ernest Baker. According to the study by Georges-Emile Giguère, it was only in the 1960s that the main dictionaries and encyclopedias defined pluralism in other than a philosophical (or, we might say, ontological) sense to denote the 'constructive coexistence of various tendencies' in religion, politics, education or work. See 'Le pluralisme à la lumière de l'histoire', in *Le pluralisme/Pluralism: Its Meaning Today*, 'Héritage et Projet' 10, Montreal 1974, pp. 67—91.

8. Léon Dion, *Société et politique: La vie des groupes*, Presses de l'Université Laval, Paris 1971.

9. See P.H. Nowell-Smith, 'Cultural Relativism', *Philosophy of Social Science*, 1, 1971, pp. 1—18.

10. See Daniel Bell, *The End of Ideology: On the Exhaustion of Political Ideas in the Fifties*, revised edn, New York 1965. At that time, it should be noted, Bell stressed that the end of ideology did not mean (and should not mean) the 'end of utopia'. Rather, the casting aside of rhetoric made it essential for us to grasp that 'the ladder to the city of Heaven' must henceforth be of an empirical character.

11. See G. Deleuze and F. Guattari, *Anti-Oedipus*, 1984. In this connection, see also L. Marcil-Lacoste, *La Raison en procès. Essais sur la philosophie et le sexisme*, Montreal/ Utrecht 1986, esp. chapter 7.

12. The term is taken from W.W. Connolly, ed., *The Bias of Pluralism*, New York 1969.

13. See M. Davis, 'Avoiding the Voter's Paradox Democratically', *Theory and Decision*, V, pp. 295—311.

14. David Easton, *The Political System: An Inquiry into the State of Political Science*, Chicago 1953.

15. See C. Wright Mills, *The Power Elite*, Oxford 1956; P. Bachrach, *The Theory of Democratic Elitism: A Critique*, Boston 1967; Robert Dahl, *Democracy in the United States: Promise and Performance*, 2nd edn, Chicago 1967.

16. See J. Habermas, 'The Public Sphere', *New German Critique* 3, 1974. For a study of Habermas's proposed alternative, see L. Marcil-Lacoste, 'Les enjeux égalitaires du consensus rationnel: Habermas et ses sources', *Laval Théologique et Philosophique*, 46, 3, 1990.

17. See Theodor U. Lowi, *The End of Liberalism*, New York 1969.

18. See L. Marcil-Lacoste, 'L'échec de l'affirmation pluraliste', *Critère: La démocratie liberée*, no. 22, 1978. CF. Ryle, *Concept of Mind*.

19. The expression is taken from John R. Searle, *Speech Act*, Cambridge 1969.

20. See André Vachet, 'La démocratie bloquée: les ambiguités du pluralisme politique', in *Le pluralisme/Pluralism: Its Meaning Today*.

21. See Karl Popper, *The Open Society and Its Enemies*, New York 1962.

22. Sée L. Marcil-Lacoste, 'Unité et pluralité de la culture: l'enjeu égalitaire', in V. Cauchy, org., *Philosophie et Culture*, Proceedings of the 17th World Congress of Philosophy, Montreal 1986, pp. 83—5.

23. See L. Marcil-Lacoste, *La Thématique contemporaine de l'égalité. Répertoire, résumés, typologie*, Montreal 1984.

24. From this point of view, it is interesting to note the contribution of two contemporary theories: that of John Rawls in *A Theory of Justice*, Harvard 1971 (which advances the 'principle of difference' in opposition to the utilitarian rule of non-differential calculation), and that of Michael Walzer in *Spheres of Justice*, Oxford 1983 (which speaks of complex equality through seriation of the various spheres of activity).

25. See L. Marcil-Lacoste, 'Cent quarante manières d'être égaux', *Philosophiques*, vol. 11, no. 2, April 1984.

26. For a first outline of this trail, see Louise Marcil-Lacoste, 'L'avenir de l'égalité', in *Doctrines et concepts. Cinquante ans de philosophie de langue française, ASPLF 1937-1987*, Paris 1988, pp. 347—61.

PART III

Hannah Arendt and the
Idea of Citizenship

Maurizio Passerin d'Entrèves

In recent years there has been a revival of the idea of citizenship both at the level of political debate and at the level of philosophical reflection on politics. In Great Britain the Conservative Party has advanced the idea of an 'active and responsible citizenship' and tied it to the notion of 'social responsibility'. The leader of the Liberal Democrats, Paddy Ashdown, has suggested that citizenship might be expanded to include a range of entitlements, such as health, education and welfare, as well as those duties and obligations that each individual owes to the community. The Labour Party has also appealed to the notion of citizenship and linked it to the idea of an 'enabling state'. In Italy the Communist Party and the trade unions have stressed the theme of 'citizenship rights' and placed it at the centre of their political programme. Citizenship has thus become a crucial theme in the European political debate and has been at the centre of conflicting interpretations with respect to its meaning, scope and political implications. The question of citizenship has also become the focus of a philosophical debate on the nature and limits of the liberal-democratic conception of politics. In this debate a number of thinkers in the communitarian tradition, such as Michael Sandel, Charles Taylor and Roberto Mangabeira Unger, have articulated and defended a conception of politics based on the civic republican ideal of citizenship, with its stress on civic engagement and active political deliberation, and used it to criticize the liberal conception which restricts citizenship to questions of legal rights and entitlements.

The purpose of this chapter is to suggest that Arendt's idea of citizenship may be highly relevant to the present discussion. Her conception of politics is in fact based on the idea of active citizenship, that is, on the value and importance of civic engagement and collective deliberation about all matters affecting the political community. The practice of citizenship is valued because it enables each citizen to exercise his or her powers of agency, to develop the capacities for judgement, and to attain by concerted action some measure of political efficacy. In what follows I will reconstruct Arendt's conception of citizenship around three major themes: (1) the public sphere, (2) political agency and collective identity, and (3) political culture. I hope in this way to show that Arendt's conception remains important for contemporary attempts to revive the idea and the practice of democratic citizenship.

Citizenship and the Public Sphere

Throughout her writings Arendt attempted to articulate the question of citizenship around the constitution of public spaces of action and political deliberation. For Arendt the public sphere refers to that sphere of appearance where citizens interact through the medium of speech and persuasion, disclose their unique identities, and decide through collective deliberation about matters of common concern. This public sphere of appearance can be established only if we share a common world of humanly created artefacts, institutions and settings, which separates us from nature and provides a relatively permanent or durable context for our activities. The constitution of public spaces of action and political discourse depends, therefore, upon the existence of a common, shared world, and upon the creation of numerous spheres of appearance in which individuals can disclose their identities and establish relations of reciprocity and solidarity.

Arendt's conception of the public sphere, of the sphere within which the activity of citizenship can flourish, has therefore two meanings, since it refers both to the space of appearance and to the world we hold in common. According to the first meaning, the public realm is that space where everything that appears

> can be seen and heard by everybody and has the widest possible publicity. For us, appearance — something that is being seen and heard by others as well as by ourselves — constitutes reality. Compared with the reality which comes from being seen and heard, even the greatest forces of intimate life —

the passions of the heart, the thoughts of the mind, the delights of the senses — lead an uncertain, shadowy kind of existence unless and until they are transformed, deprivatized and deindividualized, as it were, into a shape to fit them for public appearance.... The presence of others who see what we see and hear what we hear assures us of the reality of the world and of ourselves.[1]

Within this space of appearance, therefore, experiences can be shared, actions evaluated and identities disclosed. Indeed, Arendt maintains that 'since our feeling for reality depends utterly upon appearance and therefore upon the existence of a public realm into which things can appear out of the darkness of sheltered existence, even the twilight which illuminates our private and intimate lives is ultimately derived from the much harsher light of the public realm.'[2] In sum, the public realm as a space of appearance provides the light and the publicity which are necessary for the establishment of our public identities, for the recognition of a common reality, and for the assessment of the actions of others.

For Arendt the space of appearance is created every time individuals gather together politically, which is to say, 'wherever men are together in the manner of speech and action', and in this respect it 'predates and precedes all formal constitution of the public realm and the various forms of government'.[3] It is not restricted to a set of institutions or to a specific location; rather, it comes into existence whenever action is coordinated through speech and persuasion and is oriented towards the attainment of collective goals. However, since it is a creation of common action and collective deliberation, the space of appearance is highly fragile and exists only when actualized through the performance of deeds and the sharing of words. Its peculiarity, Arendt says, is that

unlike the spaces which are the work of our hands, it does not survive the actuality of the movement which brought it into being, but disappears not only with the dispersal of men — as in the case of great catastrophes when the body politic of a people is destroyed — but with the disappearance or arrest of the activities themselves. Wherever people gather together, it is potentially there, but only potentially, not necessarily and not forever.[4]

The space of appearance must therefore be continually recreated by action; its existence is secured whenever actors gather together for the purpose of discussing and deliberating about matters of public concern, and it disappears the moment these activities cease. It is therefore always a *potential space*, which finds its actualization in the actions and speeches of individuals who have come together to undertake some common project. It may arise suddenly, as in the case of revolutions, or it may develop slowly out of the efforts to change some specific piece of legislation or policy, i.e. saving a historic building or a natural landscape, extending the public provision of housing and health care, protecting groups from discrimination and oppression, fighting for nuclear disarmament, and so on. Historically, it has been recreated whenever public spaces of action and deliberation have been set up, from town hall meetings to workers' councils, from demonstrations and sit-ins to struggles for justice and equal rights.

The second meaning that Arendt assigns to the public realm, that which supports the space of appearance and provides action with its proper concerns, is the world, or more precisely, the world that we hold in common. This is the world which 'is common to all of us and distinguished from our privately owned place in it'.[5] It is not identical with the earth or with nature; it is related, rather, 'to the human artifact, the fabrication of human hands, as well as to the affairs which go on among those who inhabit the man-made world together'.[6] Thus 'to live together in the world means essentially that a world of things is between those who have it in common, as a table is located between those who sit around it; the world, like every in-between, relates and separates men at the same time.'[7] In this respect the public realm, as the common world, 'gathers us together and yet prevents our falling over each other, so to speak. What makes mass society so difficult to bear is not the number of people involved ... but the fact that the world between them has lost its power to gather them together, to relate and to separate them.'[8] By establishing a space between individuals, an in-between which connects and separates them at the same time, the world provides the physical context within which political action can arise. Moreover, by virtue of its permanence and durability, the world provides the temporal context within which individual lives can unfold and, by being turned into narratives, acquire a measure of immortality. As Arendt writes:

> The common world is what we enter when we are born and what we leave behind when we die. It transcends our life-span into past and future alike; it was there before we came and will outlast our brief sojourn in it. It is what we have in common not only with those who live with us, but also with those who were here before and with those who will come after us. But such a common world can survive the coming and going of the generations only to the extent that it appears in public.[9]

It is this capacity of human artifacts and institutions — i.e. the world we have in common — to endure through time and to become the common heritage of successive generations, that enables individuals to feel at home in the world and to transcend, however partially, the fleetingness of their existence. Indeed, without a measure of permanence and durability provided by the world, 'life would never be human'.[10] 'Permanence and durability [are what] human beings need precisely because they are mortals — the most unstable and futile beings we know of.'[11] For Arendt, therefore, the transitoriness of life can be overcome by constructing a lasting and stable world that allows for human re-membrance and anticipation, that is, for both memory and a measure of trust in the future. As she expressed it:

> Life in its non-biological sense, the span of time each man has between birth and death, manifests itself in action and speech, both of which share with life its essential futility. The 'doing of great deeds and the speaking of great words' will leave no trace, no product that might endure after the moment of action and the spoken word has passed. ... [Thus] acting and speaking men need the help of *homo faber* in his highest capacity, that is, the help of the artist, of poets and historiographers, of monument-builders and writers, because without them the only product of their activity, the story they enact and tell, would not survive at all.[12]

Human mortality can thus be partly transcended by the durability of the world and the public memory of individuals' deeds. By building and preserving a world that can link one generation to the next and that makes possible forms of collective memory, we are able, in Arendt's words, 'to absorb and make shine through the centuries whatever men may want to save from the natural ruin of time'.[13]

The Public Realm: Three Features

I would like now to turn to an examination of three features of the public realm and of the sphere of politics that are closely connected to Arendt's conception of citizenship. I will rely for this on an interesting essay by Margaret Canovan entitled 'Politics as Culture: Hannah Arendt and the Public Realm', in which she argues that Arendt's conception of the public realm is based on an implicit analogy between politics and culture.[14] For the purpose of exploring Arendt's conception of citizen-ship, there are three features of the public-political realm identified by

Canovan that deserve our attention: first, the artificial or constructed quality of politics and of public life in general; second, its spatial quality; third, the distinction between public and private interests.

The Artificiality of Public Life

As regards the first feature, Arendt always stressed the artificiality of public life and of political activities in general, the fact that they are man-made and constructed, rather than natural or given. She regarded this artificiality as something to be celebrated rather than deplored. Politics for her was not the result of some natural predisposition, or the realization of the inherent traits of human nature.[15] Rather, it was a cultural achievement of the first order, enabling individuals to transcend the necessities of life and to fashion a world within which free political action and discourse could flourish. It is for this reason, we might note, that Arendt's political philosophy cannot be easily located within the neo-Aristotelian tradition, notwithstanding their common emphasis on the importance of the *vita activa*. Indeed, if we take Michael Oakeshott's distinction between the tradition of political thought based on Reason and Nature and that based on Will and Artifice (characterizing respectively the ancient and the modern conception of politics), it would appear that Arendt fits more easily into the latter, since for her politics was always an artificial creation, a product of action and speech, and not the result of some natural or innate trait shared by all human beings.[16]

The stress on the artificiality of politics has a number of important consequences. For example, Arendt emphasized that the principle of political equality among citizens is not the result of some natural condition that precedes the constitution of the political realm. Political equality for Arendt is not a natural human attribute, nor can it rest on a theory of natural rights; rather, it is an artificial attribute which individuals acquire upon entering the public realm and which is secured by democratic political institutions.[17] As she remarked in *The Origins of Totalitarianism*, those who had been deprived of civil and political rights by the Nazi regime were not able to defend themselves by an appeal to their natural rights; on the contrary, they discovered that, having been excluded from the body politic, they had no rights whatsoever.[18] Political equality and the recognition of one's rights (what Arendt called 'a right to have rights') can thus be secured only by membership in a democratic political community.[19]

A further consequence of Arendt's stress on the artificiality of political life is evident in her rejection of all neo-romantic appeals to the *Volk* and to ethnic identity as the basis for political community. She maintained that one's ethnic, religious or racial identity was irrelevant to one's identity as a *citizen*, that it should never be made the basis of membership in a *political* community, and praised the American Constitution for having excluded in principle any connection between one's ethnic or religious identity and one's political status as a citizen.[20] Similarly, at the time of establishment of the state of Israel, she advocated a conception of citizenship based not on race or religion, but on the formal political rights of freedom and equality that would have extended to both Arabs and Jews.[21]

Finally, it is worth pointing out that Arendt's emphasis on the formal qualities of citizenship made her position rather distant from those advocates of participation during the 1960s who saw it in terms of recapturing a sense of intimacy, of community, of warmth and of authenticity.[22] For Arendt political participation was important because it permitted the establishment of relations of civility and solidarity among citizens. In the essay 'On Humanity in Dark Times' she wrote that the search for intimacy is characteristic of those groups excluded from the public realm, as were the Jews during the Nazi period, but that such intimacy is bought at the price of worldlessness, which 'is always a form of barbarism'.[23] Since they represent 'psychological substitutes ... for the loss of the common, visible world',[24] the ties of intimacy and warmth can never become political; the only truly political ties are those of civic friendship and solidarity, since they 'make political demands and preserve reference to the world'.[25] In other words, for Arendt the danger of trying to recapture a sense of intimacy and warmth, of authenticity and communal feelings, is that one loses the public values of impartiality, ·civic friendship, and solidarity. As Canovan has put it:

[Arendt's] conception of the public realm is opposed not only to society but also to community: to *Gemeinschaft* as well as to *Gesellschaft*. While greatly valuing warmth, intimacy and naturalness in private life, she insisted on the importance of a formal, artificial public realm in which what mattered was the people's actions rather than their sentiments; in which the natural ties of kinship and intimacy were set aside in favour of a deliberate, impartial solidarity with other citizens; in which there was enough space between people for them to stand back and judge one another coolly and objectively.[26]

The Spatial Quality of Public Life

The second feature stressed by Arendt has to do with the spatial quality of public life, with the fact that political activities are located in a public space where citizens are able to meet one another, to exchange their opinions and debate their differences, and to search for some collective solution to their problems. Politics, in this respect, is a matter of people sharing a common world and a common space of appearance in which public concerns can emerge and be articulated from different perspectives. For politics to occur it is not enough to have a collection of private individuals voting separately and anonymously according to their private opinions.[27] Rather, these individuals must be able to see and talk to one another in public, to meet in a public space so that their differences as well as their commonalities can emerge and become the subject of democratic debate.[28]

This notion of a common public space helps us to understand how political opinions can be formed which are neither reducible to private, idiosyncratic preferences, on the one hand, nor to a unanimous collective opinion, on the other. Arendt herself distrusted the term 'public opinion' since it suggested the mindless unanimity of mass society.[29] In her view representative opinions could arise only when citizens actually confronted one another in a public space, so that they could examine an issue from a number of different perspectives, modify their views, and enlarge their standpoint to incorporate that of others.[30] Political opinions, she claimed, can never be formed in private; rather, they are formed, tested and enlarged only within a public context of argumentation and debate. 'Opinions will rise wherever men communicate freely with one another and have the right to make their views public; but these views, in their endless variety, seem to stand also in need of purification and representation.[31] Where an appropriate public space exists (the example chosen by Arendt is the US Senate, at least in its original conception, but we can extend her example to all those spaces of relatively formal and structured debate that are located within civil society), these opinions can be shaped and elaborated into a sophisticated political discourse, rather than remaining the expression of arbitrary preferences or being moulded into a unanimous 'public opinion'.

Another implication of Arendt's stress on the spatial quality of politics has to do with the question of how a collection of distinct individuals can be united to form a political community. For Arendt the unity that may be achieved in a political community is neither the result of religious or ethnic affinity, nor the expression of some common value system. Rather, the unity in question can be attained by sharing a public space and a set of political institutions, and engaging in the practices and activities which are characteristic of that space and those institutions. As Christopher Lasch has remarked in an essay clearly indebted to Arendt, the assumption that 'shared values, not political institutions or a common political language, provide the only source of social cohesion ... represents a radical break from many of the republican principles on which this country was founded.'[32] What unites people in a political community is therefore not some set of common values, but the world they set up in common, the spaces they inhabit together, the institutions and practices which they share as citizens. As Canovan puts it, individuals can be united 'by the *world* which lies between them. All that is necessary is that they should have among them a common political world which they enter as citizens, and which they can hand on to their successors. It is the space between them that unites them, rather than some quality inside each of them',[33] or some set of common values and beliefs.

A further implication of Arendt's conception of the spatial quality of politics is that since politics is a public activity, one cannot be part of it without in some sense being present in a public space. To be engaged in politics means actively participating in the various public forums where the decisions affecting one's community are taken. Arendt's insistence on the importance of direct participation in politics has sometimes been interpreted to imply that individuals have an existential need for participation which they can only satisfy by engaging in public affairs. This actually represents a misunderstanding of Arendt's commitment to participatory politics, since it is based on what Canovan aptly calls a subjective or person-centred, rather than a public or world-centred, conception of politics. Although people may engage in political activity to fulfil their needs for involvement and participation, for Arendt it is not so much these personal needs as the *concerns* about the common world that constitute the substance and value of political action. Thus, as Canovan notes, 'while Arendt certainly did maintain that political participation was personally fulfilling, her fundamental argument for it was not only less subjectivist but also more simple ... it was that, since politics is something that needs a worldly location and can only happen in a public space, then if you are not present in such a space you are simply not engaged in politics.'[34]

Public and Private Interests

This public or world-centred conception of politics lies also at the basis of Arendt's distinction between public and private interests. According to Arendt, political activity is not a means to an end, but an end in itself; one does not engage in political action simply to promote one's welfare, but to realize the principles intrinsic to political life, such as freedom, equality, justice, solidarity, courage and excellence. Politics is a world with its own values and ends that are realized in public action and deliberation; it is, as Arendt says, 'concerned with the *world as such* and not with those who live in it'.[35] In a late essay entitled 'Public Rights and Private Interests' she discusses the difference between one's life as an individual and one's life as a citizen, between the life spent on one's own and the life spent in common with others. As she writes:

> Throughout his life man moves constantly in two different orders of existence: he moves within what is his *own* and he also moves in a sphere that is common to him and his fellowmen. The 'public good,' the concerns of the citizen, is indeed the common good because it is located in the *world* which we have in common *without owning it.* Quite frequently, it will be antagonistic to whatever we may deem good to ourselves in our private existence.[36]

What Arendt is claiming is that our *public* interests as citizens are quite distinct from our *private* interests as individuals. The public interest cannot be automatically derived from our private interests: indeed, it is not the sum of private interests, nor their highest common denominator, nor even the total of enlightened self-interests.[37] In fact, it has little to do with our private interests, since it concerns the world that lies beyond the self, that was there before our birth and that will be there after our death, and that finds its embodiment in activities and institutions with their own intrinsic purposes which may be often at odds with our short-term and private interests.[38] As Arendt says, 'the self *qua* self cannot reckon in terms of long-range interest, i.e. the interest of a world that survives its inhabitants.'[39] The interests of the world are not the interests of individuals: they are the interests of the public realm which we share as citizens and which we can pursue and enjoy only by going beyond our own self-interest. As citizens we share that public realm and participate in its interests: but the interests belong to the public realm, to the realm that we have in common 'without owning it', to that realm which transcends our limited lifespan and our limited private purposes.

Arendt provides an example of such public interests by examining the activity of serving on a jury. As jurors, the interests we are asked to uphold are the public interests of justice and fairness. These are not the interests of our private selves, nor do they coincide with our enlightened self-interest. They are the interests of a political community that regulates its affairs by means of constitutional laws and procedures. They are *public* interests transcending and outlasting the private interests that we may have as individuals. Indeed, the fairness and impartiality demanded of the citizens, Arendt notes, 'is resisted at every turn by the urgency of one's self-interests, which are always more urgent than the common good'.[40] The public interest in impartial justice which we share as jurors may interfere with our private affairs: it often involves inconvenience, and could sometimes involve greater risks, as when one is asked to testify against a group of criminals who have threatened retribution. According to Arendt, the only compensation for the risks and sacrifices demanded by the public interest lies in what she calls the 'public happiness' of acting in concert as citizens in the public realm. Indeed, it is only through acting in the public realm and enjoying the freedom and happiness of common deliberation that we are able to discover our public interests and to transcend, when needed, our more limited private interests.[41]

A further illustration of Arendt's distinction between public and private interests is provided by her discussion of the question of civil disobedience. At the time of the protest movement against the Vietnam War and the struggle for civil rights for blacks in the 1960s, the legitimacy of civil disobedience was often discussed in terms drawn from exemplary cases of conscience, in particular, Socrates' refusal to escape from prison after being condemned to death by the Athenians, and Thoreau's refusal to pay taxes to a government that tolerated slavery and engaged in an expansionist war against Mexico. Arendt maintained that these examples of action undertaken for the sake of one's conscience were inappropriate to characterize the struggles and protests of the 1960s, since the latter were motivated not by a concern with the integrity of one's conscience, but by a concern with the injustices taking place in the world. Thoreau's stance, as set out in his famous essay 'On the Duty of Civil Disobedience', was to avoid being implicated in the actions of the US government, rather than fighting actively for the abolition of slavery and foreign aggression. 'It is not a man's duty', he writes, 'to devote himself to the eradication of any, even the most enormous, wrong; he may still properly have other concerns to engage him; but it is his duty, at least, to wash his hands of it.'[42] Thoreau's concern, in other words, was to avoid self-reproach, to avoid being implicated in something he considered wrong, rather than fighting for the redress of injustice. Arendt's comment is the following:

> Here, as elsewhere, conscience is unpolitical. It is not primarily interested in the world where the wrong is committed or in the consequences that the wrong will have for the future course of the world. It does not say, with Jefferson, 'I tremble *for my country* when I reflect that God is just; that His justice cannot sleep forever', because it trembles for the individual self and its integrity.[43]

The rules of conscience are unpolitical, they concern the self's integrity and not the integrity of the world. They say: 'Beware of doing something that you will not be able to live with.'[44] As such, they may be effective during emergencies or when a particular atrocity is being committed, but they cannot serve as political standards; they are too much concerned with the self to serve as a basis for collective action aiming at the redress of injustice in the world.[45] One of the comments Arendt made about Rosa Luxemburg was that she 'was very much concerned with the *world* and not at all concerned with herself'. She had engaged in political action because 'she could not stand the injustice *within the world*'. Thus, for Arendt, 'the decisive thing is whether your own motivation is clear — for the world — or for yourself, by which I mean for your soul.'[46] To be sure, Arendt did not dismiss the role of conscience altogether; in her lecture 'Thinking and Moral Considerations' and in *The Life of the Mind* she argued that conscience, as the inner dialogue of me and myself, can prevent individuals from committing or participating in atrocities.[47] Conscience, however, gives no positive prescriptions; it only tells us what *not* to do, what to avoid in our actions and dealings with others; its criterion for action is 'whether I shall be able to live with myself in peace when the time has come to think about my deeds and words'.[48] It is not something that can be taken for granted — many people lack it or are unable to feel self-reproach. It cannot be generalized — what I cannot live with may not bother another person's conscience, with the result that one person's conscience will stand against another person's conscience. And, as we have seen, it directs attention to the self rather than to the world. The counsels of conscience are therefore unpolitical. They can only be expressed in purely individual, subjective form. As Arendt writes:

When Socrates stated that 'it is better to suffer wrong than to do wrong,' he clearly meant that it was better *for him*, just as it was better for him 'to be in disagreement with multitudes than, being one, to be in disagreement with himself.' Politically, on the contrary, what counts is that a wrong has been done.[49]

In sum, for Arendt there was a clear distinction to be made between the private, unpolitical stand of conscience and the public, political stance of actively caring for the affairs of the political community. Those who struggled for the extension of civil rights and the termination of the war in Vietnam were not trying to save their conscience; rather, they were struggling to improve their polity, to establish standards of universal justice and respect for national self-determination. They were acting as citizens rather than as individuals concerned with their own private integrity.[50]

Citizenship, Agency and Collective Identity

In the light of the preceding discussion, I would like now to turn to an examination of the connection between Arendt's conception of citizenship and the questions of political agency and collective identity. My aim in what follows is to argue that Arendt's participatory conception of citizenship and her theory of action provide the best starting points for addressing both the question of the constitution of collective identity and that concerning the conditions for the exercise of effective political agency.

Citizenship and Collective Identity

Let us examine first the question of collective identity. In her book *Wittgenstein and Justice* Hanna Pitkin argues that one of the crucial questions at stake in political discourse is the creation of a collective identity, a 'we' to which we can appeal when faced with the problem of deciding among alternative courses of action. In addressing the question 'what shall we do?' the 'we', she notes, is not given but must be constantly negotiated. Indeed, since in political discourse there is always disagreement about the possible courses of action, the identity of the 'we' that is going to be created through a specific form of collective action becomes the central question. As Pitkin puts it:

In political discourse's problem of 'what shall we do?' the 'we' is always called into question. Part of the issue becomes, if we pursue this or that course of action open to us, who could affirm it, who could regard it as done in his name? Who will still be with 'us' if 'we' take this course of action?[51]

Thus, 'Part of the knowledge revealed in political discourse is the scope and validity of the claim entered in saying "we": i.e., who turns out to be willing and able to endorse that claim.'[52]

Whenever we engage in action and political discourse we are thereby also engaging in the constitution of our collective identity, in the creation of a 'we' with which we are able to identify both ourselves and our actions. This process of identity-construction is never given once and for all, and is never unproblematic. Rather, it is a process of constant renegotiation and struggle, a process in which actors articulate and defend competing conceptions of cultural and political identity, and competing conceptions of political legitimacy. As Habermas has noted, if a collective identity emerges in complex societies, 'its form would be an identity, non-prejudiced in its content and independent of particular organizational types, of the community of those who engage in the *discursive* and *experimental* formation of an identity-related knowledge on the basis of a critical appropriation of tradition, as well as of the inputs from science, philosophy and the arts.'[53] In political terms this means that a collective identity under modern conditions can arise out of a process of public argumentation and debate in which competing ideals of identity and political legitimacy are articulated, contested and refined.[54] From this standpoint, Arendt's participatory conception of citizenship assumes a particular relevance, since it articulates the conditions for the establishment of collective identities. I would argue, in fact, that once citizenship is viewed as the process of active deliberation about competing identity projections, its value would reside in the possibility of establishing forms of collective identity that can be acknowledged, tested and transformed in a discursive and democratic fashion.

Such a conception of citizenship would also be able to articulate what Nancy Fraser has called 'the standpoint of the *collective concrete other*'. By this term Fraser refers to the standpoint from which specific collective identities are constructed on the basis of the specific narrative resources and vocabularies of particular groups, such as women, blacks and members of oppressed classes. The standpoint of the collective concrete other, Fraser writes, focuses on 'the specificity of the vocabularies available to individuals and groups for the interpretation of their needs and for the definitions of situations in which they encounter one another'. It would also focus on the 'specificity of the narrative resources available to individuals and groups for the construction of individual life-stories [and of] group identities and solidarities'.[55] From such a standpoint people are encountered 'less as unique individuals than as members of groups or collectivities with culturally specific identities, solidarities and forms of life ... here one would abstract *both* from unique individuality *and* from universal humanity to focalize the intermediate zone of group identity.'[56] The norms that would govern the interactions among such groups or collectivities would be 'neither norms of intimacy such as love and care, not those of formal institutions such as rights and entitlements. Rather, they would be norms of collective solidarities as expressed in shared but non-universal social practices.'[57] The value of autonomy could then be formulated in terms that would not pit it against solidarity; rather, to be autonomous would mean 'to be a member of a group or groups which have achieved a degree of collective control over the means of interpretation and communication sufficient to enable one to participate on a par with members of other groups in moral and political deliberation'.[58] The achievement of autonomy could then be considered as one of the conditions necessary to the establishment of relations of equality, mutuality and solidarity.

This formulation of the norms and values of citizenship from the standpoint of the 'collective concrete other' can be interpreted in my view as a fruitful extension of many of the themes articulated by Arendt's participatory conception of citizenship. The stress on solidarity rather than on care or compassion, on respect rather on love or sympathy, and on autonomy as a precondition of solidarity, seems to express the same concerns that animated Arendt's conception of citizenship. Indeed, as Fraser remarks, an ethic of solidarity elaborated from the standpoint of the collective concrete other

is superior to an ethic of care as a *political* ethic. It is the sort of ethic which is attuned to the contestatory activities of social movements struggling to forge narrative resources and vocabularies adequate to the expression of their self-interpreted needs. It is attuned also to collective struggles to deconstruct narrative forms and vocabularies of dominant groups and collectivities so as to show these are partial rather than genuinely shared, and are incapable of giving choice to the needs and hopes of subordinated groups. In short, an ethic of solidarity elaborated from the standpoint of the collective concrete other is more appropriate than an ethic of care for a feminist ethic, if we think of a feminist ethic as the ethic of a *social and political movement*.[59]

In this respect, Fraser concludes, an ethic of solidarity is 'just as appropriate as a *political* ethic for movements of lesbians, gays, blacks, hispanics, other people of color and subordinated classes'.[60] An ethic of solidarity is therefore not the prerogative of any specific group; rather, it is an ethic that can develop out of the struggles of all those groups who have been silenced or marginalized in the past, and who are now attempting to articulate new conceptions of cultural and political identity.[61]

Citizenship and Political Agency

The foregoing discussion has stressed the importance that political action and discourse have for the constitution of collective identities. In this section I would like to focus on a related theme, namely, the connection between political action, understood as the active engagement of citizens in the public realm, and the exercise of effective political agency. This connection represents in my view one of the central contributions of Arendt's theory of action, and underlies what I have called her 'participatory' conception of citizenship. According to Arendt, the active engagement of citizens in the determination of the affairs of their community provides them not only with the experience of public freedom and the joys of public happiness, but also with a sense of *political agency and efficacy*, the sense, in Jefferson's phrase, of being 'participators in government'. The importance of participation for political agency and efficacy is brought out clearly in the following passage from *On Revolution*. Commenting on Jefferson's proposal to institute a system of wards or local councils in which citizens would be able to have an effective share in political power, Arendt remarks that:

> Jefferson called every government degenerate in which all powers were concentrated 'in the hands of the one, the few, the well-born or the many.' Hence, the ward system was not meant to strengthen the power of the many but the power of '*every one*' within the limits of his competence; and only by breaking up 'the many' into assemblies where *every one* could count and be counted upon 'shall we be as republican as a large society can be.' In terms of the safety of the citizens of the republic, the question was how to make everybody feel 'that he is a *participator* in the government of affairs, not merely at an election one day in the year but every day.'[62]

In Arendt's view, only the sharing of power that comes from civic engagement and common deliberation can provide each citizen with a sense of effective political agency. Arendt's strictures against representation must be understood in this light. She saw representation as a substitute for the direct involvement of the citizens, and as a means whereby the distinction between rulers and ruled could reassert itself. When representation becomes the substitute for direct democracy, the citizens can exercise their powers of political agency only at election day, and their capacities for deliberation and political insight are correspondingly weakened. Moreover, by encouraging the formation of a political elite, representation means that

> the age-old distinction between ruler and ruled ... has asserted itself again; once more, the people are not admitted to the public realm, once more the business of government has become the privilege of the few, who alone may 'exercise their virtuous dispositions'.... The result is that the people must either sink into lethargy ... or preserve the spirit of resistance to whatever government they have elected, since the only power they retain is the 'reserve power of revolution.'[63]

As an alternative to a system of representation based on bureaucratic parties and state structures, Arendt proposed a federated system of councils where citizens could be actively engaged at various levels in the determination of their affairs. The relevance of Arendt's proposal for direct democracy lies in the connection it establishes between *active citizenship* and *effective political agency*. It is only by means of direct political participation, by engaging in common action and in public deliberation, that citizenship can be reaffirmed and political agency effectively exercised. As Pitkin and Shumer have remarked, 'even the most oppressed people sometimes rediscover within themselves the capacity to act. Democrats today must seek out and foster every opportunity for people to experience their own *effective* agency ... dependency and apathy must be attacked wherever people's experience centers. Yet such attacks remain incomplete unless they relate personal concerns to public issues, extend individual initiative into shared political action.'[64] In a similar vein, Sara Evans and Harry Boyte have highlighted the ways in which 'the dispossessed and powerless have again and again sought simultaneously to revive and remember older notions of democratic participation ... and ... given them new and deeper meanings and applications. Democracy, in these terms, means more than changing structures so as to make democracy possible. It means, also, schooling citizens in *citizenship* — that is, in the varied skills and values which are essential to sustaining effective participation.'[65]

Viewed in this light, Arendt's conception of participatory democracy represents an attempt to reactivate the experience of citizenship and to articulate the conditions for the exercise of effective political agency. It is worth noting, moreover, that such a conception does not imply value homogeneity or value consensus, nor does it require the dedifferentiation of social spheres. In so far as Arendt's participatory conception is based on the principle of *plurality*, it does not aim at the recovery or revitalization of some coherent value scheme, nor at the reintegration of different social spheres. As Benhabib has noted, on Arendt's participatory conception, 'the public sentiment which is encouraged is not reconciliation and harmony, but rather *political agency and efficacy*, namely, the sense that one has a say in the course of the economic, political, and civic conditions which define our lives together in the political community, and that what one does makes a difference. This can be achieved without value homogeneity among individuals, and without collapsing the various spheres into one another.'[66] Arendt's conception of participatory democracy does not, therefore, aim at value integration or at the dedifferentiation of social spheres; rather it aims at reactivating the conditions for active citizenship and democratic self-determination. As she put it in a passage of *On Revolution*:

> If the ultimate end of the Revolution was freedom and the constitution of a public space where freedom could appear … then the elementary republics of the wards, the only tangible place where everyone could be free, actually were the end of the great republic. … The basic assumption of the ward system, whether Jefferson knew it or not, was that no one could be called happy without his share in public business, that no one could be called free without his experience in public freedom, and that no one could be called either happy or free without participating and having a share in public power.[67]

Citizenship and Political Culture

The foregoing discussion has articulated Arendt's conception of citizenship around the issues of political agency and collective identity. In this last section I would like to explore the connection between Arendt's conception of participatory citizenship and the constitution of an active and democratic political culture. In her book *On Revolution* and in two essays contained in *Between Past and Future*[68] Arendt claimed that the possibility of reactivating the political capacity for impartial and responsible judgement depended upon the creation of public spaces for collective deliberation in which citizens could test and enlarge their opinions. As she put it:

> Opinions will rise wherever men communicate freely with one another and have the right to make their views public; but these views in their endless variety seem to stand also in need of purification and representation.... Even though opinions are formed by individuals and must remain, as it were, their property, no single individual ... can ever be equal to the task of sifting opinions, of passing them through the sieve of an intelligence which will separate the arbitrary and the merely idiosyncratic, and thus purify them into public views.[69]

Where an appropriate public space exists, these opinions can in fact be tested, enlarged and transformed through a process of democratic debate and enlightenment. Democratic debate is indeed crucial to the formation of opinions that can claim more than subjective validity; individuals may hold personal opinions on many subject matters, but they can form *representative* opinions only by enlarging their standpoint to incorporate those of others. In the words of Arendt:

> Political thought is representative. I form an opinion by considering a given issue from different viewpoints, by making present to my mind the standpoints of those who are absent; that is, I represent them.... The more people's standpoints I have present in my mind while I am pondering a given issue, and the better I can imagine how I would feel and think if I were in their place, the stronger will be my capacity for representative thinking and the more valid my final conclusions, my opinion.[70]

The capacity to form valid opinions therefore requires a public space where individuals can test and purify their views through a process of public argumentation and debate. The same holds true for the formation of valid judgements: as 'the most political of man's mental abilities',[71] judgement can only be exercised and tested in public, in the free and open exchange of opinions in the public sphere. As Arendt says, judgement cannot function in strict isolation or solitude; it needs the presence of others 'in whose place' it must think, whose perspectives it must take into consideration, and without whom it never has the opportunity to operate at all. As logic, to be sound, depends on the presence of the self, so judgment, to be valid, depends on the presence of others.[72]

As in the case of opinion, the validity of judgement depends on the ability to think 'representatively', that is, from the standpoint of everyone else, so that we are able to look at the world from a number of different perspectives. And this ability, in turn, can only be acquired and tested in a public setting where individuals have the opportunity to exchange their opinions and to articulate their differences through democratic discourse. As Benhabib has put it: 'To think from the standpoint of everyone else entails sharing a public culture such that everyone else can articulate indeed what they think and what their perspectives are. The cultivation of one's moral imagination flourishes in such a culture in which the self-centered perspective of the individual is constantly challenged by the multiplicity and diversity of perspectives that constitute public life.'[73] In this respect, she argues, the cultivation of enlarged thought 'politically requires the creation of institutions and practices whereby the voice and the perspective of others, often unknown to us, can become expressed in their own right.'[74] The creation and cultivation of a public culture of democratic citizenship that guarantees to everyone the right to opinion and action is therefore essential to the flourishing of the capacity to articulate and acknowledge the perspectives of others.

Conclusion

In this chapter I have argued that Arendt's conception of citizenship can be articulated around three major themes, namely, the public sphere, political agency and collective identity, and political culture.

With respect to the first theme, after having analysed Arendt's understanding of the public sphere, I have highlighted three of its major features: its artificial or constructed quality, its spaciality, and the distinction between public and private interests.

With respect to the second theme, I have argued that Arendt's participatory conception of citizenship provides the best starting point for addressing both the question of the constitution of collective identity and that concerning the conditions for the exercise of effective political agency. Drawing on some of the arguments of Pitkin and Habermas, I have shown the connection between the practice of citizenship and the constitution of collective identities. I have then examined Arendt's conception of participatory democracy and stressed the links between active citizenship and effective political agency. I have also argued that Arendt's conception of participatory democracy does not imply value homogeneity or the dedifferentiation of social spheres.

Finally, with respect to the third theme, I have explored the connection between citizenship and political culture, and have argued that the ability of citizens to enlarge their opinions and to test their judgements can only flourish in a public culture of democratic participation that guarantees to everyone the right to action and opinion.

These three themes, I would argue, are highly relevant to the present discussion on the nature and scope of democratic citizenship. The practice of citizenship depends in fact on the reactivation of a public sphere where individuals can act collectively and engage in common deliberation about all matters affecting the political community. Secondly, the practice of citizenship is essential to the constitution of a public identity based on the values of solidarity, autonomy, and the acknowledgement of difference. Participatory citizenship is also essential to the attainment of effective political agency, since it enables each individual to have some impact on the decisions that affect the well-being of the community. Finally, the practice of democratic citizenship is crucial for the enlargement of political opinion and the testing of one's judgement, and represents in this respect an essential element in the constitution of a vibrant and democratic political culture.

Notes

1. *The Human Condition*, University of Chicago Press, Chicago 1958, p. 50.
2. Ibid., p. 51.
3. Ibid., p. 199.
4. Ibid.
5. Ibid., p. 52.
6. Ibid.
7. Ibid.
8. Ibid., pp. 52–3.
9. Ibid., p. 55.
10. Ibid., p. 135.
11. *Between Past and Future*, Viking Press, New York 1968, p. 95.

12. *Human Condition*, p. 173.

13. Ibid., p. 55.

14. M. Canovan, 'Politics as Culture: Hannah Arendt and the Public Realm', *History of Political Thought*, Vol. 6, No. 3, Winter 1985, pp. 617–42.

15. For Arendt's rejection of the concept of human nature, see *Human Condition*, pp. 10–11.

16. Cf. M. Oakeshott, *Hobbes on Civil Association*, Basil Blackwell, Oxford 1975. p. 7.

17. See *Human Condition*, p. 215; *The Origins of Totalitarianism*, Harcourt Brace Jovanovich, New York 1973; *On Revolution*, Viking Press, New York 1965.

18. See *Origins of Totalitarianism*, pp. 290–302, esp. pp. 295–6.

19. Ibid., p. 296.

20. Cf. E. Young-Bruehl, *Hannah Arendt: For Love of the World*, Yale University Press, New Haven 1982, p. xiv; L. Botstein, 'Liberating the Pariah: Politics, The Jews, and Hannah Arendt', *Salmagundi* no. 60, Spring–Summer 1983, pp. 73–106; F. Feher, 'The Pariah and the Citizen: On Arendt's Political Theory', *Thesis Eleven*, no. 15, 1986, pp. 15–29.

21. Hannah Arendt, *The Jew as Pariah*, ed. R. Feldman, Grove Press, New York 1978.

22. Cf. C. Pateman, *Participation and Democratic Theory*, Cambridge University Press, Cambridge 1970; *Participation in Politics*, eds J.R. Pennock and J.W. Chapman, Atherton, New York 1975; B. Barber, *Strong Democracy: Participatory Politics for a New Age*, University of California Press, Berkeley 1984.

23. *Men in Dark Times*, Harcourt Brace Jovanovich, New York 1968, p. 13.

24. Ibid., p. 16.

25. Ibid., p. 25.

26. Canovan, 'Politics as Culture', p. 632.

27. See *On Revolution*, p. 253.

28. Cf. H. Pitkin and S. Shumer, 'On Participation', *Democracy*, vol. 2, no. 4, Fall 1982, pp. 43–54, esp. pp. 47–8.

29. See *On Revolution*, pp. 227–8.

30. See *Between Past and Future*, pp. 220–1.

31. *On Revolution*, p. 227.

32. C. Lasch, 'The Communication Critique of Liberalism', *Soundings*, vol. 69, no. 1–2, Spring–Summer 1986, p. 64.

33. Canovan, 'Politics as Culture', p. 634 (emphasis mine).

34. Ibid., p. 635.

35. H. Arendt, 'Freedom and Politics', in *Freedom and Serfdom: An Anthology of Western Thought*, ed. A. Hunold, D. Reidel, Dordrecht 1961, p. 200 (emphasis mine).

36. H. Arendt, 'Public Rights and Private Interests', in *Small Comforts for Hard Times: Humanists on Public Policy*, eds M. Mooney and F. Stuber, Columbia University Press, New York 1977, p. 104.

37. *Crises of the Republic*, Harcourt Brace Jovanovich, New York 1972, p. 175.

38. Cf. M. Markus, 'The "Anti-Feminism" of Hannah Arendt', *Thesis Eleven*, no. 17, 1987, pp. 76–87.

39. *Crises of the Republic*, p. 175.

40. Arendt, 'Public Rights and Private Interests', p. 105.

41. Ibid., p. 106.

42. H.D. Thoreau, 'On the Duty of Civil Disobedience', quoted in *Crises of the Republic*, p. 60.

43. *Crises of the Republic*, pp. 60—1.

44. Ibid., p. 64.

45. Arendt believed that the morality of conscience was too private and subjective to serve as a valid standard for political action. In place of conscience she advocated the political principle of active citizenship.

46. *Hannah Arendt: The Recovery of the Public World*, ed. M.A. Hill, St Martin's Press, New York 1979, p. 311.

47. H. Arendt, 'Thinking and Moral Considerations: A Lecture', *Social Research*, vol. 51, no. 1, Spring 1984, pp. 7—37; *The Life of the Mind*, Harcourt Brace Jovanovich, New York 1978, pp. 190—3.

48. *Life of the Mind*, p. 191.

49. *Crises of the Republic*, p. 62.

50. Canovan argues that for Arendt the important difference was between 'living as a private individual with a conscience, and living together with others in a public world for which all are jointly responsible' ('Politics as Culture', p. 639).

51. H. Pitkin, *Wittgenstein and Justice*, University of California Press, Berkeley 1972, p. 208.

52. Ibid.

53. J. Habermas, 'On Social Identity', *Telos*, no. 19, Spring 1974, p. 102.

54. Cf. C. Mouffe, 'Rawls: Political Philosophy without Politics', *Philosophy and Social Criticism*, vol. 13, no. 2, Summer 1988, pp. 105—23, esp. pp. 116—17.

55. Nancy Fraser, 'Toward a Discourse Ethic of Solidarity', *Praxis International*, vol. 5, no. 4, January 1986, p. 428.

56. Ibid.

57. Ibid.

58. Ibid.

59. Ibid., pp. 428—9 (last emphasis mine).

60. Fraser, 'Toward a Discourse Ethic of Solidarity', p. 429 (emphasis mine).

61. For a discussion of Arendt's attitude to the questions raised by the women's movement, see Markus, 'The "Anti-Feminism" of Hannah Arendt'.

62. *On Revolution*, p. 254 (emphasis mine).

63. Ibid., pp. 237—8.

64. Pitkin and Shumer, 'On Participation', p. 52 (emphasis mine).

65. S. Evans and H. Boyte, *Free Spaces: The Sources of Democratic Change in America*, Harper & Row, New York 1986, p. 17 (emphasis mine).

66. S. Benhabib, 'Autonomy, Modernity, and Community: Communitarianism and Critical Social Theory in Dialogue', in A. Honneth, T. McCarthy, C. Offe and A. Wellmer, eds, *Zwischenbetrachtungen im Prozess der Aufklaerung*, Suhrkamp, Frankfurt 1989, p. 389.

67. *On Revolution*, p. 255.

68. 'The Crisis in Culture' and 'Truth and Politics', in *Between Past and Future*, pp. 197—226, pp. 227—64.

69. *On Revolution*, p. 227.

70. *Between Past and Future*, p. 241.

71. Arendt, 'Thinking and Moral Considerations', p. 36.

72. *Between Past and Future*, pp. 220—1.

73. S. Benhabib, 'Judgment and the Moral Foundations of Politics in Arendt's Thought', *Political Theory*, vol. 16, no. 1, February 1988, pp. 47—8.

74. Ibid., p. 47.

8

Europe: A Political Community?

Etienne Tassin

The Single European Act, which was ratified in February 1986, seeks to transform the whole set of relations between Community states into a European Union. In that document, member states express their resolve to allow EC institutions to establish a common will and joint action with regard to Community interests. But political union is subordinated to the creation of a single market, defined in Article 13 as 'an area without internal frontiers in which the free movement of goods, persons, services and capital is ensured'. The single market is drawing the future contours of Europe. But what kind of union is involved? What kind of Europe?

The European idea has been slowly and arduously brought up to date since the end of the Second World War, in a process whose institutional and historical forms, and guiding principles, pose a twofold question about the nature of a political community. First, how are we to understand a *community* which gathers under a principle of unity and common identity a number of individuals and groups, which have already been defined and constituted according to territorial, ethnic, socioeconomic, cultural and other criteria of belonging, themselves forged in the course of a common history? From this perspective, we might ask in what history the unity and identity of a European community are being forced? Secondly, how are we to understand a *political* community, in so far as it is more than just an economic interest group bent on greater rationalization of the system of production and exchange? In this regard, we have to ask to what extent Europe can be something other than a market, whether common or single. To what kind of community can

Europe lay claim? What are the ideals in view? What kind of community does it represent? Such questions could also be formulated in a slightly different way. What are the cultural and historical foundations of Europe? What image of a political community does it set before it? What is the real character of the community to which it refers? The purpose of this chapter will be to explore these two interrelated problems.

What Kind of Community? What Kind of Europe?

Economic or Institutional Union?

Economic union, or the passage from a common to a single market, has been developing independently of political union. Indeed, this hiatus between the establishment of an economic and a political community has marked Europe since the end of the Second World War. In October 1972 the Paris Summit defined political union as the common ultimate goal of member states. At the same time, however, this remained contingent upon prior agreements relating to various social and economic matters — a condition which postponed political union until the indefinite future. It was not long before the problem was posed of choosing between political integration of states ('constitutional' integration, we might call it) and 'functional' economic integration. Differences in this area then connected up with a conflict between the strictly state-centred view of union (the idea of a 'confederation', advocated in France by General de Gaulle) and a federalist conception whose great champion and theorist in Europe was Denis de Rougemont. But it should be stressed that these two antitheses (constitutional or functional integration, confederation or federation) are by no means equivalent. The former is governed by a logic of facts, while the latter conforms to a choice of principle. Thus European federalists, who at first favoured constitutional integration, soon came to see the 'federal' virtues of a policy of functional integration. Moreover, the federal/confederal distinction rests upon a more general interpretation of the fate of Europe: it radically calls into question the traditional categories through which the political form of modern states has been conceptualized.

A Political Europe or a Europe of the Mind?

The European goal of political union has been developing independently of the tradition of cultural unity which initially brought it forth. This has introduced a sharp break between the new European community and Europe as a historical and cultural entity. Whatever the difficulties posed in defining a European *identity*, it is clear that the idea of Europe has denoted, and continues to denote, a common tradition of thought and culture rooted in that constant interchange over two millennia which has given this part of the world a certain unity of the mind. Until the Second World War this cultural Europe coincided with the political mapping of the continent. Yalta subsequently divided Europe in an opposition between democratic and 'socialist' systems. The political Europe in question therefore became *defined* by its democratic principle, and *circumscribed* by its reduction to five, then six, and finally ten or twelve states in the West. This outcome calls for two observations.

First, the idea of Europe is not exhausted simply in the common affirmation by member states of a political will to defend the principles of democracy, human rights and social justice. If there is to be a political community, presumably it should be rooted in a common experience and a tradition of thought and history that reside equally in all the peoples of Europe. The 'other Europe', as Eastern Europe is awkwardly called, cannot just be left out. One proof of this is the political vigour that the demand for rights and freedoms acquired in the dissident movements, Solidarity or Charter 77 — values which Europe is said to embody, and in which the countries of Central Europe have recognized themselves. Another indication is the artists and intellectuals in the East who, in claiming to belong to a common culture, reject the idea of two Europes and argue that historically there has been only one Europe of the mind.[1] Highly symbolic, too, is the character of the private seminars that the philosopher Jan Patocka organized in Prague in 1973. Starting out from a line of thought bequeathed by Husserl and reworked by Heidegger, he sought to understand how Europe, 'this two-thousand-year-old structure which raised humanity to a quite new level of reflexive consciousness and of power and vigour, and which for a long time was identified with humanity as a whole ... has definitively reached the end of its course.'[2] Europe at the end of its course? Definitively? But what is this Europe? It is the one that Platonic philosophy and its founding metaphysical move have enshrined as the Western figure of Mind. In this sense, the end of Europe might be seen as the end of philosophy, and vice versa. And yet, Patocka's philosophical ambition is precisely to show that the dissolution of 'the metaphysical way of posing the philosophical question' in no way implies the end of philosophy — nor, therefore, of the European Mind.

Now, paradoxically the idea of a European political community has been taking shape since 1944 at the very time when the most fundamental principles of western metaphysics have been shaken, and when the idea of a European Mind embodying those principles has been invalidated both factually, by the various totalitarian experiences, and at a conceptual level, by the impossibility for philosophy to assume and integrate it. The Frankfurt School critique of instrumental rationality, the existentialist rejection of any essentialist ground of values, the structuralist deconstruction of humanism, or the critique of a metaphysics of the subject, linked to the theme of the end of philosophy, which was launched by Heidegger and taken up in the different variants of contemporary deconstructivism — all these postures have impugned the philosophical move that came to merge with the idea of Europe. In short, *political Europe* saw the light of day as *the Europe of the mind* was collapsing. The idea and the necessity of a European political community emerged just after the war in a philosophical climate of almost universal indifference (the main exceptions being Karl Jaspers and Hannah Arendt, Jacques Maritain and Emmanuel Mounier). Or rather, the dominant philosopheme in Europe unified, in different forms, a radical challenging of western values amid the political crises of the time — the ordeals of Nazism and Stalinism, the decolonization drives in which western imperialist hegemony came under sharp attack, and so on — and an equally radical challenge to the Enlightenment which denied to thought its founding principle of metaphysical rationality. It is within this framework, however schematically drawn, that Patocka's position assumes its full significance. For Eastern Europe has invoked again a Europe of the mind, seeing it as the source for militant political demands on behalf of what the philosophical Europe of the West can no longer taken upon itself.

The idea of Europe-wide political unity therefore poses the philosophical question of knowing what Europe is, what it can be and wants to be. A convergence of economic interests cannot alone make a political community. This presupposes a common life which sustains itself not just on interests and cultural references but also, and above all, on a real postulated identity: real, through being woven into a history that is also a history of the mind; and postulated, since this never consummated identity is constantly changing as it projects a horizon of principles or values on which the community maintains itself without ever exhausting it.

The Foundations of the European Mind

People are constantly talking of Europe in the political sense, but they neglect to ask what exactly it is and from where it has originated. We propose to speak of the integration of Europe. But is Europe something that can be integrated? Is it a geographical or purely political concept? No. And if we wish to address the present situation, we must first understand that Europe is a concept which rests upon foundations of the mind.[3]

If Europe is not just a geographical or political concept, in what sense can one speak of European identity? We might, rather schematically, distinguish three concepts of Europe, which are deployed in three different approaches: a political concept, which involves a specifically historical approach; a cultural concept, whose meaning appears in what Braudel calls the 'grammar of civilizations'; and a philosophical concept, which sees the Greek city as the birthplace of the European mind in the shape of Platonic metaphysics.

Decline and Permanence of the Idea of Europe

It is evidently this last concept to which Patocka is referring. Only a philosophical understanding of the foundations of the European mind can restore meaning to a Community enterprise, which the twentieth century repudiated in an experience lasting some thirty years. Europe, the land of mind, science and technology, the ferment of a rational civilization *par excellence*, nevertheless 'destroyed itself with its own forces' and dragged the world into a process of general destruction.[4] How did Europe find itself on this path? For Patocka, Europe has followed a destiny which leads to the situation of modern man in general. This is defined by three components: science and technology as a knowledge of domination; the sovereign state as the concrete organization of human society; and a profusion of sovereign states in disunity. Taken together, these three dimensions account for the conflict that has turned Europe, and with it the world, upside down. The disunity among states expresses a lack of political and mental unity which allows the logic of state domination to make unparalleled technological power a slave to its own ends.

This inner logic which governed the destiny of the European mind cannot, however, be ascribed to the philosophical wellsprings of Europe. We must, Patocka argues, distinguish between the historical–political concept of Europe and the philosophical concept, and not accuse the mental source of what pertains to political history. The political birth of Europe did not coincide with its philosophical birth. In fact, it was only in the Middle Ages that Europe became a political concept designating a real political unity.

Europe was born out of the ruins of the Greek *polis* and the Roman Empire. On the one hand, the *polis* died when the Greek world of mutually destroying urban communities fell apart. The Hellenistic period unfolded through the collapse of the city-state whose political meaning was public liberty. But it also gave rise to the concept of humanity, as this expressed itself politically in the forms of a world state, religion and citizenship. These features of late Hellenism then crystal-lized in the Roman Empire.

On the other hand, the Roman Empire lived spiritually on the heritage of the Greek *polis*, as this asserted itself in a law-governed state in which civil law was based upon the rights of people. But at the same time, the imperial ambition tended towards a hegemony which could only rest upon force and create a void around it. Universalism of thought, translated into a universality of law and institutions, housed within it a contradictory, hegemonic logic which carried it into decline. And yet, Rome's imperial disaster in turn left to invaded Europe the principles of the Greek mind: universality of thought and law, and more fundamentally the metaphysical principle developed by Plato which Patocka calls 'care of the soul'. Such is the legacy which today allows us to find in the idea of Europe 'a support amid general weaknesses and acquiescence in decline'.[5]

An original combination has thus emerged through the dissociation of the historical logic that gave rise to political Europe from its spiritual or metaphysical foundation. *A theorization of Europe's decline*, as a catastrophe bound up with the establishment of nation-states and the deployment of metaphysics in the form of technological power, is conjoined to *a theorization of Europe's spiritual permanence*. Patocka, for example, could argue:

Metaphysics, which issued from the specific historical situation of the

decline of the Athens-type *polis*, gave shape to a legacy that could also
survive the decline of the Hellenistic world and contribute, after the decline
of the Roman Empire, to the formation of Europe in the proper sense of the
term. The survival of this heritage naturally also involved its transformation,
but the metaphysical basis remained.[6]

The catastrophes left intact a spiritual heritage which is 'capable of
making us conceive new hopes, allowing us not to despair of the future'.
It is no accident that this philosophical enterprise, which has striven to
preserve the meaning of Europe, is the work of a dissident thinker from
the East, a political militant seeking in philosophy the assurance that the
source of his struggle and his thought has not perished with Europe's tilt
into totalitarian systems. In this sense Patocka is Husserl's only inheritor.
Indeed, he himself asserts: 'Europe is doing everything to avoid reflection
about such things; no one is concerned about them. Since Husserl's *Krisis*
no philosopher has really reflected on the problem of Europe and the
European heritage.'[7] That no one is concerned about them is perhaps not
so surprising. For Western Europe, which sought to constitute itself as a
political community after the Second World War, was unable to do so
with the philosophical conviction that the European heritage had not
been lost. It did not fall to western philosophy to take up the questions
that Husserl posed between 1930 and 1935, to reaffirm, in the face of war
and the ordeal of genocide, the essentially Greek form of Europe. On the
contrary, Europe appeared to it to be philosophically dead, and to have
died intestate.[8]

In the lecture he gave in Vienna in 1935, Husserl tried to get to the
heart of the 'phenomenon of Europe'. What distinguished it spiritually
was its animation by a *telos* of its own: 'An entelechy is inborn in our
European civilization which holds sway throughout all the changing
shapes of Europe and accords to them the sense of development toward
an ideal shape of life and being as an eternal pole.'[9] This spiritual *telos*
governing Europe's historicity has dedicated it to universality since its
birth in Athens. The primal phenomenon or *Urphänomen* which spiritually defines Europe lies in what the Greeks called *philosophy* – a
theoretical attitude aiming at universality which confers an infinite task
upon humanity. This attitude, through which thought extricates itself
from a finite world to elaborate the truth of that world in itself, is at the
origin of that infinite construction of theoretical knowledge embodied
in European thought. But at the same time, the dedication of philosophy
to the universal gives birth to a humanity that is not bound by belonging

to any particular community. Since philosophy is not rooted in any
practical interest, it does not derive from any interest tied to the ground
of a national tradition. Rather, a pure, ideal community takes shape with
it, a community beyond nations that is based on the power of ideas. 'Ideas
are stronger than any empirical powers.'[10] 'Europe' is the proper name of
philosophy conceived as a conversion of humanity: it refers not to a
juxtaposition of different nations, but to this new ruling spirit of
humanity, this 'treasure of associated nations'. Thus, a task is finally
bestowed upon philosophy. 'Within European civilization, philosophy
has constantly to exercise its function as one which is archontic for
civilization as a whole', regulating it according to the principles of
absolute universality and the totality of truth. The European mind
merges with the spirit of philosophy which merges with the spirit of
humanity.

Europe's existential crisis should thus be understood as stemming
from an alienation of reason in the figures of objectivist, naturalist
rationality evident in science. But this crisis of rationalism is expressed
politically in the modern impossibility of grasping man at the spiritual
level of community life. The spirit of community gives way to the spirit
of national wills, distorted in the political discourse of particularities that
are set up as so many sovereignties. This compartmentalization erects the
mind against itself, and the various nations against Europe. The crisis
leaves only two possible outcomes: either Europe will disappear if it
makes itself alien to its Greek spiritual significance; or Europe will be
reborn if it is able, through 'the heroism of reason', to rediscover its faith
in the West's humanitarian mission and its conviction that 'the spirit
alone is immortal'.[11]

'Empirical Powers'

It is likely that the ordeal of Nazism and the Shoa rendered Europe alien
to its spiritual significance. Between 1935 and 1945 empirical powers
proved stronger than ideas, so that the philosophical determination of
the concept of Europe could not emerge unscathed from the Second
World War. Not only is it impossible to identify 'a pure idea of Europe
that remained intact, unscathed, unalterable, self-identical and definable
in the same way in 1936 and in 1946', as Jean Starobinski put it in the
immediate aftermath of the war.[12] It may even be that Europe's political
collapse involved a radical disavowal of a Europe grounded upon the

philosophical *Urphänomen*, so much so that the very possibility of philosophy, defined as a purely theoretical attitude, was rendered incoherent. Jean Lescure, speaking like Starobinski in Geneva in 1946, summed up the situation in a few striking sentences: 'The historical moment has passed when Europe could be presented as a philosophical problem. Today the questioning of it would seem by nature to be a matter of politics. I would say that Europe can no longer be located on the plane of the mind, but only on that of forces.'[13] If Europe can be located only on the plane of forces, if 'empirical powers' have put paid to the philosophical idea of Europe, then the question to be asked is not whether Europe can still embody humanity but whether humanity can and should still be embodied in the figure of Europe alone – and whether philosophy can still be invested with a 'directive function'. Indeed, perhaps Europe no longer denotes anything but one will to power among others, just an ordinary politics of force opposed, merely at the level of force, to what was known after the war as 'Americanism' and 'Sovietism'.

In that defeat of Europe, which principle could have offered a way out from what Lukács diagnosed in 1946 as a crisis of democracy, a crisis of the idea of progress, a crisis of belief in reason and a crisis of humanism?[14] The real blindness, the Shoa, was encapsulated in Adorno's question: 'How can we think after Auschwitz?' Patocka stands alone in having countered the theme of the end of philosophy with Husserl's idea of a Europe of the mind. But it must be noted that this reactivation is possible only if one does not go to the roots of Nazism, only if one obscures what the Jewish question has meant for Europe – or, in other words, only if one grounds Europe just on Athens and not on Jerusalem. Patocka states, for example: 'The current conception of European life as resting on twin foundations, one Jewish and one Greek, has only conditional validity inasmuch as the Jewish element passed through Greek reflection. It is Greek reflection which, by giving form to the Jewish element, enabled it to become the leaven of the new European world.'[15]

We started out from the post-war paradox that Western Europe tried to constitute itself as a political community when the values it was supposed to embody (and the philosophical concept grounding its 'directive function') had been so deeply shaken that they could not enable modern European philosophy to assume that mission once again. This faces us with two types of question.

1. If the modern idea of Europe could not sustain itself on its ancient

spiritual foundation, how did it contrive to found itself amid the
catastrophe that marked the collapse of Europe? The first point to be
made is that the modern idea of Europe did not draw its significance
from a theoretical foundation such as Husserl or Patocka assigned to the
philosophical concept of Europe, but rather sprang from the *political
experience* of resistance to Nazism, which had no equivalent in history.
The idea of a European political community drew its meaning from an
armed struggle. And so it broke both with the philosophical idea of
Europe and with a political tradition.

2. This break led to a remodelling of values, ousting at a political level
the traditional framework within which the history of Europe had
developed over six previous centuries. It has often been said that the two
world wars signalled the decline of the nation-states which had gradually
constituted Europe's political structure. A modern attempt to form a
European political community therefore had to stress that Europe
needed to leave behind the state of war by inventing a new political form
of community. The tendency within this new form to establish a federation of states was undoubtedly the great historical novelty in Europe. But
given the break with tradition, the establishment of a political Europe
raises the problem of political will. Paul Thibaud has posed it in the
following terms:

> Our political concepts and sentiments were adapted to the national frame-
> work, and Europe is now destabilizing them.... The first question no longer
> concerns the orientation of a supposedly common will (what do we want?)
> but the formation of will: how can we want things together? What is a
> political will that is shared, or called upon to cooperate, no longer out of
> practical necessity but in a radical departure at the moment of being
> conceived?[16]

Are we talking here simply of a supranational will that works itself out
within a higher-level citizenship? The crucial problem appears to be to
discover what Europe can will together, and what it can will in relation
to its recent history. Fundamentally, it seems to me, we have to know
whether Europe is still a question of *will.*

The Political Concept of Europe

The political concept of Europe has a long history. In 1814, in his book
The Reorganization of European Society, Saint-Simon wrote:

Until the end of the fifteenth century all the nations of Europe formed a single body politic at peace within itself, armed against the enemies of its constitution and independence. The Roman religion, practised from one end of Europe to the other, was the passive link of European society. The Roman clergy were its active link.[17]

That was how the first Europe took shape. This medieval Europe of the Carolingian era and the Holy Empire, inheriting the Roman *imperium* but replacing juridical with religious bonds, corresponds to what historians call *the Europe of Christendom*. Europe then flowed together with Catholicism. This was succeeded by *the Europe of sovereigns*, born with nation-states and grounded on the cultural and ideological cement of humanism. It would replace the principle of imperial integration of peoples with the principle of a concert of nations. As Bernard Voyenne puts it: 'To a hierarchical, unitary Europe, the dream of which went back to Charlemagne and Rome, Richelieu counterposed the reality of a polyphonic and collegial Europe.'[18] By wiping out the last shreds of Christendom, the Treaties of Westphalia in 1648 put an end to any attempt at hegemony and assured a peaceful equilibrium among nations. The revolutionary wars and Napoleon's project of an armed conquest of Europe issued in what is usually known as *the Europe of nationalities*, which was drawn up for the nineteenth century by the Treaty of Vienna. But the wars also showed that the idea of a united European political community was historically in contradiction with the coming of nation-states. Napoleonic Europe was less an empire, in the mode of Rome or the Holy Empire, than an expression of the essentially imperialist dimension of modern nation-states dedicated to armed confrontation. In this sense, not only were the wars of 1870 and 1914—18 national wars, but it was still the nationalities principle that was sanctioned and carried to the extreme by the Treaty of Versailles.

European Projects

Projects for a European political community were contemporaneous with the formation of the major states. Dislocation of the Holy Empire and Christian Europe, by multiplying political entities in the form of states, called forth these projects that aimed at reunification of a divided Europe.[19] But it was only with the modern reformulation of the Right of Peoples — Vittoria, Suarez's key *Tractatus de legibus et Deo legislatore* (1612) and Grotius's *De jure belli ac pacis* (1625) — that the idea of a 'league of nations', in Vittoria's words, emerged to denote a juridical institution arbitrating in assembly the disputes between nations. The dominant theme here was the regulation of war and of the conditions for the establishment of a European peace. Emeric Crucé, for instance, looking to assure perpetual peace on the basis of the Right of Peoples, proposed that a European town should house a permanent assembly of ambassadors to judge in common the differences between sovereigns.[20] Crucé's idea would influence eighteenth-century reflections on perpetual peace, from Leibniz to Kant, each of whom timidly sketched the inescapable horizon of the federative principle. But of all the eighteenth-century writers, Rousseau seems to have been alone in grasping the revolutionary import of the establishment of a European political community. Was it to be a Europe of the peoples or a Europe of the Princes? 'One can hardly imagine federative leagues being established except through revolutions,' he wrote, 'and on this principle, which of us would dare to say whether such a European league is to be desired or feared?'[21]

Now, this revolutionary character of the federalist principle dominated the way in which the idea of a United States of Europe was developed in the nineteenth century. In the aftermath of 1789, Washington could write to La Fayette: 'One day, the United States of Europe will be constituted on the model of the United States of America. The United States will be the legislator for all the nationalities.'[22] This idea of a United States detached itself with difficulty from a state-centred representation of the European community, which confounded the union of nationalities with the establishment of a great unitary and centralized state. We could say that the republican ideal was mixed up with the revolutionary principle, as Mazzini's projects or Victor Hugo's declarations testify.[23]

We owe to Proudhon the first fundamental reflection on the idea and political significance of a European political community. In analysing the failure of the Revolution, Proudhon linked it to the nation-state structure inherited from the *ancien régime*. 'If the Revolution could not resolve the social problem, this is because it could not solve the political problem.'[24] For Proudhon, then, the idea of a federative Europe had a revolutionary content. It involved a critique of the nationalities principle, which mapped nations onto the state in an attempt to make a fluid anthropological reality coincide with an administrative framework embodying the general will — a framework conceived as the only form of political expression of the various peoples. The true state, however, was the commune; the true nation was the province. The Vienna treaties would make no difference, for the nation–state framework could only carry Europe into war. The whole of Proudhon's thought was summed up in the formula: 'Federalism is the political form of humanity.'[25] But Europe could gain this political form of humanity only through a genuine revolution, an overturning of its state structures and a change in mentality. A confederation of states, being still bound up with a system of alliances between national powers, would place under the war-principle the need for a unified European monarchy.[26] Rather, the political organization of humanity had to be conceived as a federation of federations. This pointed not to a United States of Europe but to united communities of Europe — what would later be called a Europe of regions as opposed to a Europe of states. The whole post-1945 experience of developing European communities would be shot through with this opposition between the federalist principle and the national principle. But Proudhon, writing solemnly and with sharp insight, already set out the terms of the problem: 'The twentieth century will usher in the era of federations, or else humanity will again embark upon a thousand-year purgatory.'[27] It is this idea of a European federation that would eventually be forged through contacts between various Resistance movements.

The European Resistance

Since Nazism was not so much a German problem as the premeditated destruction of Europe in the name of Europe itself, the real issue in the war was not the preservation of states but the future of Europe. In 1942 a group of Italian anti-fascists launched the Movimento Federalista Europeo, arguing that the problem of international organization should supplant all other political problems. The line dividing reactionary and progressive forces no longer passed between supporters of democracy and advocates of collectivization of the means of production, but between those who limited their political horizon to national boundaries and those who wanted federal unity of Europe. In a letter sent in August 1944 to the Comité Français pour la Fédération Européenne, the Movimento wrote:

> Thanks to the resistance movements, we have at last discovered the solidarity which unites the free peoples of the continent.... *We have discovered the common destiny* whose aim is that freedom, peace and progress

should be goods that all European peoples enjoy together and all must lose together…. This awareness, awakened by the sacrifice of millions of men, is the fundamental starting point for the unity of free Europe.[28]

The Declaration of European Resistance Movements (July 1944), drawn up at secret meetings by representatives from nine European countries, proclaimed the 'necessity of rebuilding Europe on a federal basis'. This presupposed that 'the various countries of the world agree to go beyond the dogma of absolute state sovereignty and integrate themselves into a federal organization'. Noting that 'within the space of a single generation Europe has been the epicentre of two world wars whose chief cause lies in the existence of thirty sovereign states on this continent', the Declaration concluded that 'the main task is to cure this anarchy through the creation of a federal Union among the European peoples'. This union would make possible the integration of the German people and resolve the frontier problems through 'territorial demar-cations of a purely administrative character', with the goal of safe-guarding democratic institutions and rebuilding the continental economy through the elimination of national monopolies and autarkies. The federal Union would rest upon 'a declaration of civil, political and economic rights guaranteeing free development of the human person-ality and normal functioning of democratic institutions', and it would involve a government responsible to the peoples of Europe (rather than to member states), a federal army and a supreme court.[29]

In the eyes of the Resistance, it seemed impossible to rebuild Europe as an assemblage of sovereign states separated by political frontiers and customs posts: any attempt at recomposition on the model of the League of Nations or a sovereign state was doomed to bring back the conditions that led Europe into war. During the same period, a number of in-tellectuals then living in the United States, such as Jacques Maritain and Thomas Mann, argued on *Voice of America* broadcasts for the idea of a federal Europe, while Hannah Arendt drew out the revolutionary and constitutive dimension of the Resistance for the Europe to come.[30] That Europe was being born not out of Husserl's 'heroism of reason' but out of a heroism of the heart that was also a political intelligence. Such heroism, armed with the weapons of the mind, had taken up position against totalitarianism. But whereas thought would remain silent in the face of the inexplicable, the Shoa, even forbidding itself to theorize a future for Europe, the physical experience of struggle against totalitarianism would reveal, through action itself, the political resolution summoned by war.

A Europe of Federations

The idea of a federal Europe, of a union of European peoples, was grounded upon the resistance to Nazi and then Stalinist totalitarianism. But totalitarianism was itself understood by the Resistance as an expression of the dogma of absolute state sovereignty: it was the direct offspring of the nation-state, pushing its principle to its extreme consequences. As an example of this view, we can take the most acute theorist of a federal Europe, Denis de Rougemont.

'The nation-state', he wrote, 'was one of Europe's creations and must inevitably, by its inner logic, become totalitarian.'[31] Born in its modern form with the French Revolution and Empire, the nation-state derived from a combination of two social and political realities: the nation, as a cultural, spiritual and ethical reality whose compass was in no way tied to a specific political structure; and the state, as a centralized administrative apparatus built upon the principle of absolute sovereignty. Napoleon, faithful in this respect to the impetus of the revolution, carried the nation-state principle into effect by subsuming the nation under the reach of the state. The formation of the modern nineteenth-century states necessarily led through the conflict between sovereignties to the 1914–18 war. But the nation-state logic, reaffirmed by the Treaty of Versailles, brought the totalitarian state into being. For de Rougemont, the difference between the democratic states of the West and the totalitarian states of the East or Nazi Germany was only a difference of degree between two forms of the nation-state. He could therefore conclude that the same force unleashed the 1914–18 and the 1939–45 wars, namely, 'the dogma of national sovereignty and nationalism', which in the totalitarian state was driven to the extreme limits of its own inner logic, in accordance with Fichte's old utopia.

Europe could not unite, de Rougemont wrote,

> until Europeans had felt to the quick — and, one might add, at their own expense — all the possibilities of absolutism, nationalism, the royal or Jacobin unitary state, the anarchy of sovereign nations, and finally the totalitarianism that was in a way the summation of all these dementias.... There would seem to be a kind of law that reason cannot hold sway over Europeans until all the dementias have been tried out, until they have really shown themselves to be dementias and exhausted all their effects.[32]

Europe could not appear as a community until the totalitarian logic had led the states into the destruction of the Europe of nations. It was thus in its ordeal that the hope of a new Europe could find some basis. The Europe born of war could only be a federate community, grounded not on states but on regions. This was so not because regions denoted a natural form of community, but because only the region, in reproducing the human scale of the ancient Greek cities, offered a community framework favourable to the exercise of genuine citizenship within elective rather than natural, or native, communities.

This elective dimension cannot be stressed enough. Europe can be reborn only 'if possibilities are created for a human community, which is no longer defined, like the old nation, by frontiers, physical contours or civil status, but rather in terms of social, cultural or spiritual goals — communities which I shall accordingly call elective, as opposed to the old native communities.'[33] In fact, man can be free and display this freedom only within

> elective social groups — that is, groups of communities to which he can freely affiliate, communities which, by their principle, greatly overflow the small social cell of the residential unit or the satellite town. These elective social groups are defined by ideas, concerns and moral, psychological, religious or cultural needs, and no longer by birthplace, family or village traditions, territory or mere physical juxtaposition of people.[34]

For the point is not to reproduce on a smaller regional scale that constitutive principle of the nation which philosophy developed in the nineteenth century, from Herder to Fichte and Hegel. The nation was theorized as the affirmation of a purely traditional community, which found its unity in an ethnic, linguistic or 'spiritual' identity embodying the spirit of a people. This still harked back to a native community in the strict sense of the term, both a community of birth (*natio*) and a natural community. Against this perspective, de Rougemont proposed a formula of Renan's: 'Nations are not something eternal. They began, and they will end. The European confederation will probably replace them.'[35] In a way, Renan was outlining the idea of a 'nation' whose basis was more elective than natural, since it rested upon the principle of chosen citizenship. Whereas the nation has a gentile origin, which the state takes over and raises to a higher, institutional unity by giving it the 'political' reality of a national will and sovereignty, the elective community of the region defines itself through a minimax calculation: it is a problem of size, a problem of dimension and tension. For the state is a political unit whose immoderate size makes the exercise of citizenship a formal matter. The state structure generates and rests upon the apathy of citizens, because its characteristic political framework exceeds the possibilities for active participation in the management of public affairs. In this sense, the state introduces within society the principle of necessary *depoliticization* of the citizenry. The city, by contrast, as embodied in the *polis*, the *civitas* or the free commune of the late Middle Ages, set the frame for an active citizenship that the development of nation-states rendered obsolete. It is not a question, then, of restoring communal freedoms — an idea found in the principle of European associations like the Council of Communes of Europe or the Union of towns and local authorities[36] — but rather of understanding that beyond the nation-state framework which brought Europe to catastrophe, the basic political unit has to be redefined. This unit cannot be the commune; it is the Region federating the communes. In the dialectic of the particular (commune) and the universal (state), the federation of regions involves a reconciliation of communal interests raised to the higher power of Europe. It is reconciliation and not transcendence, a measure and not a middle term. For the federal principle maintains the *human* scale of active political citizenship within a local community, while raising it beyond the national framework and allowing a genuine European community to be constituted. Europe, de Rougemont tells us, has to be built in Proudhonian style from the bottom up — not in order to destroy the state, as Proudhon imagined, but to redistribute it.[37]

Denis de Rougemont, along with Dandieu and Mounier, was the founder of *personalism* in the 1930s. Federalism was its corresponding politics. A federative regime, by optimally combining the tension between collective power and individual liberties, would reflect the tension within each person between individual autonomy and responsibility to the community. It is the only remedy to the twin evils of modern politics: individualism, which denies responsibility to the community; and collectivism, which denies individual liberties. By expressing this dialectical tension at the level of institutions, federalism makes it possible to take up two contradictory maxims: autonomy of the parts, and unity of the whole. It is in this sense that Europe can only be a federation of federations. 'The region is the true socio-economic unit of present-day Europe.'[38]

The Dangers in Building Europe

The failure of the immediate post-war attempt to build Europe should be attributed to the fact that Europe was to be unified on the basis of nation-states. Breakdown was inevitable once the political negotiations reduced the possibility of a united Europe to a single alternative: on the one hand, the supranationality principle, which posited a European super nation-state operating over European nations a unitary reduction similar to that which the French state imposed on the regions during the Revolution: on the other hand, the nationalism principle involved in tactical cooperation between states pursuing strictly national ends. This latter conception was the one embraced by de Gaulle in his famous press conference of 5 September 1960 on the building of Europe: 'In such an area', he stated, 'it is necessary to act not on dreams but in accordance with realities. What are the realities of Europe? What are the pillars on which it can be built? The fact is that they are states, ... the only entities which have the right to issue orders and to be obeyed.' De Gaulle, then, had in mind a Europe that would be no more than an 'organized, regular harmony of responsible governments', involving cooperation between states. This is what is known as 'L'Europe des Patries', and what de Rougemont called the 'Association of Misanthropes'.[39] Faced with this alternative, federalism required a politics. But whereas the community momentum flowing out of the Resistance sought immediate institutional expression, the existing states, still governed by the rule of national sovereignty, found this impossible to accept. Two tendencies thus emerged from the various post-war European movements: a 'unionist' tendency that was firmly attached to the principle of national sovereignty; and a federalist tendency, varying in its radicalism, which called for a federal authority and, in some cases, envisaged an immediate change in the internal structures of European states.

This antithesis has continued right up to the present day to mark political efforts to build the European community. But it has itself undergone various shifts as existing states have shown themselves more or less reticent, and as economic necessities have come into play. The Council of Europe, which was founded in 1949, set itself the goal of 'creating a European political authority endowed with limited functions but real powers'.[40] The federal path was described as a 'constitutional' solution involving a general reform of state structures. And in opposition to this, the method of so-called functional integration was put forward, whereby specialized supranational authorities would be established to carry out particular limited tasks. Believing that it would be a delusion to expect sovereign states to renounce their sovereignty, the architects of Europe — including the federalists — rallied to the principle of functional integration. The most effective way of building Europe seemed to be to take each problem that could not be solved within a national framework and to appoint a limited authority that would try to solve it at a European level. This principle led to the European Coal and Steel Community in 1950 and the EEC in 1957; and it underlay the failure of the EDC in 1954, since the idea of a defence community was subordinated to the prior establishment of a policy community that would call national sovereignty into question.

The history of the Europe of Twelve thus displays a shifting antithesis. As early as 1950 it was no longer a question of counterposing a political community to an economic community. It appeared that political Europe could be born, if at all, only out of a common market, according to the pragmatic (but also technocratic) viewpoint that presided over its formulation. But this shift left in abeyance the political choice between confederation, as desired by de Gaulle as well as Kohl or Mitterrand, and a genuine federation. A pragmatic (and realist?) perspective therefore carried the day. But should we count on a knock-on effect such that the lifting of customs barriers and frontier restrictions, the free circulation of goods, capital and persons, will slowly but surely weave a community that is no longer merely economic but a speech community in which the cultural figures common to Europeans will be redeployed? Should we expect that a common identity of minds will be recognized beyond the symbolic marks of physical and cultural territoriality, language and conventions? Will the hallmarks of national belonging, far from disappearing, combine to form a cultural cement for a transnational identity that will be capable of turning the 'Association of Misanthropes' into a community of philanthropes? Above all, will this cement be capable of giving the peoples of Europe a will to 'think together' instead of remaining content with a convergence of interests? We can certainly hope and wish so, and work towards it! But does this hold out the promise of a *political community*?

National Will or Common Citizenship: The Public Space

Whatever the future of political Europe, the achievement of a single market already indicates the need to overstep the strictly national

framework of European states, as well as the impossibility of imagining a
Europe-wide political community in the present or the near future. Does
the establishment of a political community therefore depend, as Thibaud
argues, on the 'formation of a will' common to the states and peoples of
Europe?

The idea of a European community cannot be viable if it refers to a
community structured like the classical state, in which a general will is
embodied in the national will. Whatever political shape it may assume,
no *will* — be it common, unitary, general, national or supranational —
can define the European community or lay its foundations of possibility.
This community cannot be a communion of will — on the contrary, it
displays a complementarity of heterogeneous, non-generalizable wills, of
disparate particularities resistant to any 'common union'. Since in reality
it objects to the individuation principle of a general or national will, it
suggests that a common space of European peoples should be protected
both from the chimera of an original common identity to be reconstituted for the planned union, and from the phantasm of a unitary will to
be forced out of nothing so that a common politics should become
possible. In short, it calls on us to shake off the organicist imagery bound
up with the idea of will, to stop thinking of community in terms of *the
body* or of politics in terms of sovereignty and domination. Just as the
institutionalized community cannot fall under the statist logic of the
monopoly of legitimate violence, so its constituent parts cannot establish
themselves against each other in a relationship of domination. The
principle indicated here is rather that of 'participation in government'
(Arendt), which can only be guaranteed by a *public space* such that the
community institutions assure its durability without reflecting any
common will.

If political union was supposed to derive from a pre-existing common
identity and will, the rupture of European identity and the plurality of
political wills have rendered the project fanciful. But in reality, the idea
of a European political community can overturn this political schema
inherited from the nation-states. Instead of being the precondition for a
public space, the European community is actually its result: it is a
community resting not upon an amalgamation of interests, feelings and
wills, but on the contrary upon a politically constituted public space in
which the plurality of political initiatives stand face to face. The political
institutions cutting across states actually mark out a public space which
does not have to express a supposedly common identity or will. Far from
being created by a general will and becoming its expression, they give

birth to a public space of plural judgements, decisions and actions in which not only states or ad hoc commissions but all citizens, by virtue of common citizenship, are called upon to participate. The public character of this space therefore replaces the generality of will, making possible joint participation in the community's affairs. For these institutions do not embody the volitions of any organism. Europe is no longer, as Valéry put it, the brain of a huge body — not because this body now lacks a spirit, but because the spirit can no longer seek for bodily form. The geographical, geopolitical and geocultural extension of the European idea has doubtless ruled this out as a possibility. More important, however, is the fact that this European spirit can no longer be conceived as the *Subject* structuring human history whose ostensible will is embodied in a community.

With no general will or supranational identity, with no individualized European body and mind, the political ambiguity of Europe can be resolved only through the development of a European fellow-citizenship appropriate to the public space that it opens up. The republican (nation-state) principle of citizenship is based on a deliberate conflation of general will and national will or, in other words, on an amalgamation of nationality and citizenship. The prospect of a Europe of fellow-citizens is shattering this dogma of nation-states. It requires citizenship to be broken away from nationality. The right of foreign residents (including non-Europeans) to vote in local elections is, for example, an essential and obligatory step in the formation of this new community citizenship. It indicates that participation in the life of public institutions takes precedence over nationality; that, whatever the citizen's cultural or national identity, his or her insertion in public political space is elective and not 'native'; that it derives from a political choice and not from birth (*natio*) or an identity passed on by history; that the idea of a European fatherland has to be replaced by that of a public space of disparate communities. A European political community will be born not so much from an *idea* of Europe as from the idea of a public space of fellow-citizenship which is alone capable of giving meaning to a non-national political community. A community identity cannot give birth to a politically organized public space; rather, a common citizenship of European peoples can emerge from the political institution of this space. In this sense, we could say that the struggle for Europe begins with a struggle inside each nation. Europe can only spring from a 'denationalization' of states. A European fatherland cannot exist, or it is not a *political* community. A Europe of fatherlands cannot exist, or it is not a political *community*. In large part, therefore, the political future of Europe lies in the establishment of a transnational public space and in the creation of a joint citizenship.

Translated by Patrick Camiller

Notes

1. See the lecture by I. Boldiszar in *Les XXXièmes Rencontres Internationales de Genève* (1985), Neuchâtel 1986.

2. Jan Patocka, *Platon et l'Europe*, Paris 1983, p. 16.

3. Ibid., p. 191.

4. Ibid., pp. 16–17. 'Europe really was master of the world. As economic master, it developed capitalism and the commercial network of the global economy. As political master, it held a monopoly of power deriving from science and technology, all of which was linked to its level of reflection and to the rational civilization that it alone possessed. Europe was all of that. And this colossal reality was wiped out for good in the space of some thirty years, in two wars which left nothing of its world-dominating power. It destroyed itself with its own forces. Of course, it drew the whole world into this process, just as before it had appropriated it materially. It forced the whole world to join in these destructive enterprises, with the result that successors came forward who would never again accept that Europe should be what it once was.'

5. Patocka, *Platon et l'Europe*, p. 21.

6. Ibid., p. 139.

7. Ibid., p. 163.

8. It was in this sense that Hannah Arendt quoted René Char's remark that 'our heritage did not come from any testament'. However, seeing the experience of the Resistance discussed by Char as an attempt to refound Europe politically, Arendt interprets it as a revolutionary moment which laid the bases for a new European political community. See below 'La Résistance européenne'.

9. E. Husserl, 'Philosophy and the Crisis of European Humanity', in idem, *The Crisis of European Sciences and Transcendental Phenemenology*, Evanston, Ill 1970, p. 275.

10. Ibid., p. 288.

11. Ibid., p. 299.

12. Jean Starobinski, in *L'Esprit européen*, Premières Recontres Internationales de Genève (1946), Paris 1947, p. 237.

13. Jean Lescure, in ibid., p. 119.

14. G. Lukàcs, in ibid., p. 165.

15. Patocka, *Platon et l'Europe*, p. 138.

16. Paul Thibaud, 'L'Europe et la crise des valeurs politiques', *Esprit*, January 1989, pp. 34–5.

17. Henri Saint-Simon, *Selected Writings*, London 1975, p. 130.

18. Bernard Voyenne, *Histoire de l'idée européenne*, Paris 1964, p. 81. In all that follows, I am greatly indebted to this work. For another point of view, see Jean-Baptiste Duroselle, *L'Idée d'Europe dans l'histoire*, Paris 1965. A collection of texts on Europe was edited by Denis de Rougemont under the title *Vingt-huit Siècles d'Europe*, Paris 1961.

19. Early in the fourteenth century, Pierre Dubois drew up for Philip IV of France a 'Treatise on General Politics' (*De Recuperatione Terrae Sanctae*), in which he developed the principle of a confederation of kingdoms free from any pontifical or imperial tutelage.

20. In 1623 Emeric Crucé published *Le nouveau Cynée ou Discours des Occasions et Moyens d'établir une Paix générale et la Liberté de Commerce par tout le Monde.* He expressed his wish 'to see men go freely here and there, and to communicate together with no scruple as to country, ceremonies or suchlike diversities, as if the earth was — which it indeed is — a city common to all.' Quoted in Voyenne, *Histoire*, p. 75.

21. Jean-Jacques Rousseau, 'Jugement sur le projet de paix perpétuelle' [the project of Abbé de Saint-Pierre], in *Oeuvres complètes*, vol. 3, Paris 1964, p. 600.

22. Quoted in Voyenne, *Histoire*, p. 101.

23. Victor Hugo, in his opening speech to the peace congress organized by Mazzini in 1847, predicted: 'A day will come when you France, you Russia, you Italy, you England, you Germany, all you nations of the continent, without losing your distinct qualities and your glorious individuality, shall dissolve in a higher unity and constitute the European brotherhood.... A day will come when cannon-balls and bombs shall be replaced by votes, universal popular suffrage, and the genuine arbitration of a sovereign Senate which shall be to Europe what the Diet is to Germany, what the Legislative Assembly is to France.... A day will come when people will see ... the United States of Europe.'

24. Voyenne, *Histoire*, p. 135.

25. Proudhon, *Du Principe fédératif* (1863), Editions Rivière, Paris, p. 335. Quoted in Voyenne, *Histoire*, p. 142.

26. 'There has often been talk, among the democrats of France, of a European confederation — in other words, the United States of Europe. Under this designation, nothing else ever seems to have been understood than an alliance of all the states, large and small, presently existing in Europe, under the standing presidency of a Congress. It is implied that each state would preserve the form of government which suited it best. Now, if each state disposed in the Congress of a number of votes proportional to its population and territory, the small states would soon find themselves, in this supposed confederation, enthralled to the large states; indeed, were it possible for this new Holy Alliance to be animated by a principle of collective evolution, we would rapidly see it degenerate, after an internal conflagration, into a single power or a great European monarchy.' Ibid., p. 336.

27. Ibid., p. 335, quoted in Voyenne, *Histoire*, p. 143.

28. Cf. *L'Europe de demain*, published by the Centre d'action pour la fédération européenne, Neuchâtel 1945, a collection of documents relating to the Declaration of European Resistance Movements. The Movimento letter is quoted from p. 79. See also, for example, the article from *Combat* No. 53, December 1954: 'Resistance Europe — that is where France's place is. There is its mission. Not in the theoretical Europe that "great power" diplomats are carving up on green cloth, but in that Europe of suffering which is anxiously rising at daybreak, in that underground Europe of masks and false papers, in that Europe of blood which is struck and gives blow for blow. There is our fraternity. There is our future.... The European Resistance will remake Europe. A free Europe of free citizens, because we have all known slavery. A Europe united both politically and economically, because we have paid the price of division. An armed

Europe, because we have paid the price of weakness.' Ibid., pp. 94–5.

29. 'Projet de Déclaration des Résistances européennes', in ibid., pp. 68–75.

30. See in particular Hannah Arendt, 'Approaches to the German Problem', *Partisan Review* 12/1, Winter 1945, and 'Organized guilt and universal responsibility', *Jewish Frontier*, January 1945.

31. Denis de Rougemont, *Inédits*, Neuchâtel 1988, p. 82.

32. Ibid., p. 97.

33. Ibid., p. 32.

34. Ibid.

35. *Qu'est-ce qu'une nation?*, Paris 1880.

36. De Rougemont, *Inédits*, p. 41. The fault of these two institutions is that they 'cling to the village or small-town model we have inherited from the Middle Ages'.

37. Ibid., p. 174.

38. Ibid., p. 195.

39. Ibid., p. 126.

40. Voyenne, *Histoire*, pp. 192 and *passim*.

9

Eastern Europe's
Republics of Gilead

Slavoj Žižek

Why is the West so fascinated by the recent events in Eastern Europe? The answer seems obvious: what fascinates the Western gaze is the *re-invention of democracy*. It is as if democracy, which in the West shows increasing signs of decay and crisis, lost in bureaucratic routine and publicity-style election campaigns, is being rediscovered in Eastern Europe in all its freshness and novelty. The function of this fascination is thus purely ideological: in Eastern Europe the West looks for its own lost origins, for the authentic experience of 'democratic invention'. In other words, Eastern Europe functions for the West as its Ego-Ideal: the point from which the West sees itself in a likeable, idealized form, as worthy of love. The real object of fascination for the West is thus the *gaze*, namely the supposedly naive gaze by means of which Eastern Europe stares back at the West, fascinated by its democracy. It is as if the Eastern gaze is still able to perceive in Western societies its *agalma*, the treasure that causes democratic enthusiasm and which the West has long lost the taste of.

The reality now emerging in Eastern Europe is, however, a disturbing distortion of this idyllic picture of the two mutually fascinated gazes. It is best illustrated by the strange destiny of a well-known Soviet joke about Rabinovitch, a Jew who wants to emigrate. The bureaucrat at the emigration office asks him why. Rabinovitch answers: 'There are two reasons why. The first is that I'm afraid that the Communists will lose power in the Soviet Union, and the new forces will blame us Jews for the Communist crimes ...' 'But', interrupts the bureaucrat, 'this is pure nonsense, the power of the Communists will last forever!' 'Well,' responds Rabinovitch calmly, 'that's my second reason.' In *The Sublime Object of Ideology*, published in 1989,[1] it was still possible to count on the efficacy of this joke; however, according to the latest information, the main reason cited by Jews emigrating from the Soviet Union is Rabinovitch's *first* reason. They fear, in effect, that, with the disintegration of Communism and the emergence of nationalistic forces openly advocating anti-Semitism, the blame will again be put on them. So today we can easily imagine the reversal of the joke, with Rabinovitch answering the bureaucrat's question thus: 'There are two reasons why. The first is that I know that Communism in Russia will last forever, nothing will really change here, and this prospect is unbearable for me ...' 'But,' interrupts the bureaucrat, 'this is pure nonsense, Communism is disintegrating all around!' 'That's my second reason!' responds Rabinovitch.

The dark side of the processes current in Eastern Europe is thus the gradual retreat of the liberal-democratic tendency in the face of the growth of corporate national populism with all its usual elements, from xenophobia to anti-Semitism. The swiftness of this process has been surprising: today, we find anti-Semitism in East Germany (where one attributes to Jews the lack of food, and to Vietnamese the lack of bicycles) and in Hungary and in Romania (where the persecution of the Hungarian minority also continues). Even in Poland we can perceive signs of a split within Solidarity: the rise of a nationalist-populist faction that imputes to the 'cosmopolitan intellectual' (the old regime's code-word for Jews) the failure of the recent government's measures.

The Nation-Thing

To explain this unexpected turn, we have to rethink the most elementary notions about national identification — and here, psychoanalysis can be of help. The element that holds together a given community cannot be reduced to the point of symbolic identification: the bond linking its members always implies a shared relationship toward a Thing, toward Enjoyment incarnated.[2] This relationship towards the Thing, structured by means of fantasies, is what is at stake when we speak of the menace to our 'way of life' presented by the Other: it is what is threatened when, for example, a white Englishman is panicked because of the growing presence of 'aliens'. What he wants to defend at any price is *not* reducible to the so-called set of values that offer support to national identity. National identification is by definition sustained by a relationship toward the Nation *qua* Thing. This Nation-Thing is determined by a series of contradictory properties. It appears to us as 'our Thing' (perhaps we could say *cosa nostra*), as something accessible only to us, as something 'they', the others, cannot grasp, but which is none the less constantly menaced by 'them'. It appears as what gives plenitude and vivacity to our life, and yet the only way we can determine it is by resorting to different versions of an empty tautology: all we can say about it is, ultimately, that the Thing is 'itself', 'the real Thing', 'what it really is about', and so on. If we are asked how we can recognize the presence of this Thing, the only consistent answer is that the Thing is present in that elusive entity called 'our way of life'. All we can do is enumerate disconnected fragments of the way our community organizes its feasts, its rituals of mating, its initiation ceremonies — in short, all the details by which is made visible the unique way a community *organizes its enjoyment*. Although the first, so to speak, automatic, association that arises here is of course that of the reactionary, sentimental *Blut und Boden*, we should not forget that such a reference to a 'way of life' can also have a distinctive 'leftist' connotation. Note George Orwell's essays from the war years, in which he attempted to define the contours of an English patriotism opposed to the official, puffy-imperialist version of it: his points of reference were precisely those details that characterize the 'way of life' of the working class (the evening gathering in the local pub, and so forth).[3]

This paradoxical existence of an entity that 'is' only in so far as the subjects believe (in the other's belief) in its existence, is the mode of being proper to ideological Causes: the 'normal' order of causality is here inverted, since it is the Cause itself that is produced by its effects (the ideological practices that it animates). However, it is precisely at this point that the difference separating Lacan from 'discursive idealism' emerges most forcefully: Lacan is far from reducing the (national, etc.) Cause to a performative effect of the discursive practices that refer to it. The pure discursive effect doesn't have enough 'substance' to exert the attraction proper to a Cause; and the Lacanian term for the strange 'substance' that must be added to enable a Cause to obtain its positive ontological consistency — the only 'substance' acknowledged by psychoanalysis — is, of course, *enjoyment* (as Lacan states explicitly in his *Le Séminaire XX — Encore*). A nation exists only as long as its specific enjoyment continues to be materialized in certain social practices, and transmitted in national myths that structure these practices. To emphasize, in a 'deconstructivist' mode, that the Nation is not a biological or transhistorical fact but a contingent discursive construction, an overdetermined result of textual practices, is thus misleading: it overlooks the role of a remainder of some real, non-discursive kernel of enjoyment which must be present for the Nation *qua* discursive-entity-effect to achieve its ontological consistency.[4]

It would, however, be erroneous simply to reduce the national Thing to the features composing a specific 'way of life'. The Thing is not directly a collection of these features; there is 'something more' in it, something that *is present* in these features, that *appears* through them. Members of a community who partake in a given 'way of life' *believe in their Thing*, where this belief has a reflexive structure proper to the intersubjective space: 'I believe in the (national) Thing' is equal to 'I believe that others (members of my community) believe in the Thing.' The tautological character of the Thing — its semantic void, the fact that all we can say about it is that it is 'the real Thing' — is founded precisely in this paradoxical reflexive structure. The national Thing exists as long as members of the community believe in it; it is literally an effect of this belief in itself. The structure here is the same as that of the Holy Spirit in Christianity. The Holy Spirit *is* the community of believers in which Christ lives after his death; to believe in Him is to believe in belief itself — to believe that I'm not alone, that I'm a member of the community of believers. I do not need any external proof or confirmation of the truth of my belief: by the mere act of my belief in others' belief, the Holy Spirit is here. In other words, the whole meaning of the Thing consists in the fact that 'it means something' to people.

Theft of Enjoyment

Nationalism thus presents a privileged domain of the eruption of enjoyment into the social field. The national Cause is ultimately nothing but the way subjects of a given ethnic community organize their enjoyment through national myths. What is therefore at stake in ethnic tensions is always the possession of the national Thing. We always impute to the 'other' an excessive enjoyment; he wants to steal our enjoyment (by ruining our way of life) and/or has access to some secret, perverse enjoyment. In short, what really bothers us about the 'other' is the peculiar way it organizes its enjoyment: precisely the surplus, the 'excess' that pertains to it — the smell of their food, their 'noisy' songs and dances, their strange manners, their attitude to work (in the racist perspective, the 'other' is either a workaholic stealing our jobs or an idler living on our labour; and it is quite amusing to note the ease with which one passes from reproaching the other with a refusal to work, to reproaching him for the theft of work). The basic paradox is that our Thing is conceived as something inaccessible to the other, and at the same time threatened by it; this is also the case with castration, which, according to Freud, is experienced as something that 'really cannot happen', but we are none the less horrified by its prospect. The ground of incompatibility between different ethnic subject positions is thus not exclusively the different structure of their symbolic identifications. What categorically resists universalization is rather the particular structure of their relationship towards enjoyment:

> Why does the Other remain Other? What is the cause for our hatred of him, for our hatred of him in his very being? It is hatred of the enjoyment in the Other. This would be the most general formula of the modern racism we are witnessing today: a hatred of the particular way the Other enjoys ... The question of tolerance or intolerance is not at all concerned with the subject of science and its human rights. It is located on the level of tolerance or intolerance toward the enjoyment of the Other, the Other as he who essentially steals my own enjoyment. We know, of course, that the fundamental status of the object is to be always already snatched away by the Other. It is precisely this theft of enjoyment that we write down in short-hand as minus-Phi, the matheme of castration. The problem is apparently unsolvable as the Other is the Other in my interior. The root of racism is thus hatred of my own enjoyment. There is no other enjoyment but my own. If the Other is in me, occupying the place of extimacy, then the hatred is also my own.[5]

What we conceal by imputing to the Other the theft of enjoyment is the traumatic fact that *we never possessed what was allegedly stolen from us*: the lack ('castration') is original; enjoyment constitutes itself as 'stolen', or, to quote Hegel's precise formulation from his *Science of Logic*, it 'only *comes to be* through being *left behind*'.[6] Yugoslavia today is a case-study of such a paradox, in which we are witness to a detailed network of 'decantations' and 'thefts' of enjoyment. Every nationality has built its own mythology narrating how other nations deprive it of the vital part of enjoyment the possession of which would allow it to live fully. If we read all these mythologies together, we obtain Escher's well-known visual paradox of a network of basins where, following the principle of *perpetuum mobile*, water pours from one basin into another until the circle is closed, so that by moving the whole way downstream we find ourselves back at our starting point. These fantasies are structured in a complementary, symmetrical way. Slovenes are being deprived of their enjoyment by 'Southerners' (Serbians, Bosnians) because of their proverbial laziness, Balkan corruption, dirty and noisy enjoyment, and because they demand bottomless economic support, stealing from Slovenes their precious accumulation by means of which Slovenia could already have caught up with Western Europe. The Slovenes themselves, on the other hand, are supposed to rob Serbs because of their unnatural diligence, stiffness and selfish calculation; instead of yielding to simple life pleasures, Slovenes perversely enjoy constantly devising means of depriving Serbs of the results of their hard labour, by commercial profiteering, by reselling what they bought cheaply in Serbia. Slovenes are afraid that Serbs will 'inundate' them, and that they will thus lose their national identity. Serbs reproach Slovenes with their 'separatism', which means simply that Slovenes are not prepared to recognize themselves as a sub-species of Serb. To mark their difference from the 'Southerners', recent Slovenian popular historiography has been obsessed with proving that Slovenes are not really Slavs but in fact of Etruscan origin. Serbs, on the other hand, excel in proving how Serbia was a victim of 'Vatican–Comintern conspiracy': their *idée fixe* is that there was a secret joint plan of Catholics and Communists to destroy Serbian statehood. The basic premiss of both is of course 'We don't want anything foreign, we just want what rightfully belongs to us.' In both cases, the root of these fantasies is clearly hatred of one's own enjoyment. Slovenes, for example, repress their own enjoyment by means of obsessional activity, and it is this very enjoyment which returns in the real, in the figure of the dirty and easy-going 'Southerners'.[7]

This logic is, however, far from being limited to 'backward' Balkan conditions. The way that 'theft of enjoyment', or — to use a Lacanian technical term — imaginary castration, is an extremely useful notion for analysing today's ideological processes, can be further exemplified by a feature of the American ideology of the 1980s: its obsession with the idea that there might still be some American POWs alive in Vietnam, leading a miserable existence, forgotten by their own country. This obsession articulated itself in a series of macho adventures of a hero undertaking a solitary rescue mission (*Rambo II: Missing In Action*). The fantasy-scenario supporting it is, however, far more interesting. It is as if down there, far away in the Vietnamese jungle, America has lost a precious part of itself, has been deprived of an essential element of its very life-substance, the essence of its potency; and as if this was the ultimate cause of its decline and impotence in the post-Vietnam War, Carter years, so that recapturing this stolen, forgotten part became a component of the Reaganesque reaffirmation of a strong America.[8]

Antagonism and Enjoyment

What sets in motion this logic of the 'theft of enjoyment' is of course not immediate social reality — the reality of different ethnic communities living closely together — but the *inner antagonism inherent to these communities*. It is possible to have a multitude of ethnic communities living side by side without racial tensions (like today's California); on the other hand, one does not need a lot of 'real' Jews to impute to them some mysterious enjoyment that threatens us (it is well known that in Nazi Germany anti-Semitism was most ferocious in those parts where there were almost no Jews; in today's East Germany the anti-Semitic skinheads outnumber Jews by ten to one). Our perception of 'real' Jews is always mediated by a symbolic-ideological structure which tries to cope with social antagonism: the real 'secret' of the Jew is our own antagonism. In today's America, for example, a role resembling that of the Jew is being played more and more by the *Japanese*. Witness the obsession of the American media with the idea that the Japanese don't know how to enjoy themselves. The reason for Japan's increasing economic superiority over the United States is located in the somewhat mysterious fact that the Japanese don't consume enough, that they accumulate too much wealth. If we look closely at the logic of this accusation, it is clear that what American 'spontaneous' ideology really reproaches the Japanese for is not simply their inability to take pleasure, but the fact that their very relationship between work and enjoyment is strangely distorted. *It is as if they find enjoyment in their excessive renunciation of pleasure*, in their zeal, in their inability to 'take it easy', to relax and enjoy; and it is this attitude that is perceived as a threat to American supremacy. Which is why the American media report with such evident relief how the Japanese are finally learning to consume, and why American television depicts with such self-satisfaction Japanese tourists staring at the wonders of the American pleasure industry: they are finally 'becoming like us', learning our way to enjoy.

It is too easy to dispose of this problematic by pointing out that this is simply the transposition, the ideological displacement, of the effective socio-economic antagonisms of today's capitalism. The problem is that, while this is undoubtedly true, *it is precisely through such a displacement that desire is constituted.* What we gain by transposing the perception of inherent social antagonisms into this fascination by the Other (Jew, Japanese) is the fantasy-organization of desire. The Lacanian thesis that enjoyment is ultimately always enjoyment of the Other — enjoyment supposed, imputed to the Other — and that, conversely, the hatred of the Other's enjoyment is always the hatred of one's own enjoyment, is perfectly exemplified by this logic of the 'theft of enjoyment'. What are fantasies about the Other's special, excessive enjoyment — about the Black's superior potency and sexual appetite, about the special relation-ship of Jews or Japanese towards money and work — if not precisely *so many ways, for us, to organize our own enjoyment*? Do we not find enjoyment precisely in fantasizing about the Other's enjoyment, in this ambivalent attitude towards it? Do we not obtain satisfaction by means of the very supposition that the Other enjoys in a way inaccessible to us? Is not the reason for the Other's enjoyment to exert such a powerful fascination, that in it we represent to ourselves our own innermost relationship with enjoyment? And, conversely, is the anti-Semitic capitalist's hatred of the Jew not the hatred of the excess that pertains to capitalism itself, that which is produced by its inherent antagonistic nature? Is capitalism's hatred of the Jew not the hatred of its own innermost, essential feature? For this reason, it is not sufficient to point out how the racist's Other presents a threat to our identity. We should rather invert this proposi-tion: the fascinating image of the Other personifies our own innermost split — what is already 'in us more than ourselves' — and thus prevents us from achieving full identity with ourselves. *The hatred of the Other is the hatred of our own excess of enjoyment.*

How the Real 'Returns to its Place'

The national Thing thus functions as a kind of *'particular Absolute' resisting universalization*, bestowing its special 'tonality' upon every neutral, universal notion. It is for this reason that the eruption of the national Thing in all its violence has always taken by surprise the devotees of international solidarity. Perhaps the most notable case was the disastrous collapse of international solidarity within the worker's movement in the face of 'patriotic' euphoria at the outbreak of the First World War. Today, it is difficult to imagine what a traumatic shock it was for the leaders of all currents of social democracy and socialism, from Eduard Bernstein to Lenin, when the social-democratic parties of all countries (with the exception of the Bolsheviks in Russia and Serbia) gave way to chauvinist outbursts, and stood 'patriotically' behind 'their' respective governments, oblivious of the proclaimed solidarity of the working class 'without country'. This shock, the *powerless fascination* felt by its participants, bears witness to an encounter with the Real of enjoyment. That is to say, the basic paradox is that these chauvinist outbursts of 'patriotic feeling' were far from unexpected. Years before the actual outbreak of the war, social democracy drew the attention of workers to the fact that imperialist forces were preparing for a new world war, and warned against yielding to 'patriotic' chauvinism. Even at the very outbreak of hostilities, in the days following the Sarajevo assassination, the German social democrats cautioned workers that the ruling class would use the assassination as an excuse to declare war. Furthermore, the Socialist International adopted a formal resolution obliging all its members to vote against war credits. When war broke out, international solidarity vanished into thin air. An anecdote showing how this overnight reversal took Lenin by surprise is significant: when he saw the daily newspaper of German social democracy announcing on its front page that the social-democratic deputies had voted for the war credits, he was at first convinced that the issue had been fabricated by German police to lead workers astray!

And it is the same in today's Eastern Europe. The 'spontaneous' presupposition was that what is 'repressed' there, what will burst out once the lid of 'totalitarianism' is removed, will be *democratic desire* in all its forms, from political pluralism to flourishing market economy. What we are getting instead, now that the lid *is* removed, are more and more ethnic conflicts, based upon the constructions of different 'thieves of enjoyment': as if, beneath the Communist surface, there glimmered a wealth of 'pathological' fantasies, waiting for their moment to arrive – a perfect exemplification of the Lacanian notion of communication, where the speaker gets back from the addressee his own message in its true, inverted form. The emergence of ethnic causes breaks the narcissistic spell of the West's complacent recognition of its own values in the East: Eastern Europe is returning to the West the 'repressed' truth of its democratic desire. And what we should point out is, again, the *powerless fascination* of (what remains of) the critical leftist intellectuals when faced with this outburst of national enjoyment. They are, of course, reluctant to embrace fully the national Cause; they are desperately trying to maintain a kind of distance from it. This distance is, however, false: a disavowal of the fact that their desire is already *implied*, caught in it.

Far from being produced by the radical break in Eastern Europe, an obsessive adherence to the national Cause is precisely what *remains the same* throughout this process — what, for example, Ceausescu and the now ascendant radical rightist-nationalist tendencies in Romania have in common. Here we encounter the Real, that which 'always returns to its place' (Lacan), the kernel that persists unchanged in the midst of the radical change in society's symbolic identity. It is therefore wrong to conceive this rise of nationalism as a kind of 'reaction' to the alleged Communist betrayal of national roots: the common idea that because Communist power ripped out the entire traditional fabric of society, the only remaining point on which to base resistance is national identity. It was already Communist power which *produced* the compulsive attachment to the national Cause, an attachment that became more exclusive the more totalitarian the power structure. The most extreme cases are to be found in Ceausescu's Romania, in Cambodia under the Khmer Rouge, in North Korea and in Albania.[9] The ethnic Cause is thus the leftover that persists once the network of Communist ideological fabric disintegrates. We can detect it in the way the figure of the Enemy is constructed in today's Romania, for example: Communism is treated as a foreign body, as the Intruder which poisoned and corrupted the sane Body of the Nation; as something that really could not have its origins in our own ethnic tradition, and which therefore has to be cut off for the sanity of the Nation's Body to be restored. The anti-Semitic connotation is here unmistakable: in the Soviet Union, the Russian nationalist organization, *Pamyat*, likes to count the number of Jews in Lenin's Politburo, in order to prove its 'non-Russian' character. A popular pastime in Eastern Europe is no longer simply to put all the blame on Communists, but to play the game 'who was *behind* the Communists?' (Jews for Russians and Romanians; Croatians and Slovenes for Serbs; and so on). This construction of the Enemy reproduces in its pure — so to speak, distilled — form, the way the Enemy was constructed in the late Communist nationalist-totalitarian regimes: what we get, once we overthrow the Communist symbolic form, is the underlying relation to the ethnic Cause, stripped of this form.

Mastering the Excess

So, why this unexpected disappointment? Why does authoritarian nationalism overshadow democratic pluralism? Why the chauvinist obsession with the 'theft of enjoyment', instead of openness towards ethnic diversity? Because, at this point, the Left's standard analysis of the causes of ethnic tensions in the 'real socialist' countries proved to be wrong. Its thesis was that ethnic tensions were instigated and manipulated by the ruling Party bureaucracy as a means of legitimizing their hold on power. In Romania, for example, the nationalist obsession, the dream of Great Romania, the forceful assimilation of Hungarian and other minorities, created a constant tension which legitimized Ceausescu's hold on power. In Yugoslavia, the growing tensions between Serbs and Albanians, Croats and Serbs, Slovenes and Serbs, and so on, illustrate how corrupted local bureaucracies can prolong their power by presenting themselves as sole defenders of national interests. This hypothesis was refuted, however, in a most spectacular way by the recent events: once the rule of the Communist bureaucracies was broken, ethnic tensions emerged even more forcefully. So, why does this attachment to the ethnic Cause *persist* even after the power structure that produced it has collapsed? Here, a combined reference to the classical Marxist theory of capitalism and to Lacanian psychoanalysis might be of help.

The elementary feature of capitalism consists in its *inherent structural imbalance*, its innermost antagonistic character: the constant crisis, the incessant revolutionizing of its conditions of existence. Capitalism has no 'normal', balanced state: its 'normal' state is the permanent production of an excess — the only way for it to survive is to expand. Capitalism is thus caught in a kind of loop, a vicious circle, that was clearly designated already by Marx: It produces more than does any other socio-economic formation to satisfy needs, but the result is the creation of even more needs to be satisfied; the more wealth it creates, the greater is the need to create even more wealth. It should be clear from that why Lacan designated capitalism the reign of the *discourse of the Hysteric*: this vicious circle of a desire, whose apparent satisfaction only widens the gap of its dissatisfaction, is what defines hysteria. There exists effectively a kind of structural homology between capitalism and the Freudian notion of superego. The basic paradox of the superego also concerns a certain structural imbalance: the more we obey its command, the more we feel guilty; so that renunciation entails only a demand for more renunciation, repentance more guilt — as in capitalism, where a growth of production to fill out the lack, only increases the lack.

It is against this background that we should grasp the logic of what Lacan calls the (discourse of the) *Master*: its role is precisely to introduce *balance,* to *regulate the excess.* Pre-capitalist societies were still able to dominate the structural imbalance proper to the superego in so far as their dominant discourse was that of the Master. In his last works, Michel Foucault showed how the ancient Master embodied the ethics of self-mastery and 'just measure': the entire tradition of pre-capitalist ethics aimed at preventing the excess proper to the human libidinal economy from exploding. With capitalism, however, this function of the Master is suspended, and the vicious circle of the superego revolves freely.

Now, it should also be clear where the corporatist temptation comes from; that is, why this temptation in the necessary reverse of capitalism. Let us take the ideological edifice of fascist corporatism: the fascist dream is simply to have *capitalism without its 'excess', without the antagonism that causes its structural imbalance.* Which is why we have, in fascism, on one hand, the return to the figure of the Master – Leader – who guarantees the stability and balance of the social fabric, who again saves us from the society's structural imbalance; and, on the other hand, the reason for this imbalance is projected into the figure of the Jew whose 'excessive' accumulation and greed are deemed the cause of social antagonism. The dream is thus that, since the excess was introduced from outside – the work of an alien intruder – its elimination would enable us to obtain once again a stable social organism whose parts form a harmonious corporate body, where, in contrast to capitalism's constant social *displacement,* everybody would again occupy *their own place.* The function of the Master is to dominate the excess by locating its cause in a clearly de-limited social agency: 'It is *they* who steal our enjoyment, who, by means of their excessive attitude, introduce imbalance and antagonism.' With the figure of the Master, the antagonism *inherent* to the social structure is transformed into the relationship of power, in the struggle for *domination* between *us* and *them,* the cause of antagonistic imbalance.

Capitalism without Capitalism

Perhaps this matrix helps us also to grasp the re-emergence of national chauvinism in Eastern Europe as a kind of 'shock absorber' against the sudden exposure to capitalist openness and imbalance. It is as if, in the very moment when the bond, the chain, preventing the free develop-ment of capitalism – a deregulated production of the excess – was broken, it was countered by a *demand for a new Master* to bridle it. The demand is for the establishment of a stable and clearly defined social

Body that will restrain capitalism's destructive potential by cutting off the 'excessive' element; and since this social Body is experienced as that of a Nation, the cause of imbalance 'spontaneously' assumes the form of a 'national enemy'.

When the democratic opposition was still fighting against Communist power, it united under the sign of 'civil society' all the 'anti-totalitarian' elements, from the Church to the leftist intellectuals. Within the 'spontaneous' experience of the unity of this fight, the crucial fact passed unnoticed: that the same words used by all participants refer to two fundamentally different languages, to two different worlds.[10] Now that the opposition has won, this victory necessarily assumes the shape of a split: the enthusiastic solidarity of the fight against Communist power has lost its mobilizing potential; the fissure separating the two political universes cannot be concealed anymore. This fissure is of course that of the well-known couple *Gemeinschaft/Gesellschaft*: traditional, organically linked community versus 'alienated' society which dissolves all organic links. The problem of Eastern Europe's nationalist populism is that it perceived Communism's 'threat' from the perspective of *Gemeinschaft* — as a foreign body corroding the organic texture of the national community; it thereby actually imputes to Communism the crucial feature of capitalism itself. In its moralistic opposition to the Communist 'depravity', the nationalist-populist moral majority unknowingly *prolongs* the thrust of the previous Communist regime toward state qua organic community. The desire at work in this symptomatic substitution of Communism for capitalism is a desire for capitalism-*cum-Gemeinschaft*: a desire for capitalism without the 'alienated' civil society, without the formal-external relations between individuals. Fantasies about the 'theft of enjoyment', the re-emergence of anti-Semitism, and so on, are the price to be paid for this impossible desire.

Paradoxically, we could say that what Eastern Europe needs most now is *more alienation*: the establishment of an 'alienated' state that would maintain its distance from civil society, that would be 'formal', 'empty', embodying no particular ethnic community's dream (and thus keeping the space open for them all). Otherwise, the vision depicted by Margaret Atwood in her *The Handmaid's Tale*, the vision of a near-future 'Republic of Gilead' where a moral-majority fundamentalism reigns, will come closer to being realized in Eastern Europe than in the United States itself.

Notes

The author wishes to thank Perry Anderson, Fredric Jameson, Peter Wollen and Robin Blackburn for their helpful suggestions.

1. Slavoj Žižek, *The Sublime Object of Ideology*, Verso, London 1989, pp. 175–6.

2. For a detailed elaboration of this notion of the Thing, see Jacques Lacan, *Le Séminaire vii—L'éthique de la psychanalyse*, Paris 1986. Note here that enjoyment (*jouissance*) is not to be equated with pleasure: enjoyment is precisely 'pleasure in unpleasure'; it designates the paradoxical satisfaction procured by a painful encounter with a Thing that perturbs the equilibrium of the 'pleasure principle'. In other words, enjoyment is located 'beyond the pleasure principle'.

3. The way these fragments persist across ethnic barriers can be sometimes quite affecting: as, for example, with Robert Mugabe who, when asked by a journalist what was the most precious legacy of British colonialism to Zimbabwe, answered without hesitation, 'cricket' – a senselessly ritualized game, almost beyond the grasp of a Continental, in which the prescribed gestures (or, more precisely, gestures established by an unwritten tradition) – the way to throw a ball, for example – appear grotesquely 'dysfunctional'.

4. The fact that a subject fully 'exists' only through enjoyment – that is, the ultimate coincidence of 'existence' and 'enjoyment' – was indicated in Lacan's early *Seminars* by the ambiguously traumatic status of existence: 'By definition, there is something so improbable about all existence that one is in effect perpetually questioning oneself about its reality' (*The Seminars of Jacques Lacan, Book II*, Cambridge 1988, p. 226). This proposition becomes much clearer if we simply replace 'existence' with 'enjoyment' thus: 'By definition, there is something so improbable about all enjoyment that one is in effect perpetually questioning oneself about its reality.' The fundamental subjective position of a *hysteric* consists precisely in such a questioning about one's existence *qua* enjoyment, while a sadistic *pervert* avoids this questioning by transposing the 'pain of existence' on to the other (his victim).

5. Jacques-Alain Miller, 'Extimité', unpublished lecture, Paris, 27 November 1985.

6. G.W.F. Hegel, *The Science of Logic*, Oxford 1975, p. 402.

7. The mechanism at work here is of course that of paranoia. At its most elementary, paranoia consists in this very externalization of the function of castration in a positive agency appearing as the 'thief of enjoyment'. By means of a somewhat risky generalization of the foreclosure of the Name-of-the-Father (the elementary structure of paranoia, according to Lacan), we could perhaps sustain the thesis that Eastern Europe's national paranoia stems precisely from the fact that Eastern Europe's nations are not yet fully constituted as 'authentic states': it is as if the failed, foreclosed state's symbolic authority 'returns in the real' in the shape of the Other, the 'thief of enjoyment'.

8. I am indebted for this idea to William Warner's paper 'Spectacular Action: Rambo, Reaganism, and the Cultural Articulation of the Hero', presented at the colloquium 'Psychoanalysis, Politics and the Image', at New York State University, Buffalo, on 8 November 1989. Incidentally, *Rambo II* is in this respect far inferior to *Rambo I*, which accomplishes an extremely interesting ideological rearticulation: it

condenses in the same person the 'leftist' image of a lone hippy vagrant threatened by the small town atmosphere embodied in a cruel sheriff, and the 'rightist' image of a lone avenger taking the law into his own hands and doing away with the corrupt bureaucratic machinery. This condensation implies, of course, the hegemony of the *second* figure, so that *Rambo I* succeeded in including in the 'rightist' articulation one of the crucial elements of the American 'leftist' political imaginary.

9. This attachment is not without its comical side effects. Because of his Albanian origins, John Belushi, the very embodiment of Hollywood 'decadence', who died of a drugs overdose, enjoys today a cult status in Albania: the official media praise him as a 'great patriot and humanist' who was 'always ready to embrace the just and progressive causes of humanity'!

10. What we have here can be grasped by means of the Lacanian opposition, 'subject of the enunciated/subject of the enunciation' (*sujet d'énoncé/sujet d'énonciation*): the same enunciated (demands for freedom and democracy, and so forth) is supported by a totally different position of the enunciation, is spoken from a totally different horizon of meaning. In Slovenia today, this fissure appears in an exemplary way apropos of the motto 'national reconciliation' proposed by the opposition: the desire to overcome old traumas of national division that result from Communist rule. Now that the opposition has won, it has become clear that this motto functions in two opposed ways. Both sides agree that the only way to cut short the circle of revenge, the wild *acting out* of old hatreds, is a 'working through' of the traumatic past: one should confront in broad daylight the demons of the past; long-repressed memories should become part of the nation's history-narrative. The aims to be achieved via such a 'working through', however, differ radically. One conceives 'reconciliation' as a means to achieve new national unity, organic solidarity, the recognition of all Slovenes in a new 'dream' of a common destiny. Within this perspective, past victims of the Communist oppression function like ritual animals whose sacrifice guarantees present unity; those who oppose this unity *eo ipso* betray their sacrifice. Whereas for the others 'reconciliation' means precisely reconciliation with the fact that there is no organic unity of Slovenes; that the multitude of 'dreams' is irreducible; that nobody has the right to enforce his/her own dream on the others. One must accept the traumatic fact that past victims were utterly unnecessary, that there was no 'meaning' in them. Referring to the conceptual apparatus articulated by Ernesto Laclau and Chantal Mouffe in their *Hegemony and Socialist Strategy* (Verso, London 1985), we could say that perhaps the crucial hegemonic fight in Slovenia today is the fight for 'national re-conciliation', for the appropriation of this 'floating signifier'.

PART IV

10

On Justice, the Common Good and the Priority of Liberty

Quentin Skinner

I

A surprising feature of recent debates about the theory of justice has been the renewed vigour displayed by the venerable concept of the social contract. The main influence upon this development has undoubtedly been exercised by John Rawls. When he published *A Theory of Justice* in 1971, he characterized his approach at the outset as an attempt 'to present a conception of justice which generalises and carries to a higher level of abstraction the familiar theory of the social contract as found, say, in Locke, Rousseau and Kant'.[1]

Rawls employs the device of an imagined contract as a means of trying to show us how rational individuals would, he thinks, arrive at an agreed account of distributive justice, and hence an agreed set of principles for the proper treatment of individuals within society. The starting point for this exercise is the observation that, within any society, there will always be conflicts of interest between individual citizens. The reason Rawls gives is that 'persons are not indifferent as to how the greater benefits produced by their collaboration are distributed, for in order to pursue their ends they each prefer a larger to a lesser share.' It follows that 'a set of principles is required for choosing among the various social arrangements which determine this division of advantage'. These, Rawls adds, 'are the principles of social justice'.[2]

The essence of such principles is that they should offer a means 'for assigning basic rights and duties', and for ensuring 'the proper distribution of the benefits and burdens of social co-operation'.[3] The outcome of imposing them will be to establish a range of institutions which guarantee that 'no arbitrary distinctions are made between persons in the assigning of basic rights and duties'.[4] When this position is reached, according to Rawls, the traditional Aristotelian ideal of distributive justice will also have been attained, the ideal according to which the doing of justice is a matter of rendering *ius suum cuique*, to each what he is due.[5]

Rawls next turns to explain why he believes that the actual content of these principles can best be elucidated by thinking in terms of an imagined social contract. His crucial suggestion is that the agreement we are to conceive of ourselves as making with each other at the birth of our society must be concluded under what he calls a veil of ignorance.[6] When we all agree to the principles that will later bind us, we are to imagine doing so in ignorance of many important facts about ourselves, including our good or ill fortune in the matter of our social position and the range of our natural abilities. Rawls's fundamental thesis is that, since no one knows what standing he or she will enjoy in the society whose rules are being drawn up, and since everyone will primarily be concerned to ensure that they are not themselves disadvantaged, we can safely treat as principles of just distribution whatever agreement is reached under such circumstances by 'free and rational persons concerned to further their own interests'.[7]

Rawls thus introduces the idea of the social contract essentially as a device for enabling us to test our intuitions about the ideal of distributive justice. But his main concern is of course with the contents of these intuitions, and thus with the actual set of principles which, he argues, rational egoists would in fact espouse as principles of justice under such a veil of ignorance. His conclusion, as is well known, is that such principles would amount to a view of distributive justice as essentially equivalent to a certain kind of fairness and equality of treatment. It is accordingly this ideal of 'justice as fairness', as Rawls labels it,[8] which it becomes the main purpose of his book to analyse and commend.

Rawls opens his analysis by proclaiming that 'justice is the first virtue of social institutions, as truth is of systems of thought'. But if justice is to be secured, he at once adds, the principle that must above all be respected is that of the absolute autonomy and separateness of individuals. 'Each person possesses an inviolability founded on justice that even the welfare of society as a whole cannot override.'[9] Taking up the same point at the end of Part I, Rawls restates his commitment by invoking and ratifying

Kant's requirement 'that the principles of justice [should] manifest in the basic structure of society men's desire to treat one another not as means only but as ends in themselves'.[10]

If justice is to be done to individuals within society, it follows that what must basically be respected is a certain set of individual rights. As Rawls initially puts it, 'in justice as fairness the concept of right is prior to that of the good'. By this he means not only that 'a just social system defines the scope within which individuals must develop their aims'; he also means that 'it provides a framework of rights and opportunities and the means of satisfaction within and by the use of which these ends may be equitably pursued'.[11]

As Rawls later emphasizes, the enjoyment of these rights and opportunities can in turn be viewed as equivalent to the enjoyment by each individual citizen, to the maximum possible degree, of his or her individual liberty. For the rights of citizens consist of certain 'basic liberties', above all a liberty from unnecessary interference, and hence a liberty to pursue one's own ends as far as is compatible with the enjoyment of an equal right by others.[12]

This in turn means that, if justice is to be secured, the highest priority must be assigned to the protection of individual liberty in this sense. This Rawls duly acknowledges in the definitive statement of what he calls his 'first principle' of justice in Part II. The first principle states that 'each person is to have an equal right to the most extensive total system of basic liberties compatible with a similar system of liberty for all'. To this Rawls adds his 'first priority rule', which secures what he calls 'the priority of liberty' by requiring that 'liberty can be restricted only for the sake of liberty'.[13]

To summarize: I have argued that two claims are embodied in Rawls's view of rights and liberty in relation to justice. The first is that the ideal of justice can properly be described in traditional terms as a matter of rendering to each his due. The second is that what *is* due to individuals is an equal right to maximize their own individual liberty, a right assured by minimizing any unjust interference with their pursuit of their chosen ends.

Rawls's avowed aim in defending this conception of justice as fairness is, as he expresses it, 'to work out a theory of justice that represents an alternative to utilitarian thought'.[14] As he makes clear, however, he intends this contrast to be a very general one. His account of distributive justice is designed to stand in opposition to any theory which assigns priority not to the liberty (and thus to the rights) of the individual, but rather to the common good or 'the welfare of the group'.[15]

This does not mean that Rawls refuses to invoke the concept of the common good. But it does mean that, when he invokes it, he employs the term to refer only to the idea of a sum total of individual goods.[16] As he repeatedly makes clear, what he opposes more than anything is the view that the concept can ever be justifiably applied in such a way as to give priority to the common good or general welfare over the good — and especially the liberty — of individual citizens.

Rawls's invocation of the idea of the social contact enables him to state his objection to such theories in an extraordinarily strong form. What he claims is that it could never be *rational* to espouse any social philosophy founded on the priority of the common good. 'It hardly seems likely', as he puts it,

> that persons who view themselves as equals, entitled to press their claims upon one another, would agree to a principle which may require lesser life-prospects for some simply for the sake of a greater sum of advantages enjoyed by others. Since each desires to protect his interests, his capacity to advance his conception of the good, no one has a reason to acquiesce in an enduring loss for himself in order to bring about a greater net balance of satisfaction.... Thus it seems that the principle of utility is incompatible with the conception of social cooperation among equals for mutual advantage.[17]

Rawls writes mainly as a moral rather than a legal or political philosopher. Nevertheless, his theory of social justice clearly implies a certain view about the proper relations between individuals and the state. As we have seen, it is Rawls's belief that, if justice is to be upheld, the liberty of every individual citizen must be equally respected. But he also believes that, if equal liberty is to be maximized, there must be a minimum of external interference with the lives of such citizens. In the words of his 'first principle', there must be an equal right to the enjoyment of such liberties. The political implications are clear: there must be a corresponding duty on the part of the state, in the name of the ideal of justice, to respect so far as possible this equal liberty of all citizens to pursue their own chosen goals in their own chosen way.

At this point Rawls is simply restating a standard liberal view of the proper relationship between the powers of the state and the freedom of individual citizens. The same assumption can already be found, for example, in a work such as Isaiah Berlin's classic essay, *Two Concepts of Liberty*, where it is expressed in the form of a forthright demand for 'a maximum degree of non-interference compatible with the minimum demands of social life'.[18] It can also be found in a number of more recent writings sympathetic to Rawls's theory of justice. Ronald Dworkin, for example, reiterates the same assumption in *Taking Rights Seriously* in the form of the claim that 'rights are trumps'. They take moral priority, that is, over any calls of social duty, as a result of which they are said to ensure that our freedom to pursue our own chosen ends is maximized in the manner required by the dictates of distributive justice.[19]

To summarize again. I have now argued that Rawls's analysis of social justice in terms of the priority of liberty appears to imply two claims about the role of the state. The first is that, since justice is the first virtue of social institutions, the state must above all seek to ensure that justice is done. The second is that, since the doing of justice requires the maximizing of individual liberty, the basic duty of the state must be to keep its own demands upon its citizens to an agreed minimum.

At the heart of Rawls's theory of justice there is thus a claim about the ideal of political liberty and how best to sustain it. It is this claim that I should like to examine in the second half of these remarks. The question I should like to raise is simply whether the basic assumption made by Rawls and, even more clearly, by such followers as Dworkin is justified. Is it clear that the best way for citizens to maximize and guarantee their individual liberty is to minimize the demands made upon them by the calls of social duty?

II

Rawls's key assumption about individual liberty has already been widely criticized by those who wish to uphold a view of the state in which the importance of shared meanings and common purposes is accorded more emphasis.[20] I have no wish, however, to criticize Rawls's argument from that standpoint. On the contrary, I fully endorse his sense that the right way to think about the relationship between individual citizens and the powers of the state is to emphasize the equal right of all citizens to pursue their chosen goals so far as possible. I merely wish to question whether Rawls and (especially) his more enthusiastic followers are right to assume that the best way to secure and maximize that value is necessarily to treat the calls of social duty as so many 'interferences'.

The way in which I shall pursue this doubt is by focusing on a strongly contrasting way of thinking about the relations between liberty and the common good, one that not only predates modern liberalism but has largely been obliterated by its triumph. The strand of thought I have in mind is that of classical republicanism.[21] Within this tradition, the discussion of political liberty is generally embedded in an analysis of what it means to live 'in a free state'. This approach was largely derived from Roman moral philosophy, and especially from those writers whose greatest admiration had been reserved for the doomed Roman republic: Livy, Sallust and above all Cicero. Within modern political theory, their line of argument was at first taken up in Renaissance Italy as a means of defending the traditional liberties of the city-republics against both the *signori* and the powers of the Church.[22] Among the many writers who espoused the cause of the *vivere libero* at this formative stage, undoubtedly the greatest was Machiavelli in his *Discourses* on the first ten books of Livy's *History of Rome*. Later a similar defence of 'free states' was mounted – with extensive acknowledgements to Machiavelli's influence – by James Harrington, John Milton and other English republicans in the course of the constitutional revolution of the seventeenth century. Still later, many elements of the same outlook came to be embodied – again with acknowledgements to Machiavelli's inspiration – in the opposition to the absolutism in eighteenth-century France, and above all in Montesquieu's analysis of republican virtue in *De l'Esprit des Lois*.[23]

By this stage, however, the classical republican ideal of citizenship had largely been swallowed up by a more familiar and very different style of theorizing centred on the concept of natural rights. If we wish to investigate the heyday of classical republicanism, accordingly, we need to turn back to the period before the concept of rights attained the hegemony it has never subsequently lost. This means turning back to the moral and political philosophy of the Renaissance, as well as to the Roman moral philosophers on whom the Renaissance theorists placed such overwhelming weight. It is with these sources, therefore, that I shall mainly be concerned. And it is from Machiavelli's *Discourses* – by far the most compelling presentation of the case – that I shall mainly cite.

As I have already intimated, the significance of this strand of thought for my present purposes stems from its analysis of the relationship between the maximizing of individual liberty and the pursuit of the common good. As we have seen, it is vital to recent contractarian accounts of social justice to insist that, if we wish to maximize our liberty, it is actually irrational to assign the common good a higher priority. But it is precisely this assumption which is challenged by classical republican theories of citizenship. The republican theorists are so far from arguing that the maximizing of liberty requires us to treat our rights as trumps that they barely mention the concept of rights at all. Instead they maintain that, if we wish to maximize our liberty, we must devote ourselves wholeheartedly to a life of public service, placing the ideal of the common good above all considerations of individual advantage.

Ever since Hobbes satirized this commitment in *Leviathan*, liberal theorists of natural rights have generally treated it as blankly paradoxical.[24] This is why it seems to me of such importance to try to retrieve and understand the classical republican case. Not only does it seem to me to succeed in resolving the paradox; it does so in a way that enables us, I shall argue, to perceive some unfamiliar yet plausible connections between the ideals of justice, liberty and the common good. In doing so it offers us a way of connecting these concepts which, although decidedly non-liberal in its orientation, is not I think in the least anti-liberal in its values.

To understand how the paradox can be resolved, we need to begin by reverting to the point I stressed at the outset: that the analysis of individual liberty in the republican tradition of thought is embedded within a wider discussion of the *vivere libero*, the ideal of the 'free state' and its 'free way of life'. We first need to ask what these writers mean by predicating freedom in this way of entire communities.

To grasp their answer, we need only recall that these writers take the metaphor of the body politic as seriously as possible. A political body, like a natural one, is said to be at liberty if and only if it is unconstrained. Like a free person, a free state is one that is able to act according to its own will in pursuit of its chosen ends.[25] To say that a community possesses a free constitution, and is therefore able to follow a free way of life, is thus to say that its constitution enables the will of the citizens — the general will of the whole body politic — to choose and determine whatever ends are pursued by the community as a whole. As Machiavelli, for example, summarizes the point at the beginning of his *Discourses*, free states are those 'which are far from all external servitude, and are thus able to govern themselves according to their own will'.[26]

One of the questions with which these writers are most preoccupied is accordingly the following: what jeopardizes the freedom of such communities, what endangers the capacity of free states to sustain their free and independent way of life?

The answer they generally give — one that Machiavelli constantly emphasizes, for example, throughout the *Discourses* — is based on a sense that personal ambition almost always poses a lethal threat to the proper conduct of public life. Most men, it is conceded, merely desire not to be dominated. But a few display an insatiable thirst for power, a restless desire to rule and dominate others.[27] And as Machiavelli puts it, it is this ambition on the part of the powerful, directed against the populace, which constitutes the gravest and least easily neutralized danger to free governments.[28]

The ambitions of the powerful are said to be capable of undermining the freedom of communities in two distinct ways. If a state has ambitious leaders, they will be sure to seek to conquer and dominate their neighbouring states. A writer like Machiavelli assumes, indeed, that no community can ever hope 'to succeed in standing still and enjoying its liberties'.[29] The natural ambitions of political leaders, allied with the mutual hatreds to be expected from neighbouring communities, will always ensure that, unless one's own community stands ready to attack and conquer, it will almost certainly be attacked and conquered.[30] To be conquered, however, is to be made subject to the will of a conqueror. And as we have seen, for a community to be a subject in this sense is held by these writers to be equivalent to the condition of slavery. Hence it is that conquest is always treated as equivalent to the total destruction of free government.[31]

The other way in which the ambitions of the powerful are said to bring about the collapse of free states is by undermining their free way of life from within. This danger is generally treated by the classical republican writers at much greater length. The issue occupies Machiavelli, for example, throughout Book I of his *Discourses*, in the course of which he develops what became by far the most influential analysis of this further and more insidious threat.

Machiavelli sees two main sources of danger to free constitutions arising from the political machinations of the *grandi* and others who may have 'a great longing to rule'.[32] One is that they may be able to engineer positions of overwhelming power for themselves within the community, especially if they are able to get themselves elected to important military commands.[33] The other is that they may be able to use their wealth to bribe and corrupt their fellow citizens into doing their bidding, even if what they wish to see done is contrary to the laws.[34] The outcome in either case is that the will of such powerful and unscrupulous leaders, as opposed to the will of the community itself, increasingly determines how the community acts. As we have seen, however, to say of a community that its actions are determined by a force other than its own will is to say, according to the writers I am considering, that the community has been enslaved. For any body — human or political — which is moved to act by a will other than its own must obviously be acting under constraint. Hence it is that, as Machiavelli repeatedly insists, whenever 'the ambitions of the powerful' result in 'the establishment of a government according to their own will', we may say that 'they have taken away the people's liberty'.[35]

The main concern of these writers is thus to ask how these dangers can be offset and a free way of life secured. They answer with a strong theory of civic duty. What is held to be indispensable to the maintenance of free government is that the whole body of the citizens should be imbued with such a powerful sense of civic virtue that they can neither be bribed nor coerced into allowing either external threats or factional ambitions to undermine the common good.

This is generally held to require that citizens should commit them-selves to serving and upholding the good of their community in two distinct ways. They must first of all be willing to defend it against the external threat of conquest and enslavement. A political body, no less than a natural one, which entrusts itself to be defended by others instead of learning the arts of self-defence will be gratuitously exposing itself to the loss of its liberty and even its life. For no one can be expected to care as much for our own liberties as we care ourselves. It follows that a willingness to serve one's community in a military capacity — the ideal of military service — is indispensable to the preservation of free govern-ment. By contrast, the employment of standing or mercenary armies is invariably treated, throughout this tradition of thought, as one of the gravest threats to free government.

The other aspect of civic duty which all the republican writers emphasize is the need to prevent the government of one's community from falling into the hands of ambitious individuals or self-interested groups. As Machiavelli explains in a recurring metaphor, this in turn requires that everyone should be prepared to keep guard, to remain on the watch, in order to prevent the powerful from gaining undue in-fluence.[36] But this is to say that the maintenance of a free way of life requires continual supervision of, and participation in, the political processes by the whole body of citizens. In the words of the famous epigram coined in 1790 by the radical Irish judge and politician John Curran to summarize this aspect of republican ideology, 'the condition on which God hath given liberty to man is eternal vigilance.'[37]

It may well seem — and this has generally been argued by

contractarian writers — that this conception of the duties of citizenship stands in the strongest possible contrast to the contractarian emphasis on the liberty of individual citizens and their consequent right to remain as free as possible from external interference. The classic statement of this objection appears in Hobbes's *Leviathan.* 'The liberty whereof there is so frequent and honourable mention in the histories and philosophy of the ancient Greeks and Romans ... is not the liberty of particular men, but the liberty of the Commonwealth.' This limitation becomes obvious, Hobbes adds, as soon as we reflect on the fact that the preservation of a so-called 'free government' requires the exaction of so many services from its citizens. For we can only say of a 'particular man' that he possesses 'more liberty' if he enjoys 'immunity from service to the commonwealth'.[38]

There is a sense in which Hobbes's objection is well judged. Classical republican theorists generally place less emphasis than contractarian writers on individual liberties. And even when they connect the maintenance of such liberties with the pursuit of the common good, they make it clear that this is not their principal reason for insisting that the common good should be pursued. Instead they argue, as we have seen, that the pursuit of the common good is mainly to be valued as the indispensable means of upholding the ideal of 'free government'.

Nevertheless, the classical republican writers never doubt that the majority of citizens in any polity can safely be assumed to have it as their fundamental desire to lead a life of personal liberty. It is true that, as we have seen, a few ambitious souls are said to desire this liberty — this freedom from interference — mainly as a means to the end of ruling and dominating others. But most individuals, as Machiavelli puts it, 'simply want not to be ruled'; they want to be left to live as free individuals, pursuing their own ends as far as possible without insecurity or interference. They want in particular to be left at liberty to live together as they choose; to bring up their families without having to fear for their honour or welfare; and to possess the freedom to hold their own property. This is what it means, according to Machiavelli, for individuals to enjoy *la libertà*; and this is what enables them to recognize 'that they have been born in liberty and not as slaves'.[39]

Moreover, the essence of the classical republican case can be stated as a claim about how to preserve and maximize this familiar ideal of 'negative' liberty. For the central thesis of these writers is that, if we ourselves wish to live in a condition of personal liberty — to live 'in a free state' it is indispensable that we should live under a free constitution, one that we serve and uphold to the best of our civic abilities.

This is not of course presented as the basic reason we have for wishing to live under such a constitution. As Machiavelli, for example, stresses in a deeply influential passage at the beginning of Book II of his *Discourses*, the main reason we have for wishing to do so is that such states are alone capable of growing to greatness both in power and wealth.[40] Nevertheless, it is clearly stated that one consequence of living under such a constitution is that our own individual liberty to pursue our chosen goals will thereby be secured and maximized. As Machiavelli puts it, 'the common benefit' of living in such a free state is that everyone enjoys 'the power of enjoying at liberty' his own possessions and his own chosen way of life.[41]

The apparent paradox on which these writers wish above all to insist is thus that we can only hope to enjoy a maximum of our own individual liberty if we do not place that value above the pursuit of the common good. To insist on doing so is — to adopt their terminology — to be a corrupt as opposed to a virtuous citizen; and the price of corruption is always slavery. The sole route to individual liberty is by way of public service.

The point on which I wish to insist, and my reason for having outlined this theory of citizenship, is that the republican writers seem to me to offer strong reasons for concluding that this apparently paradoxical conclusion deserves to be taken literally.

Consider first their account of the consequences to be expected from any failure or refusal to serve one's community by defending it against external aggression. Given the natural rivalries between states, this is to invite invasion and conquest. But when a free state is conquered, it not only forfeits its free constitution by becoming subject to an external power. Its citizens also forfeit their own individual liberty to pursue their chosen goals. For they now become liable, as subjects of their conquerors, to be used simply as means to their ends. But to have one's ends determined by someone else's will is to be in a condition of servitude. There is thus held to be an intimate connection between the defence of free communities and the capacity of individual citizens to secure and maximize their own liberty. Paradoxical as it may appear, the one is a necessary condition of the other.[42]

The same applies to any refusal to serve one's community by guarding and upholding its free constitution. The natural ambitions of the powerful are such that this will invite its subversion by unscrupulous leaders or factional interests. Again, however, the effect will not merely be to destroy the liberty of the community to pursue its own goals. It will also be to subordinate the ends of individual citizens to the ends and purposes of those in power. But this again is equivalent to reducing them to a condition of servitude. Once again, the key contention is that public service, paradoxically enough, constitutes our only means of ensuring and maximizing our own personal liberty.

By way of concluding, I should like to underline my reasons for having excavated this pre-liberal stratum of thought about civic and personal liberty. Contemporary liberalism, especially in its so-called libertarian form, is in danger of sweeping the public arena bare of any concepts save those of self-interest and individual rights. Those moralists who have protested against this impoverishment have generally concluded that the best alternative must be to revive the Aristotelian view that citizenship is essentially a matter of shared moral purposes. As Alasdair MacIntyre has recently remarked, for example, in *After Virtue*, 'the crucial moral opposition is between liberal individualism in some version or other and the Aristotelian tradition in some version or other.'[43]

I have sought to argue that this is a false dichotomy. The Aristotelian assumption that a healthy public life needs to be founded on some objective conception of the Good is by no means the only alternative available to us if we wish to challenge the presuppositions and hence engage with the limitations of contemporary liberalism. It is also open to us to meditate on the potential relevance of a theory which tells us that, if we wish to maximize our personal liberty, we must not place our trust in princes; we must instead take charge of the political arena ourselves.

It will be objected that this is the merest nostalgic anti-modernism. We have no realistic prospect of taking direct control of the political process in any large-scale contemporary nation-state. But the objection is too crudely formulated. There are many areas of public life, short of directly controlling the actions of the executive, where greater public participation might serve to improve the accountability of our *soi disant* representatives, if only by pressuring them into taking greater account of the actual beliefs and aspirations of the majority of citizens.

Even if the objection is valid, however, it misses the point. The reason for wishing to bring the republican vision of civic virtue back into view is not that it directly shows us how to construct a genuine democracy, one in which government is for the people as a result of being by the people. It is certainly arguable that it gestures more effectively in that direction than much contemporary liberalism. But the actual construction of such a model, suitable for current conditions, remains of course our own task. My reason for undertaking this act of excavation is a more general one. Politics is a profession; unless politicians are persons of exceptional altruism, they will always face the temptation of making decisions in line with their own interests and those of powerful pressure-groups instead of in the interests of the community at large. Given this predicament, the republican argument conveys a warning which, while we may wish to dismiss it as unduly pessimistic, we can hardly afford at the present juncture to ignore: that unless we act to prevent this kind of political corruption by giving our civic duties priority over our individual rights, we must expect to find our individual rights themselves undermined.

Notes

1. John Rawls, *A Theory of Justice*, Cambridge, Mass. 1971, p. 11.
2. Ibid., p. 11.
3. Ibid., p. 5.
4. Ibid.
5. Ibid., p. 10.
6. Ibid., p. 12.
7. Ibid., p. 11.
8. Ibid.
9. Ibid., p. 3.
10. Ibid., p. 179.
11 Ibid., p. 31.
12. Ibid., pp. 60—1. On Rawls's apparent equivocation at this point between 'liberty' and 'liberties', see H.L.A. Hart, 'Rawls on Liberty and its Priority', in *Reading Rawls*, ed. Norman Daniels, revised edn, Stanford, Cal. 1989, pp. 230—52.
13. Rawls, *Theory of Justice*, p. 302.
14. Ibid., p. 22.
15. Ibid., p. 23.
16. Ibid., p. 246.
17. Ibid., p. 14.
18. Isaiah Berlin, *Four Essays on Liberty*, Oxford 1969, p. 161.
19. Ronald Dworkin, *Taking Rights Seriously*, Cambridge, Mass. 1977, esp. pp. xi, xv, 170-7. Cf. also Ronald Dworkin, *A Matter of Principle*, esp. the chapter on Liberalism in Part III, pp. 181—204.
20. See, for example, the criticisms of Rawls in Michael Sandel, *Liberalism and the Limits of Justice*, Cambridge 1982. Rawls has replied in 'Justice as Fairness: Political not Metaphysical', *Philosophy and Public Affairs* 14, 1985. See also John Rawls, 'The Priority of Right and Ideas of the Good', *Philosophy and Public Affairs* 17, 1988, pp. 151—76, which includes a discussion of the principles of classical republicanism.

21. My argument at this point draws heavily on earlier papers I have published on this theme: 'Machiavelli on the Maintenance of Liberty', *Politics* 18, 1983, pp. 3–15; 'The Idea of Negative Liberty: Philosophical and Historical Perspectives', in *Philosophy in History*, ed. Richard Rorty, J.B. Schneewind and Quentin Skinner, Cambridge 1984, pp. 193–221; and 'The Paradoxes of Political Liberty', in *The Tanner Lectures on Human Values*, vol. VII, ed. S. McMurrin, Cambridge 1986, pp. 225–50, an essay in which I already attempt to draw out some of the broader implications of the 'republican' argument. For a full statement of a 'republican' theory of justice and liberty, see now the impressive (and, to me, very congenial) analysis in John Braithwaite and Philip Pettit, *Not Just Deserts*, Oxford 1990, esp. pp. 54–85.

22. I have already tried to illustrate this theme in my book, *The Foundations of Modern Political Thought*, vol. I, *The Renaissance*, Cambridge 1978, esp. pp. 3–48, 69–112, 139–89.

23. The classic study of these later phases in the development of republican ideology is J.G.A. Pocock, *The Machiavellian Moment*, Princeton 1975.

24. For Hobbes's scornful dismissal of Italian republicanism, see *Leviathan*, ed C.B. Macpherson, Penguin Classics edn, Harmondsworth 1985, esp. p. 266.

25. For a classic statement to the effect that the concept of liberty must be understood in this way as a triadic relationship between agents, constraints and ends, see Gerald C. MacCallum Jr, 'Negative and Positive Freedom', in *Philosophy, Politics and Society*, series IV, ed. Peter Laslett, W.G. Runciman and Quentin Skinner, Oxford 1972, pp. 174–93.

26. Niccolo Machiavelli, *Il Principe e Discorsi*, ed. Sergio Bertelli, Milan 1960, p. 129. In this and in all subsequent citations from Machiavelli's *Discorsi*, all references are to Bertelli's edition and all translations are my own. The similarity between Machiavelli's position and Rousseau's doctrine of the *volonté générale* needs no emphasis.

27. Machiavelli, *Discorsi*, e.g. at pp. 216, 257, 272.

28. Ibid., p. 298.

29. Ibid., p. 379.

30. Ibid., and cf. also p. 460.

31. Ibid., e.g., at pp. 296, 386.

32. Ibid., p. 204.

33. Ibid., p. 270; cf. also p. 485.

34. Ibid., pp. 290–9; cf. also p. 493.

35. Ibid., p. 293; cf. also pp. 242, 251, 274.

36. Ibid., pp. 203, 283.

37. John Curran, Speech of 10 July 1790 on the right of election of the Lord Mayor of Dublin.

38. Hobbes, *Leviathan*, p. 266.

39. Machiavelli, *Discorsi*, pp. 232, 332.

40. Ibid., pp. 329–30.

41. Ibid., p. 236.

42. For these arguments see Machiavelli, *Discorsi*, pp. 450–1, 461, 519.

43. Alasdair MacIntyre, *After Virtue*, London 1981, p. 241.

Democratic Citizenship
and the Political Community

Chantal Mouffe

The themes of 'citizenship' and 'community' are being discussed in many quarters of the Left today. It is no doubt a consequence of the crisis of class politics and indicates the growing awareness of the need for a new form of identification around which to organize the forces struggling for a radicalization of democracy. I do indeed agree that the question of political identity is crucial and I consider that to attempt to construct 'citizens'' identities should be one of the important tasks of democratic politics. But there are many different visions of citizenship and central issues are at stake in their contest. The way we define citizenship is intimately linked to the kind of society and political community we want.

How should we understand citizenship when our goal is a radical and plural democracy? Such a project requires the creation of a chain of equivalence among democratic struggles, and therefore the creation of a common political identity among democratic subjects. For the interpellation 'citizens' to be able to fulfil that role, what conditions must it meet?

These are the problems that I will address and I will argue that the key question is how to conceive of the nature of the political community under modern democratic conditions. I consider that we need to go beyond the conceptions of citizenship of both the liberal and the civic republican tradition while building on their respective strengths.

To situate my reflexions in the context of the current discussions, I will begin by engaging with the debate between Kantian liberals and the

226 DIMENSIONS OF RADICAL DEMOCRACY

so-called 'communitarians'. In this way I hope to bring to the fore the specificity of my approach both politically and theoretically.

Liberalism versus Civic Republicanism

What is really at stake between John Rawls and his communitarian critics is the issue of citizenship. Two different languages in which to articulate our identity as citizens are confronting each other. Rawls proposes representing the citizen of a constitutional democracy in terms of equal rights expressed by his two principles of justice. He affirms that once citizens see themselves as free and equal persons, they should recognize that to pursue their own different conceptions of the good, they need the same primary goods, i.e. the same basic rights, liberties and opportunities, as well as the same all-purpose means such as income and wealth and the same social bases of self-respect. This is why they should agree on a political conception of justice that states that 'all social primary goods — liberty and opportunity, income and wealth and the bases of self-respect — are to be distributed equally, unless an unequal distribution of any or all of these goods is to the advantage of the least favored.'[1] According to that liberal view, citizenship is the capacity for each person to form, revise and rationally pursue his/her definition of the good. Citizens are seen as using their rights to promote their self-interest within certain constraints imposed by the exigency to respect the rights of others. The communitarians object that it is an impoverished conception that precludes the notion of the citizen as one for whom it is natural to join with others to pursue common action in view of the common good. Michael Sandel has argued that Rawls's conception of the self is an 'unencumbered' one, which leaves no room for a 'constitutive' community, a community that would constitute the very identity of the individuals. It only allows for an 'instrumental' community, a community in which individuals with their previously defined interests and identity enter in view of furthering those interests.[2]

For the communitarians the alternative to this flawed liberal approach is the revival of the civic republican view of politics that puts a strong emphasis on the notion of a public good, prior to and independent of individual desires and interests. Such a tradition has almost disappeared today because it has been displaced by Liberalism, though it has a long history. It received its full expression in the Italian republics at the end of the Middle Ages but its origins go back to Greek and Roman thought. It was reformulated in England in the seventeenth century by James Harrington, John Milton and other republicans. Later it travelled to the New World through the work of the neo-Harringtonians, and recent studies have shown that it played a very important role during the American Revolution.[3]

There are indeed serious problems with the liberal conception of citizenship but we must be aware of the shortcomings of the civic republican solution, too. It does provide us with a view of citizenship much richer than the liberal one, and its conception of politics as the realm where we can recognize ourselves as participants in a political community has obvious appeal for the critics of liberal individualism. Nevertheless there is a real danger of coming back to a pre-modern view of politics, which does not acknowledge the novelty of modern democracy and the crucial contribution of liberalism. The defence of pluralism, the idea of individual liberty, the separation of church and state, the development of civil society, all these are constitutive of modern democratic politics. They require that a distinction be made between the private and the public domain, the realm of morality and the realm of politics. Contrary to what some communitarians propose, a modern democratic political community cannot be organized around a single substantive idea of the common good. The recovery of a strong participatory idea of citizenship should not be made at the cost of sacrificing individual liberty. This is the point where the communitarian critique of liberalism takes a dangerous conservative turn.

The problem, I believe, is not that of replacing one tradition by the other but drawing on both and trying to combine their insights in a new conception of citizenship adequate for a project of radical and plural democracy. While liberalism did certainly contribute to the formulation of the idea of a universal citizenship, based on the assertion that all individuals are born free and equal, it also reduced citizenship to a mere legal status, setting out the rights that the individual holds against the state. The way these rights are exercised is irrelevant as long as their holders do not break the law or interfere with the rights of others. Social cooperation aims only to enhance our productive capacities and facilitates the attainment of each person's individual prosperity. Ideas of public-mindedness, civic activity and political participation in a community of equals are alien to most liberal thinkers.

Civic republicanism, on the contrary, emphasizes the value of political participation and attributes a central role to our insertion in a political community. But the problem arises with the exigency of conceiving the political community in a way that is compatible with modern democracy and liberal pluralism. In other words, we are faced with the old dilemma of how to reconcile the liberties of the ancients with the liberties of the moderns. The liberals argue that they are incompatible and that today ideas about the 'common good' can only have totalitarian implications. According to them, it is impossible to combine democratic institutions with the sense of common purpose that pre-modern society enjoyed, and the ideals of 'republican virtue' are nostalgic relics which ought to be discarded. Active political participation, they say, is incompatible with the modern idea of liberty. Individual liberty can only be understood in a negative way as absence of coercion.

This argument, powerfully restated by Isaiah Berlin in 'Two Concepts of Liberty',[4] is generally used to discredit any attempt to recapture the civic republican conception of politics. However it has recently been challenged by Quentin Skinner, who shows that there is no basic necessary incompatibility between the classical republican conception of citizenship and modern democracy.[5] He finds in several forms of republican thought, particularly in Machiavelli, a way of conceiving liberty which though negative — and therefore modern — includes political participation and civic virtue. It is negative because liberty is conceived as the absence of impediments to the realization of our chosen ends. But it also asserts that it is only as citizens of a 'free state', of a community whose members participate actively in the government, that such individual liberty can be guaranteed. To ensure our own liberty and avoid the servitude that would render its exercise impossible, we must cultivate civic virtues and devote ourselves to the common good. The idea of a common good above our private interest is a necessary condition for enjoying individual liberty. Skinner's argument is important because it refutes the liberals' claim that individual liberty and political participation can never be reconciled. This is crucial for a radical democratic project, but the kind of political community adequate for such an articulation between the rights of the individual and the political participation of the citizen then becomes the question to be addressed.

Modern Democracy and Political Community

Another way to approach the debate between Kantian liberals like Rawls and the communitarians is via the question of the priority of the right over the good, this has a direct relevance to the issue of the modern democratic political community.

For Rawls such a priority indicates that individual rights cannot be sacrificed for the sake of the general welfare, as is the case with Utilitarianism, and that the principles of justice impose restrictions on what are the permissible conceptions of the good that individuals are allowed to pursue. This is why he insists that the principles of justice must be derived independently of any particular conception of the good, since they need to respect the existence of a plurality of competing conceptions of the good in order to be accepted by all citizens. His aim here is to defend liberal pluralism which requires not imposing upon individuals any specific conception of well-being or particular plan of life. For liberals those are private questions bearing on individual morality, and they believe that the individual should be able to organize his/her life according to his/her own wishes, without unnecessary interventions. Hence the centrality of the concept of individual rights and the assertion that principles of justice must not privilege a particular conception of the good life.

I consider this an important principle, which needs defending because it is crucial for modern democratic societies. Indeed, modern democracy is precisely characterized by the absence of a substantive common good. This is the meaning of the democratic revolution as analysed by Claude Lefort,[6] who identifies it with the dissolution of landmarks of certainty. According to Lefort, modern democratic society is a society where power has become an empty space and is separated from law and knowledge. In such a society it is no longer possible to provide a final guarantee, a definite legitimation, because power is no longer incorporated in the person of the prince and associated to a transcendental instance. Power, law and knowledge are therefore exposed to a radical indeterminacy: in my terms, a substantive common good becomes impossible. This is also what Rawls indicates when he affirms that 'We must abandon the hope of a political community if by such a community we mean a political society united in affirming a general and comprehensive doctrine.'[7] If the priority of the right over the good were restricted to that, there would not be anything for me to disagree with. But Rawls wants to establish an absolute priority of the right over the good because he does not recognize that it can only exist in a certain type of society with specific institutions and that it is a consequence of the democratic revolution.

To that the communitarians reply, with reason, that such an absolute priority of the right cannot exist and that it is only through our

participation in a community which defines the good in a certain way that
we can acquire a sense of the right and a conception of justice. Charles
Taylor correctly points out that the mistake with the liberal approach is
that

> it fails to take account of the degree to which the free individual with his
> own goals and aspirations whose just rewards it is trying to protect, is
> himself only possible within a certain kind of civilization; that it took a long
> development of certain institutions and practices, of the rule of law, of rules
> of equal respect, of habits of common deliberation, of common association,
> of cultural development and so on, to produce the modern individual.[8]

Where the communitarians lost their way is when some of them, such
as Sandel, conclude that there can never be a priority of the right over the
good, and that we should therefore reject liberal pluralism and return to
a type of community organized around shared moral values and a
substantive idea of the common good. We can fully agree with Rawls
about the priority of justice as the principal virtue of social and political
institutions and in defending pluralism and rights, while admitting that
those principles are specific to a certain type of political association.

There is, however, another aspect of the communitarian critique of
liberalism which we should not abandon but reformulate. The absence
of a single substantive common good in modern democratic societies
and the separation between the realm of morality and the realm of
politics have, no doubt, signified an incontestable gain in individual
freedom. But the consequences for politics have been very damaging. All
normative concerns have increasingly been relegated to the field of
private morality, to the domain of 'values', and politics has been stripped
of its ethical components. An instrumentalist conception has become
dominant, concerned exclusively with the compromise between already
defined interests. On the other side, liberalism's exclusive concern with
individuals and their rights has not provided content and guidance for
the exercise of those rights. This has led to the devaluation of civic
action, of common concern, which has caused an increasing lack of social
cohesion in democratic societies. The communitarians are right to
criticize such a situation and I agree with their attempt to revive some
aspects of the classical conception of politics. We do need to re-establish
the lost connection between ethics and politics, but this cannot be done
by sacrificing the gains of the democratic revolution. We should not
accept a false dichotomy between individual liberty and rights on one

side and civic activity and political community on the other. Our only choice is not one between an aggregate of individuals without common public concern and a pre-modern community organized around a single substantive idea of the common good. Envisaging the modern democratic political community outside of this dichotomy is the crucial challenge.

I have already pointed out how Quentin Skinner indicates a possible form of articulation between individual freedom and civic participation. But we must also be able to formulate the ethical character of modern citizenship in a way that is compatible with moral pluralism and respects the priority of the right over the good. What we share and what makes us fellow citizens in a liberal democratic regime is not a substantive idea of the good but a set of political principles specific to such a tradition: the principles of freedom and equality for all. Those principles constitute what we can call, following Wittgenstein, a 'grammar' of political conduct. To be a citizen is to recognize the authority of those principles and the rules in which they are embodied; to have them informing our political judgement and our actions. To be associated in terms of the recognition of the liberal democratic principles, this is the meaning of citizenship that I want to put forward. It implies seeing citizenship not as a legal status but as a form of identification, a type of political identity: something to be constructed, not empirically given. Since there will always be competing interpretations of the democratic principles of equality and liberty there will therefore be competing interpretations of democratic citizenship. I will inquire into the nature of a radical demo-cratic citizenship, but before I do, I must return to the question of the political association or community.

The Political Community: Universitas or Societas?

As I indicated previously, we need to conceive of a mode of political association, which, although it does not postulate the existence of a substantive common good, nevertheless implies the idea of common-ality, of an ethico-political bond that creates a linkage among the par-ticipants in the association, allowing us to speak of a political 'community' even if it is not in the strong sense. In other words, what we are looking for is a way to accommodate the distinctions between public and private, morality and politics which have been the great contribution of liberalism to modern democracy, without renouncing the ethical nature of the political association.

I consider that, if we interpret them in a certain way, the reflections on civil association proposed by Michael Oakeshott in *On Human Conduct* can be very illuminating for such a purpose. Oakeshott shows that *societas* and *universitas*, which were understood in the late Middle Ages as two different modes of human association, can also represent two alternative interpretations of the modern state. *Universitas* indicates an engagement in an enterprise to pursue a common substantive purpose or to promote a common interest. It refers therefore to 'persons associated in a manner such as to constitute them a natural person, a partnership of persons which is itself a Person, or in some important respects like a person'.[9]

Contrary to that model of association of agents engaged in a common enterprise defined by a purpose, *societas* or 'civil association' designates a formal relationship in terms of rules, not a substantive relation in terms of common action.

> The idea *societas* is that of agents who, by choice or circumstance, are related to one another so as to compose an identifiable association of a certain sort. The tie which joins them, and in respect of which each recognizes himself to be *socius*, is not that of an engagement in an enterprise to pursue a common substantive purpose or to promote a common interest, but that of loyalty to one another.[10]

It is not a mode of relation, therefore, in terms of common action but a relation in which participants are related to one another in the acknowledgement of the authority of certain conditions in acting.

Oakeshott insists that the participants in a *societas* or *cives* are not associated for a common enterprise nor with a view to facilitating the attainment of each person's individual prosperity; what links them is the recognition of the authority of the conditions specifying their common or 'public' concern, a 'practice of civility'. This public concern or consideration of *cives* Oakeshott calls *respublica*. It is a practice of civility specifying not performances, but conditions to be subscribed to in choosing performances. These consist in a complex of rules or rule-like prescriptions, which do not prescribe satisfactions to be sought or actions to be performed but 'moral considerations specifying conditions to be subscribed to in choosing performances'.[11]

It seems to me that Oakeshott's idea of the civil association as *societas* is adequate to define political association under modern democratic conditions. Indeed it is a mode of human association that recognizes the disappearance of a single substantive idea of the common good and makes room for individual liberty. It is a form of association that can be enjoyed among relative strangers belonging to many purposive associations and whose allegiances to specific communities is not seen as conflicting with their membership in the civil association. This would not be possible if such an association were conceived as *universitas*, as purposive association, because it would not allow for the existence of other genuine purposive associations in which individuals would be free to participate.

To belong to the political community what is required is that we accept a specific language of civil intercourse, the *respublica*. Those rules prescribe norms of conduct to be subscribed to in seeking self-chosen satisfactions and in performing self-chosen actions. The identification with those rules of civil intercourse creates a common political identity among persons otherwise engaged in many different enterprises. This modern form of political community is held together not by a sub-stantive idea of the common good but by a common bond, a public concern. It is therefore a community without a definite shape or a definite identity and in continuous re-enactment.

Such a conception is clearly different from the pre-modern idea of the political community, but it is also different from the liberal idea of the political association. For liberalism also sees political association as a form of purposive association, of enterprise, except that in its case the aim is an instrumental one: the promotion of self-interest.

Oakeshott criticizes the liberal view of the state as a conciliator of interests, which he considers to be as remote from civil association as the idea of the state as promoter of an interest, and he declares 'it has been thought that the "Rule of Law" is enough to identify civil association whereas what is significant is the kind of law: "moral" or "instru-mental"'.[12] His conception should therefore not be confounded with the liberal doctrine of the Rule of Law. He stresses the moral character of the *respublica* and affirms that political thought concerns the *respublica* in terms of *bonum civile*. He declares 'Civility, then, denotes an order of moral (not instrumental) considerations, and the so-called neutrality of civil prescriptions is a half truth, which needs to be supplemented by the recognition of civil association as itself a moral and not a prudential condition.'[13] By 'moral' he obviously refers not to a comprehensive view but to what I have proposed calling the 'ethico-political', since he asserts that what is civilly desirable cannot be inferred or derived from general moral principles and that political deliberation is concerned with moral considerations of its own. 'This *respublica* is the articulation of a common concern that the pursuit of all purposes and the promotion of all interests, the satisfaction of all wants and the propagation of all beliefs shall be in subscription to conditions formulated in rules indifferent to the merits of any interest or the truth or error of any belief and consequently not itself a substantive interest or doctrine.'[14]

We could say, using Rawls's vocabulary, that in a civil association or *societas* there exists a priority of the right over the good, but in Oakeshott's case, the principles that specify the right, the *respublica*, are conceived not in a Kantian manner as in Rawls, but in a Hegelian way, since for him, to be associated in terms of the recognition of the *respublica* is to enjoy a *sittlich* relation. What I find useful in this approach is that, while allowing for the recognition of pluralism and individual liberty, the notion of *societas* does not relinquish all normative aspects to the sphere of private morality. This mode of association, which Oakeshott traces back to Machiavelli, Montesquieu and Hegel, permits us to maintain a certain idea of the political community in the sense of a non-instrumental, an ethical, type of bond among *cives*, while severing it from the existence of a substantive common good.

I mentioned at the outset that to be useful to a radical democratic project Oakeshott's reflexions needed to be interpreted in a certain way. I am, of course, perfectly aware of the conservative use he makes of the distinction between *societas* and *universitas*, but I believe that it is not the only and necessary one.[15] To be sure, Oakeshott's conservatism resides in the content he puts in the *respublica*, and that can obviously be solved by introducing more radical principles, as I will indicate later. But more fundamentally, it lies in his flawed idea of politics. For his conception of politics as a shared language of civility is only adequate for one aspect of politics: the point of view of the 'we', the friend's side. However, as Carl Schmitt has rightly pointed out, the criteria of the political is the friend/enemy relation. What is completely missing in Oakeshott is division and antagonism, that is, the aspect of the 'enemy'. It is an absence that must be remedied if we want to appropriate his notion of *societas*.

To introduce conflict and antagonism into Oakeshott's model, it is necessary to recognize that the *respublica* is the product of a given hegemony, the expression of power relations, and that it can be challenged. Politics is to a great extent about the rules of the *respublica* and its many possible interpretations, it is about the constitution of the political community, not something that takes place inside the political community as some communitarians would have it. Political life concerns collective, public action; it aims at the construction of a 'we' in a context of diversity and conflict. But to construct a 'we' it must be distinguished from the 'them' and that means establishing a frontier, defining an 'enemy'. Therefore, while politics aims at constructing a political community and creating a unity, a fully inclusive political community and a final unity can never be realized since there will permanently be a 'constitutive outside', an exterior to the community that makes its existence possible. Antagonistic forces will never disappear and politics is characterized by conflict and division. Forms of agreement can be reached but they are always partial and provisional since consensus is by necessity based on acts of exclusion. We are indeed very far from the language of civility dear to Oakeshott!

A Radical Democratic Citizenship

What becomes of the idea of citizenship in such a perspective? If we understand citizenship as the political identity that is created through identification with the *respublica*, a new conception of the citizen becomes possible. First, we are now dealing with a type of political identity, a form of identification, no longer simply with a legal status. The citizen is not, as in liberalism, someone who is the passive recipient of specific rights and who enjoys the protection of the law. It is not that those elements become irrelevant but the definition of the citizen shifts because the emphasis is put on the identification with the *respublica*. It is a common political identity of persons who might be engaged in many different purposive enterprises and with differing conceptions of the good, but who accept submission to the rules prescribed by the *respublica* in seeking their satisfactions and in performing their actions. What binds them together is their common recognition of a set of ethico-political values. In this case, citizenship is not just one identity among others — as in liberalism — or the dominant identity that overrides all others — as in civic republicanism. It is an articulating principle that affects the different subject positions of the social agent (as I will show when I discuss the public/private distinction) while allowing for a plurality of specific allegiances and for the respect of individual liberty.

Since we are dealing with politics, however, there will be competing forms of identification linked to different interpretations of the *respublica*. In a liberal democratic regime we can conceive of the *respublica* as constituted by the political principles of such a regime: equality and liberty for all. If we put such a content in Oakeshott's notion of *respublica* we can affirm that the conditions to be subscribed to and taken into account in acting are to be understood as the exigency of treating the others as free and equal persons. This is clearly open to potentially very radical interpretations. For instance, a radical democratic interpretation will emphasize the numerous social relations where relations of domination exist and must be challenged if the principles of liberty and equality are to apply. It should lead to a common recognition among different groups struggling for an extension and radicalization of democracy that they have a common concern and that in choosing their actions they should subscribe to certain rules of conduct; in other words, it should construct a common political identity as radical democratic citizens.

The creation of political identities as radical democratic citizens depends therefore on a collective form of identification among the democratic demands found in a variety of movements: women, workers, black, gay, ecological, as well as in several other 'new social movements'. This is a conception of citizenship which, through a common identification with a radical democratic interpretation of the principles of liberty and equality, aims at constructing a 'we', a chain of equivalence among their demands so as to articulate them through the principle of democratic equivalence. For it is not a matter of establishing a mere alliance between given interests but of actually modifying the very identity of these forces. This is something that many pluralist liberals do not understand because they are blind to power relations. They agree on the need to extend the sphere of rights in order to include groups hitherto excluded but they see that process as a smooth one of progressive inclusion into citizenship. This is the typical story as told by T.H. Marshall in his celebrated article 'Citizenship and Social Class'. The problem with such an approach is that it ignores the limits imposed on the extension of pluralism by the fact that some existing rights have been constituted on the very exclusion or subordination of the rights of other categories. Those identities must first be deconstructed if several new rights are to be recognized.

To make possible a hegemony of the democratic forces, new identities are therefore required, and I am arguing here in favour of a common political identity as radical democratic citizens. By that I understand a collective identification with a radical democratic interpretation of the principles of the liberal-democratic regime: liberty and equality. Such an interpretation presupposes that those principles are understood in a way that takes account of the different social relations and subject positions in which they are relevant: gender, class, race, ethnicity, sexual orientation, etc.

Such an approach can only be adequately formulated within a problematic that conceives of the social agent not as a unitary subject but as the articulation of an ensemble of subject positions, constructed within specific discourses and always precariously and temporarily sutured at the intersection of those subject positions. Only with a non-essentialist conception of the subject which incorporates the psycho-analytic insight that all identities are forms of identification can we pose the question of political identity in a fruitful way. A non-essentialist perspective is also needed concerning the notions of *respublica, societas* and political community. For it is crucial to see them not as empirical referents but as discursive surfaces. Failure to do so would make the type of politics which is posited here completely incomprehensible.

On this point a radical democratic conception of citizenship connects with the current debates about 'postmodernity' and the critique of rationalism and universalism. The view of citizenship I am proposing rejects the idea of an abstract universalist definition of the public, opposed to a domain of the private seen as the realm of particularity and difference. It considers that, although the modern idea of the citizen was indeed crucial for the democratic revolution, it constitutes today an obstacle to its extension. As feminist theorists have argued, the public realm of modern citizenship has been based on the negation of women's participation.[16] This exclusion was seen as indispensable to postulate the generality and universality of the public sphere. The distinction public/private, central as it was for the assertion of individual liberty, also led to identifying the private with the domestic and played an important role in the subordination of women.

To the idea that the exercise of citizenship consists in adopting a universal point of view, made equivalent to Reason and reserved to men, I am opposing the idea that it consists in identifying with the ethico-political principles of modern democracy and that there can be as many forms of citizenship as there are interpretations of those principles.

In this view the public/private is not abandoned but reformulated. Here again Oakeshott can help us to find an alternative to the limitations of liberalism. *Societas* is, according to him, a civil condition in which every enterprise is 'private' while never immune from the 'public' conditions specified in *respublica*. In a *societas* 'every situation is an encounter between "private" and "public", between an action or an utterance to procure an imagined and wished-for substantive satisfaction and the conditions of civility to be subscribed to in performing it; and no situation is the one to the exclusion of the other.'[17] The wants, choices and decisions are private because they are the responsibility of each individual but the performances are public because they are required to subscribe to the conditions specified in *respublica*. Since the rules of the *respublica* do not enjoin, prohibit or warrant substantive actions or utterances, and do not tell agents what to do, this mode of association respects individual liberty. But the individual's belonging to the political community and identification with its ethico-political principles are manifested by her acceptance of the common concern expressed in the *respublica*. It provides the 'grammar' of the citizen's conduct.

In the case of a radical democratic citizen, such an approach allows us to visualize how a concern with equality and liberty should inform her actions in all areas of social life. No sphere is immune from those concerns, and relations of domination can be challenged everywhere. Nevertheless we are not dealing with a purposive kind of community affirming one single goal for all its members, and the freedom of the individual is preserved.

The distinction private (individual liberty)/public (*respublica*) is maintained as well as the distinction individual/citizen, but they do not correspond to discrete separate spheres. We cannot say: here end my duties as a citizen and begins my freedom as an individual. Those two identities exist in a permanent tension that can never be reconciled. But this is precisely the tension between liberty and equality that characterizes modern democracy. It is the very life of such a regime and any attempt to bring about a perfect harmony, to realize a 'true' democracy can only lead to its destruction. This is why a project of radical and plural democracy recognizes the impossibility of the complete realization of democracy and the final achievement of the political community. Its aim is to use the symbolic resources of the liberal democratic tradition to struggle for the deepening of the democratic revolution, knowing that it is a never-ending process. My thesis here has been that the ideal of citizenship could greatly contribute to such an extension of the principles of liberty and equality. By combining the ideal of rights and pluralism with the ideas of public spiritedness and ethico-political concern, a new modern democratic conception of citizenship could restore dignity to the political and provide the vehicle for the construction of a radical democratic hegemony.

Notes

1. John Rawls, *A Theory of Justice*, Oxford 1971, pp. 302—3.

2. Michael Sandel, *Liberalism and the Limits of Justice*, Cambridge 1982.

3. For a general presentation of the debate see my article 'American Liberalism and its Critics: Rawls, Taylor, Sandel and Walzer', *Praxis International* 8, 2, July 1988.

4. Isaiah Berlin, 'Two Concepts of Liberty', in *Four Essays on Liberty*, Oxford 1969.

5. Quentin Skinner, 'The Idea of Negative Liberty: Philosophical and Historical Perspective', in R. Rorty, J.B. Schneewind and Q. Skinner, eds. *Philosophy in History*, Cambridge 1984.

6. Claude Lefort, *The Political Forms of Modern Society*, Oxford 1986, p. 305ff.

7. John Rawls, 'The Idea of an Overlapping Consensus', *Oxford Journal of Legal Studies* 7, 1, Spring 1987, p. 10.

8. Charles Taylor, *Philosophy and the Human Sciences*, Philosophical Papers 2, Cambridge 1955, p. 200.

9. Michael Oakeshott, *On Human Conduct*, Oxford 1975, p. 203.

10. Ibid., p. 201.

11. Ibid., p. 182.

12. Ibid., p. 318.

13. Ibid., p. 175.

14. Ibid., p. 172.

15. One of Oakeshott's targets is undoubtedly the idea of redistributive justice and the forms of state intervention that such an idea renders legitimate, but I do not believe that the distinction between *universitas* and *societas* necessarily commits us to reject state intervention as being inherently linked to a conception of the state as a purposive common enterprise. One can perfectly justify state intervention on the basis of a certain interpretation of the *respublica*.

16. See, for instance, Carole Pateman, *The Sexual Contract*, Stanford 1988; and Geneviève Fraisse, *Muse de la raison*, Aix-en-Provence 1989.

17. Oakeshott, *On Human Conduct*, p. 183.

What Revolutionary
Action Means Today

Sheldon Wolin

One of the chapters in Tocqueville's *Democracy in America* is entitled 'Why Great Revolutions will become Rare'. His thesis was that once a society becomes democratized in its political system and more egalitarian in its social institutions, it is unlikely that it will ever undergo the type of revolutionary upheavals experienced by France in 1789 and England in the 1640s. The great revolutions had resulted from gross political and social inequalities. Thanks to its system of equal political rights (i.e. for white males), and to the ready availability of land, American democracy had eliminated the causes of revolution. He claimed that the revolutionary impulse would wither because for the first time in western history the masses of ordinary human beings had a tangible stake in defending the status quo.

Tocqueville's conclusions have been restated in many ways. Democracy, it has been said, is the form of government that has had its revolution. Others claim that for the people to rebel against democracy is for them to rebel against themselves, or that a revolution against democracy in the name of democracy is a contradiction in terms. In each of these formulations the implication is that as long as a political system is democratic, it makes no sense to think of revolutionary activity as an appropriate or obligatory form of action for the democratic citizen. But the real problem is, is it right for the democratic citizen to undertake revolutionary action when the political system retains some of the formal features of democracy but is clearly embarked on a course that is progressively anti-democratic without being crudely repressive? What are the precise ways in which a system that is formally democratic conceals its anti-democratic tendencies? Are pseudo-democratic substitutes introduced that create the illusion of democracy? Was the idea of a democratic citizen partially skewed at the outset so that its development in America was truncated? And, finally, does it make sense even to discuss the possibility of revolution under the circumstances of an advanced, complex society? In what terms would it make sense to talk of revolution today — what would revolutionary action by democratic citizens be?

Our starting point is with a significant silence. Although the United States has been repeatedly described as being in a condition of crisis, no one seems to have suggested that there is a crisis at the centre of American democracy, in the idea of citizenship itself. While there are many voices, with varying degrees of good faith, ready to testify for democracy — especially when the purpose is to contrast the US with the USSR — there is virtually no one who is given to reflecting about the democratic citizen, to asking what it is to be one, or why, if each of us is one and there are so many of us, the society seems to have so many anti-democratic tendencies.

In a speech in June 1981 to the British Parliament, Ronald Reagan announced that the United States was about to throw its prestige and resources behind a programme launched to strengthen 'democracy throughout the world', but he made no reference to the idea of democratic citizenship or any suggestion that democracy might need strengthening at home. The silence on the subject is not peculiar to conservatives or reactionaries. The democratic citizen does not appear in any substantial form in the writings of Barry Commoner, the titular leader of the Citizens' Party, or Michael Harrington, the theoretician of Democratic Socialism of America. Most Marxists are interested in the 'masses' or the workers, but they dismiss citizenship as a bourgeois conceit, formal and empty, although Marx himself was much preoccupied with the idea in his early writings.

The present silence is a symptom of a crisis that has been in the making since the beginning of the republic. Its origins are in the one-sided conception of citizenship that was reflected in the Constitution. Beginning with the movement for a bill of rights, which was mounted in the midst of the controversy over ratification of the original Constitution (1787–89), and extending through the era of Jacksonian Democracy, the battle over slavery, and the adoption of Amendments 13, 14, 15, 17 (providing for the direct election of senators), and 19 (prohibiting the denial of suffrage on the basis of sex), a distinct pattern emerged in which each extension of rights was assumed to be an advance toward the realization of democracy. In actuality, the ideal of rights was usurping the place of civic activity. A liberal conception of citizenship was becoming predominant.

A democratic conception of citizenship, if it means anything at all, means that the citizen is supposed to exercise his rights to advance or protect the kind of polity that depends on his being involved in its common concerns. The liberal view was that citizenship is democratic in the United States because every citizen, regardless of cultural, social, economic and biological differences, can equally claim the right to vote, speak, worship, acquire property and have it protected and be assured of the elements of a fair trial. Unfortunately, the liberal civic culture never supplied any content to rights. A citizen was no less a citizen for espousing Ku Klux Klan doctrines than he was for joining the NAACP. To possess rights was to be free to do anything or say anything as long as one did not break the law or interfere with the rights of others.

How could a democratic conception of citizenship be said to be fulfilled — as a liberal conception would be — by having rights exercised for anti-democratic ends, as the KKK choice would be? It is not that a liberal view of rights disposes one toward the Klan, only that liberalism is fulfilled by protecting those who are so disposed. The American Civil Liberties Union, with its commitment to defending the entire range of opinion, from the most liberal to the most illiberal, was, one might say, immanent in the historical failure of liberalism to create a vision of civic commitments and of common action that could furnish both content and guidance to the exercise of rights.

This failure was inevitable, given the nature of the original liberal project, which was to protect rights by limiting governmental power. That project was written into the Constitution. The Constitution was not designed to encourage citizen action but to prevent arbitrary power, especially the form of power represented by the will of the majority. Among several of the states, the majority principle was being actively tested in the period from the outbreak of the Revolution in 1776 to the ratification of the Constitution in 1789. The Constitution was intended to shatter the majoritarian experiment at the national level by incorporating several devices that were supposed to frustrate the natural form of democratic action: separation of powers, checks and balances, federalism, the Supreme Court, indirect election of the president and Senate, and brief tenure for representatives. At the same time, the Constitution made no reference to the right to vote or hold office or to the principle of equality. Save for a somewhat enigmatic clause which was later interpreted to prevent a state from discriminating against citizens of other states, citizenship hardly figured as a basic institution. When the first ten amendments were quickly added to the Constitution, the outline of the citizen began to emerge, but it was primarily as a bearer of rights rather than as a participant in a collective undertaking. Several rights in the original Bill of Rights were couched in language that was less suggestive of what a citizen might actively do than what government was prohibited from doing. ('Congress shall make no law ... abridging the freedom of speech....' 'No person shall ... be deprived of life, liberty, or property, without due process of law ...')

The present silence about democratic citizenship is a sign of the disintegration of the liberal conception of rights and, necessarily, of the idea of citizenship dependent upon it. What happened is that in the twentieth century the liberal practice of politics rapidly undermined the liberal conception of rights. The theory of rights enshrined in the Bill of Rights conceived of special forms of freedom and protection that were to be beyond the ordinary reach of legislative or executive power. Once they had been given constitutional status, rights were not only beyond the scope of positive law, they were assumed to be 'above' politics. Whenever an historical controversy arose about rights, the point was made repeatedly that constitutional guarantees were intended to protect rights against 'transient majorities' and 'temporary gusts of passion'.

At almost the exact moment when the liberal theory of rights was about to be given the material form of the first ten amendments to the Constitution, James Madison, who was the prime mover of that effort, also produced what came to be the classical formulation of the liberal theory of politics. In Letter 10 of the *Federalist* papers he argued that one of the sternest tests for the proposed Constitution would be whether it could control 'factions', the distinctive form of politics in a society founded on freedom. A faction was a group organized to promote its interests by political means. Inevitably, factions would be in continual conflict with each other, not only over property rights but over political and religious beliefs as well. Thus the liberal conception of politics, with its conception of groups as pursuing interests that would conflict with other interests protected by legal rights, carried the presumption that politics was an activity that, by nature, posed a threat to rights. The task, as Madison and later liberals saw it, was to encourage institutional

244 DIMENSIONS OF RADICAL DEMOCRACY

devices that would control the effects of politics, not to reconstitute politics. Citizens would be engrossed in private actions, for when men and women are given freedom they use it to promote their self-interests, and it would be unjust and oppressive to limit that pursuit in the name of encouraging common action for common ends.

There were at least two further respects in which the liberal conception of politics was at odds with liberal rights. First, the protection of rights presupposed that government would be their defender, intervening to prevent interest groups from violating the rights of other groups or individuals. For this presupposition to work, government itself would have to withstand effectively the pressures generated by interest-group politics, pressures that were guaranteed to be unrelenting by the system of elections, campaign contributions and lobbying. The presupposition collapsed because once politics was reduced to interest groups, there was no general constituency to support government in its role of impartial defender of rights. Instead of playing the role of defender of rights, government assumed a function more consistent with the politics of interest groups, that of 'balancing' rights against certain overriding matters of state. Thus when wider latitude was given to the CIA and FBI to conduct surveillance, or when First Amendment rights of the press were limited by the prohibition against disclosing the names of CIA agents, the government's justification was that there had to be a balancing of national security needs with civil liberties, as though the setting were simply another instance of having to weigh the demands of conflicting groups.

Interest politics discourages as well the development of a civic culture favourable to the defence of rights and to the acceptance of integrative action as the activity definitive of citizenship. Interest politics dissolves the idea of the citizen as one for whom it is natural to join together with other citizens to act for purposes related to a general community and substitutes the idea of individuals who are grouped according to conflicting interests. The individual is not first and foremost a civic creature bound by pre-existing ties to those who share the same history, the same general association, and the same fate. He or she is instead a business executive, a teamster, a feminist, office worker, farmer or homosexual whose immediate identity naturally divides him or her from others. As a member of an interest group, the individual is given an essentially anticivic education. He is taught that the first duty is to support the self-interest of the group because politics is nothing but a struggle for advantage. In contrast, the citizen has to decide what to do,

Despite the deepening unemployment, the irrational level of defence expenditures, the utter hopelessness for millions of blacks and many Hispanics, and the brazenly business-oriented bias of the Reagan administration, there has been an astonishing passivity among those who have been hurt most by recent economic policies. All of the elements for radical political protest appear to be present. And yet there has been no general mobilization of outrage, only a few parades.

There are, of course, many reasons for the political passivity of the unemployed and the permanently poor, but one of the most important is the depoliticization to which they have been subjected. For more than three decades the thinking behind as well as the substance of public policies dealing with the poor, the unemployed and racial minorities, have treated them as having a pariah status quite unlike other interests. The tacit assumption of interest-group politics has always been that there was one common element among farmers, workers, employers and teachers, etc.: they were all productive in one way or another. They might receive subsidies, benefits or protections from the government, but, after all, it was they who in the last analysis were contributing to what they were receiving. This is why farmers and businessmen have always been outraged whenever the federal government has attempted to use government aid as a justification for government regulation and intervention. Farmers and businessmen have never conceived of themselves as receiving handouts and therefore as being dependants. As a result, they have been able to retain a strong sense of dignity and have been able to act with others who share their interests.

Those who are poor, unemployed or members of racial minorities can be treated differently, in ways that are divisive, that render them incapable of sustained political action. They are 'targeted' by specialized programmes that, in effect, fragment their lives. One agency handles medical assistance, another job training, a third food stamps, and so on *ad infinitum.* If a person's life is first flensed by bureaucrats whose questionnaires probe every detail of it, and that life is reorganized into categories corresponding to public programmes that are the means of one's existence, the person becomes totally disabled as a political being, unable to grasp the meaning of common concerns of even so small a totality as a neighbourhood. This is because he or she has been deprived of the most elemental totality of all, the self.

Depoliticization is more extreme among the poor and racial minorities because they are the most helpless of all groups in the political economy, the new social form that is replacing the older form of the political order. The political economy has taken the liberal idea of the citizen one apolitical step farther. The conception of the citizen as a bearer of rights, who in principle could exercise his capacities to speak, petition, write and associate, gave way to a conception of a wholly new kind of being whose existence consisted of indices which told him what his condition was objectively: an index for prices, another for wages, inflation, unemployment, consumer spending, and, most grandly, 'a misery index'.

However useful indices may be for those who have the power to make decisions, they are simultaneously a symbol of powerlessness and a persuasive force toward further depoliticization for those who cannot. An index, such as one representing inflation rates, does not tell the individual what he is *doing*, but rather what is *happening to him*. It registers forces that are beyond his ability to influence or control.

Perhaps there is no more striking indication of the extent of de-politicization than the level of popular awareness concerning how the political system really works. Most people understand that our system makes it relatively easy for wealth and economic power to be translated into political power and influence, which are then retranslated into legislative enactments, Treasury rulings, defence contracts, export licences, and the like. They also know that money, especially corporate money, buys candidates, finances campaigns, hires lobbyists, and keeps a legion of experts, especially academic ones, on long retainers and short leashes. What is so striking is not that people know these things, but that the dominant groups in the political economy are now so confident of their control that they encourage rather than suppress public knowledge of their enormous power. It becomes the interest of corporate power, not simply that ordinary citizens should perceive how money buys politicians and legislation, but that they should perceive how *much* money it takes. That knowledge provides an invaluable lesson in powerlessness. Lurid accounts of political scandals are doubly useful in this regard, especially when large sums are involved; they teach how much money it takes to purchase favours and how purchasable public officials are, and how utterly cynical it has all become when government corrupts its own members.

Corporate politics has perverted the forms of politics that meant to connect the institutions of government with the citizens. These changes have been recognized but not frontally challenged because — at the most obvious level — the political economy developed over the past century has been a spectacular success. The very functioning of a successful economy seems to transform political categories and expectations into economic ones, and thereby creates an illusion of 'economic democracy'. If we do not participate as citizens we do participate as consumers, exercising our freedom to choose our satisfactions whenever we wish — and as if by magic when new products suddenly materialize on the store shelves, we feel that the economy is responding to our every impulse and desire — which is more than we can say about our elected representatives and non-elected public administrators.

About seventy-five years ago, Elihu Root, a representative public figure of the age, remarked after surveying the state of American politics that 'in the whole field of popular government I am convinced that one of the plainest duties of citizenship is hopefulness, and that pessimism is criminal weakness.'[1] In a land where optimism is virtually a patriotic duty, pessimism is still taken as a symptom of resignation and despair. But pessimism is, I think, something else: the sign of suppressed revolutionary impulses. Pessimism is the mood inspired by a reasoned conviction that only a revolutionary change can ward off the consequences that are implicit in the tendencies in contemporary American society, but that such a revolution, while politically and morally justified by democratic standards for legitimate authority, is neither possible nor prudent — if by revolution we mean launching a campaign of violent insurrection or civil war. Revolutions of that nature are plainly pathological under contemporary conditions of interdependency.

Democrats need a new conception of revolution. Its text should be John Locke not Karl Marx, because the problem is not to show that a social class should seize power — no social class in an advanced society can pretend to the universality of right which Marx presupposed in the workers of his day — but to reinvent the forms and practices that will express a democratic conception of collective life.

Locke is best remembered for the argument that when those who rule seem bent on acquiring 'Absolute Power over the Lives, Liberties, and Estates of the People', their power, which they hold on trust from the people, reverts, and the people are free to fashion new institutions. The right to revolution is not solely a right to overturn and destroy institutions but to fashion new ones because those who rule have perverted the old ones. The right to revolution is the right to create new forms.

Locke insisted that if that right were to be meaningful, people were not required to wait submissively until absolute power had been established:

... the State of Mankind is not so miserable that they are not capable of using
this Remedy till it be too late to look for any.... Men can never be secure
from Tyranny if there be no means to escape it, till they are perfectly under
it ... they have not only a right to get out of it, but to prevent it.[2]

When the right to revolution is conceived as justifying political creativity rather than violence, it is easy to understand why Locke was so
insistent that people should and would not revolt over 'every little
mismanagement in publick affairs'. Establishing new institutions was
justified only after the rulers had engaged in a long train of Abuses,
Prevarications, and Artifices, all tending the same way'. Elsewhere he
alluded to a 'general course and tendency of things' and to 'a settled
Design'. Given the complex judgement required, Locke's discussion was
remarkable for its democratic implications. At various times he referred
to the right to revolt as an option that belonged to the 'people', to 'the
majority', and even to individuals; but he never implied that it was so
weighty a matter that only a high-minded elite could be entrusted with
it. This last point is crucial, for if the right to revolt is about devising new
institutions, citizenship is more than a matter of being able to claim
rights. It is about a capacity to generate power, for that is the only way
that things get established in the world. And it is about a capacity to
share in power, to cooperate in it, for that is how institutions and
practices are sustained.

Under contemporary conditions, the Lockean question is: are there signs
of rebellion, symptoms of disaffection but also examples of political
creativity? For some years now social scientists have uncovered widespread civic apathy and pollsters have reported on the low esteem in
which politicians and major political institutions are held. Now in a
society where the official rhetoric and the rituals of political socialization
are still heavily democratic, *incivisme* of the kind documented by voting
studies is a serious matter. It is not alienation but disaffection and
rejection. I want to suggest that 'rejectionism' pervades our society and
that its presence and intensity represents a form of rebellion, a gesture of
defiance in the face of a system that is immovable and so interconnected
as to be unreformable as a totality. We see rejectionism in the vast
underground economy of illicit transactions; in the chronic insubordina-
tion that plagues the armed forces; and even, I would hazard, in the
patriotic zeal of the Moral Majority: for if one looks at their rhetoric and
actions, one finds a profound loathing for the current condition of the

body politic. We see it among professional groups where the obsession with money and status seems inspired less by greed than by the inability to find any moral point to serving a society so wholly dominated by the corporate ethos. And it is present in its most exaggerated form among high school achievers and undergraduates who are convinced that if they can transform themselves into technical functions — law, medicine, public administration and business management — they will be hermetically sealed off from the cynicism and corruption of society.

The origins of rejectionism lie in the 1960s. The turmoil of those years was not solely about the Vietnam War: it was about racism, imperialism, professionalism, affluence, moral codes, orthodox notions of sexuality and gender, and much more, from junk food to slick culture. It was revolutionary not because it was violent — the violence was exaggerated by the media — but because it was uncivil and yet civil: uncivil in withdrawing from and condemning the bourgeois forms of civility, but civil in inventing new ones, many of them bearing the marks of an obsession with participation and equality as well as an intoxication with the first experience of power, the experience of cooperation, common sacrifice, and common concern. 'Sharing' threatened suddenly to lose its sentimental overtones and become a political word.

The truth of rejectionism is that it recognizes that it is naive to expect the initiative for reform of the state to issue from the political process that serves the interests of political capitalism. This structure can only be reduced if citizens withdraw and direct their energies and civic commitment to finding new life forms. Towards these ends, our whole mode of thinking must be turned upside-down. Instead of imitating most other political theories and adopting the state as the primary structure and then adapting the activity of the citizen to the state, democratic thinking should renounce the state paradigm and, along with it, the liberal-legal corruption of the citizen. The old citizenship must be replaced by a fuller and wider notion of being whose politicalness will be expressed not in one or two modes of activity — voting or protesting — but in many.

A political being is not to be defined as the citizen has been, as an abstract, disconnected bearer of rights, privileges and immunities, but as a person whose existence is located in a particular place and draws its sustenance from circumscribed relationships: family, friends, church, neighbourhood, workplace, community, town, city. These relationships are the sources from which political beings draw power — symbolic, material and psychological — and that enable them to act together. For true political power involves not only acting so as to effect decisive changes; it also means the capacity to receive power, to be acted upon, to change, and be changed. From a democratic perspective, power is not simply force that is generated; it is experience, sensibility, wisdom, even melancholy distilled from the diverse relations and circles we move within. Democratic power, accordingly, bears the marks of its diverse origins — family, school, church, workplace, etc. — and, as a result, everything turns on an ability to establish practices whose form will not distort the manifold origins of power.

The practical task is to nurture existing movements that can provide constructive forms for rejectionism and make it genuinely political. The most important of these are the grassroots movements that have become epidemic throughout the country. Their range and variety are astonishing. They include rent control, utility rates and service, environmental concerns, health care, education, nuclear power, legal aid, workers' ownership of plants, and much more. Their single most important feature is that they have grown up outside the state-corporate structure and have flourished despite repeated efforts to discredit them.

While it is of the utmost importance that democrats support and encourage political activity at the grassroots level, it is equally necessary that the political limitations of such activity be recognized. It is politically incomplete. This is because the localism that is the strength of grassroots organizations is also their limitation. There are major problems in our society that are general in nature and necessitate modes of vision and action that are comprehensive rather than parochial. And there are historical legacies of wrong and unfairness that will never be confronted and may even be exacerbated by exclusive concern with backyard politics.

During the last year hopeful signs of discontent have emerged at this more general level in the anti-nuclear movement, the opposition to an imperialistic foreign policy, and the defence of human rights. These developments are suggestive because they represent the first steps ever towards systematic popular intervention in the sacrosanct domain of state secrets and national security. This is new terrain for democratic politics and it is genuinely political, for the problems of war, rights, and imperialism concern us all, not only because our survival is at stake but also because our bodies, our labour, and our legitimating name are frequently used for purposes that implicate us in shameful actions.

Notes

1. Elihu Root, *Addresses on Government and Citizenship*, Harvard University Press, Cambridge, Mass. 1916, p. 59.
2. John Locke, *Two Treatises of Government*, II.220.

Contributors

Mary Dietz is a member of the Department of Politics, University of Minnesota at Minneapolis.

Maurizio Passerin d'Entrèves is a member of the Department of Politics at the University of Manchester.

Jean Leca is a member of the Institut d'études politiques in Paris.

Louise Marcil-Lacoste is a member of the Département de philosophie at the Université de Montréal.

Kirstie McClure is a member of the Department of Political Science, Johns Hopkins University.

Chantal Mouffe is a member of the Collège international de philosophie, Paris.

Quentin Skinner is Professor of Political Science at the University of Cambridge.

Etienne Tassin is a member of the Université de Paris—Dauphine.

Bryan Turner is Professor of Sociology at the University of Essex.

Michael Walzer is Professor of Social Science at the Institute for Advanced Studies, Princeton.

Sheldon Wolin was formerly Professor of Political Science at the University of Princeton.

Slavoj Žižek is a member of the Institute for Sociology, Ljubljana.